Acknowledgements and thanks to ...

KU-260-785

All the inspirational teachers from my UK and US action research teams since 2009:

Worthing, Surrey, Lincoln, Kettering, Doncaster, Hampshire, Essex, Rotherham, Ellesmere Port, Tower Hamlets London, Hertfordshire, Sheffield, Warwickshire, Brighton and Hove, Reading, Kentucky and Wisconsin. *Many teachers gave me samples without giving me their names and schools. If your work appears in this book without your name, please let me know, so it can appear in subsequent print runs!*

All the teachers on my first DVD, *The Power of Formative Assessment*, and the following from the DVD who appear in videoclips in this book:

Helen Quincey, Barton Seagrave Primary School, Northants; Alice Hewins, Broadwater C of E First and Middle School, West Sussex; Jen Bullard, Dunholme St Chad's Primary School, Lincoln; Natasha Boult, Vale First and Middle School, West Sussex; and Katie Bartle, Cherry Wilingham Primary School, Lincoln

Special thanks to Seamus Gibbons, St Stephen's R.C. Primary School, Westminster, now at St Luke's C of E Primary School, Westminster, London, for being the sole subject of my second DVD, *Outstanding Formative Assessment*, and for everything you have contributed to my work

Gary Wilkie and the teachers from Sheringham Primary School, Newham, for extensive contributions to this book

Paula Hill, Milby Primary School, Nuneaton, Warwickshire

Katherine Muncaster, Ludworth Primary School, Stockport

Charlotte Rollinson, Thameside Primary School, Reading

Ben Massey and Jenny Aldridge, Rudyard Kipling Primary School, Brighton and Hove

Celia Thatcher, Wescott Infant School, Wokingham

Danielle Abbott, St Thomas of Canterbury R.C. Primary School, Salford

Catherine Thorp, St Thomas of Canterbury R.C. Primary School, Salford

Lorraine Sutton, Kingfisher Primary School, Doncaster

Debbie Smith, Hexthorpe Primary School, Doncaster

Graham Rhodes, Mexborough Highwoods Primary School, Doncaster

Sue Sparrow and Claire Carroll, Blagdon Nursery School and Children's Centre, Reading

Liza Craggs, Tannerswood JMI School, Hertfordshire

Charis Fletcher, St Nicholas Primary School, Hertfordshire

Chater Infant School, Hertfordshire

Kirstin Greygoose, Bidford-on-Avon Primary School, Warwickshire

Katie Walton, St Michael's C of E Primary School, Warwickshire

Emma Hancock, Brenchley and Matfield C of E Primary School, Tunbridge Wells

Phillipa Hampton and Kate Smith, Windhill Primary School, Hertfordshire

Sue Teague, Caddington Village School, Luton

Lori Riney, Washington County Elementary School, Kentucky, USA

Holly Medley, Washington County High School, Kentucky, USA

Rita Messer, Washington County High School, Kentucky, USA

Stephanie Harmon, Rockcastle County High School, Kentucky, USA

Pie Corbett for inviting me to be on the steering committee for his *Talk for writing with formative assessment* project and for providing welcome expert commentary to Chapter 7.

Moira Raynor, Principal Primary Advisor, Stockport Local Authority, and Angela Cale, Strategic Lead Assessment/School Improvement Adviser (retired), for much appreciated comments on the draft of this book.

My love and gratitude to my husband, John, and Katy, my daughter, for letting me get on with the book in peace – and thanks too, John, for all the footage for the DVDs, all your help with realia and a million other things.

Last but definitely not least, my soon-to-retire editor, Chas Knight. You have been a joy to work with and your editing is exemplary. I am delighted that this book is your swansong! I will miss you....

Contents

Introduction vi

PART ONE: Background to Formative Assessment

1 Why do we need it and what is it? 2

PART TWO: Lesson Culture and Structure

Laying the foundations

2 The spirit of formative assessment in the learning
   culture of the school and classroom. .10

3 Involving children at the planning stage. 47

4 Talk and talk partners 57

Effective starts to lessons

5 Questions and activities. 72

6 Learning objectives and success criteria. 79

7 Developing excellence... for all subjects, and beyond
   the success criteria for Writing. 95

Developing the learning

8 Ongoing questioning. 114

9 Feedback. 120

Effective ends to lessons

10 Summarising the learning. 148

PART THREE: Whole-school Development

11 Lesson study: definitions and practice. 152

12 Whole-school accounts 157

13 The impact of formative assessment, and conclusion 194

References and resources. 198

Introduction

I wrote my last book, *Active Learning through Formative Assessment*, in 2008, with a clear vision of what I wanted it to do. I have always tried to answer the needs, as I perceive them at the time, of teachers on my courses and in my action research teams. I had, in my previous books, introduced the basic principles of formative assessment as a response to the initial confusion about it; woven the elements together in whole-lesson accounts to help teachers see how the bits fitted together; written in depth about effective feedback (as it was in 2003...) and produced a book for secondary teachers. *Active Learning through Formative Assessment* featured hundreds of examples across the age ranges, including nursery and special schools: exactly what teachers were telling me they needed at that point.

By 2010, I was inundated with teachers asking for copies of the videoclips in my presentations, and the idea of creating a DVD began to form. I took ten teachers from my action research teams and filmed them demonstrating formative assessment in the classroom. Gradually the successful implementation of formative assessment was becoming clearer, as a range of excellent examples was shown. Now we could see success criteria being generated across the age ranges, with talk partners, self- and peer evaluation in action with 5 year olds and 11 year olds.

Last year, although tempted to write this book then, I decided to create another DVD. 'Lesson study' (see Chapter 11) was becoming more significant in my thinking about staff development and I believe that video is the next best thing. I found an extraordinary Inner London teacher working in challenging circumstances whose formative assessment practice is exemplary and whose children's achievements and test results were amazing. Any in-depth study of one excellent teacher is enough to promote in-depth thinking and discussion about how the teaching impacts the learning and lead to implications for one's own thinking about facilitating children's learning. Videoclips from his classroom and from other teachers are provided throughout this book, illustrating key points made.

What I have learnt from my own close observation of excellent teachers and their impact on the learning is central to my own thinking and development, and I make reference to teachers and their anecdotes and strategies throughout this book.

The rationale for the book is as usual to update the key strategies, with excellent examples, but also to introduce more whole-school development examples and issues. Most of all, this book includes more of *my* thoughts than I have ever included before about the often complex issues involved in formative assessment. I have learnt, and continue to learn, so much in my years of experience in this field, mainly from the hundreds of teachers in my action research teams, in discussion with them, hearing their feedback and in watching many of them and their children in action. My very own lesson study experience! I am indebted to those teachers for allowing me that privilege.

Outstanding Formative Assessment

Culture and Practice

SHIRLEY CLARKE

HODDER
EDUCATION
AN HACHETTE UK COMPANY

This book is dedicated to my parents:

my beloved father (1929–2010), who gave me my love of children, of learning, of equality and justice. You still live on in my heart and in my work;

my wonderful, strong, wise, unflappable mother, who provides the voice of reason and calm steadiness.

Although every effort has been made to ensure that website addresses are correct at time of going to press, Hodder Education cannot be held responsible for the content of any website referenced here.

Orders: please contact Bookpoint Ltd, 130 Milton Park, Abingdon, Oxon OX14 4SB. Telephone: (44) 01235 827827. Fax: (44) 01235 400454. Lines are open 9.00–5.00, Monday to Saturday, with a 24-hour message answering service. Visit our website at www.hoddereducation.co.uk

First published 2014 by Hodder Education, part of Hachette UK, Carmelite House, 50 Victoria Embankment, London EC4Y 0DZ

Impression number   10 9 8 7 6 5 4
Year   2018 2017 2016 2015

Typeset in ITC Stone Informal Std Medium 10.5/14 in India.

Printed in Dubai.

A catalogue record for this title is available from the British Library.

ISBN 978 1 471 82947 5

I am always surprised at how far the practical strategies to fulfil the principles of formative assessment evolve each time I write a new book, and this book contains updated thinking and examples. This time, however, there have also been some shifts about our understanding of schooling. The work of John Hattie (see Chapter 1 and throughout) has been highly significant in helping us see, through his rigorous, long-term synthesis of research findings, what we have been wasting our time with and what really matters. Top of the list of effect-sizes is of course formative assessment – the single most important factor in raising achievement and enabling children to become lifelong learners.

My books have so far all followed the same basic pattern: a journey though the various aspects of formative assessment with principles, thoughts and examples. For the first time I am linking the various elements in a different way – a way which I believe is more helpful for a teacher to work with, focusing more on the structure of a lesson.

The first chapter describes the background to formative assessment and where it is now, giving the various definitions and hopefully some cutting through them to give clarity.

The main body of the book is then split into four sections, each colour-coded for easy reference:

- **Laying the foundations**, in which the conditions for pupils to be active learners, constant reviewers and self-assessors are set up: a learning culture, involvement in the planning and talk partners.

- **Effective starts to lessons**, in which questioning strategies, exploratory activities and examples of pupil work are used to establish prior knowledge, capture interest, co-construct success criteria and discuss excellence.

- **Developing the learning**, in which dialogue is key, establishing and helping children articulate their understanding so far and focusing on constant review and improvement.

- **Effective ends to lessons**, in which various techniques are described which help to encourage pupil reflection and find out what has been learnt so far and what needs to be rethought or developed.

The final section focuses on whole-school development, including lesson study.

There are many excellent teachers practising formative assessment in their classrooms, but in this book, for the first time, I have been able to include schools in which every teacher practices formative assessment and the school as a whole has embedded its spirit as well as the practice. A number of excellent schools share their stories and it is enlightening to see the common threads and key factors that have contributed to whole-school success. In Chapter 2 there are accounts from three schools about how they established a whole-school growth mindset learning culture. In Chapter 12, on whole-school development I have included the fascinating and inspirational journeys of three other excellent schools and included some useful examples of school documents. Those stories are rich with expertise and wisdom and should be extremely helpful to senior managers who have formative assessment as a vision for their schools.

Through all the changes in education and curriculum, it is heartening to know that formative assessment remains immune. In the UK at this moment, teachers are concerned about assessment without levels, soon to be enforced. Good formative assessment focuses around successes and improvement for each learner, against their own previous achievement (*ipsative* assessment), so grading or other benchmarks are irrelevant. Summative assessment summarises what the learner knows or understands at that moment – again, with or without any benchmarking. Whatever the learner's age, the curriculum demands, the subject, the educational setting or testing arrangements, formative assessment is always relevant, as it revolves around the only focus that makes any sense: the empowerment of the learner. Once this becomes the prime focus of every teacher and pupil, with formative assessment as the driving and guiding force, *outstanding* achievement is not only possible, but highly probable.

Using the QR codes

The **videoclip tasters** throughout this book originate from Shirley's two DVDs, which can be purchased via her website: www.shirleyclarke-education.org

You can access and view the videoclips using a QR code reader on your smartphone/tablet. There are many free readers available, depending on the smartphone/tablet you are using.

Once you have downloaded a QR code reader, simply open the reader app and use it to take a photo of the code. The file will then load on your smartphone/tablet.

If you cannot read the QR code or you are using a computer, type the URLs into your internet browser.

PART ONE
Background to Formative Assessment

Why do we need it and what is it?

Why keep improving?

It seems that, no matter how hard teachers try, there is always a drive for even greater achievement for our pupils. Each generation of teachers sees the targets as somehow unreachable and yet, over time, we see how much more we actually have achieved, more than we ever thought possible. It is the human condition to want to keep learning, to progress and develop and, when I look for successful teachers, I know I will always see one linking characteristic: *passion* – passion about children's learning, about moving forward, about learning as much about your teaching as you want for your children's learning. Without that passion, teaching is merely a job, not a mission, and your children will, I believe, never reach their full potential while they are placed in your hands. So my first reason for wanting to be 'even better' (see Chapter 9) is that we are teachers, and that is our job, always.

Secondly, although it is now an old chestnut that to be economically competitive we need to be continually raising standards of achievement, we must pay attention to this political perspective, routinely stated by our political leaders:

> What really matters is how we're doing compared with our international competitors. That is what will define our economic growth and our country's future. The truth is, at the moment we are standing still while others race past.

Michael Gove (DfE White Paper, 2010)

It is good to know that there are some alternative views – not to diminish the pursuit of excellence, but to look at it in a different way:

> This is not a time to bring up yet another generation of teachers and students in the belief that the only route to success is competition and the only worthwhile outcome is increased profit. It is critical that we design UK educational provision from the perspective of global, not national citizenship.

Paul Ginnis (December 2010)

Teachers are better than ever before and children are higher achievers than they used to be, as Wiliam (2011) points out, looking at years of PISA testing (Programme for International Student Assessment) and Wechsler intelligence tests, but we have a changing workplace which dictates, more than anything else, that we need to strive for ever higher achievement. With technology replacing even highly skilled jobs at an alarming rate, and a global recession setting the tone, we already hear too many stories of highly qualified graduates without job prospects.# Why do we need it and what is it?

Why keep improving?

It seems that, no matter how hard teachers try, there is always a drive for even greater achievement for our pupils. Each generation of teachers sees the targets as somehow unreachable and yet, over time, we see how much more we actually have achieved, more than we ever thought possible. It is the human condition to want to keep learning, to progress and develop and, when I look for successful teachers, I know I will always see one linking characteristic: *passion* – passion about children's learning, about moving forward, about learning as much about your teaching as you want for your children's learning. Without that passion, teaching is merely a job, not a mission, and your children will, I believe, never reach their full potential while they are placed in your hands. So my first reason for wanting to be 'even better' (see Chapter 9) is that we are teachers, and that is our job, always.

Secondly, although it is now an old chestnut that to be economically competitive we need to be continually raising standards of achievement, we must pay attention to this political perspective, routinely stated by our political leaders:

> What really matters is how we're doing compared with our international competitors. That is what will define our economic growth and our country's future. The truth is, at the moment we are standing still while others race past.

Michael Gove (DfE White Paper, 2010)

It is good to know that there are some alternative views – not to diminish the pursuit of excellence, but to look at it in a different way:

> This is not a time to bring up yet another generation of teachers and students in the belief that the only route to success is competition and the only worthwhile outcome is increased profit. It is critical that we design UK educational provision from the perspective of global, not national citizenship.

Paul Ginnis (December 2010)

Teachers are better than ever before and children are higher achievers than they used to be, as Wiliam (2011) points out, looking at years of PISA testing (Programme for International Student Assessment) and Wechsler intelligence tests, but we have a changing workplace which dictates, more than anything else, that we need to strive for ever higher achievement. With technology replacing even highly skilled jobs at an alarming rate, and a global recession setting the tone, we already hear too many stories of highly qualified graduates without job prospects.

So, the third reason: we must continually strive to predict the unknown: what will today's pupils need in tomorrow's world? Tim Birkhead, from the University of Sheffield, says:

The most striking thing about some undergraduates is their dependence, their lack of initiative and their reluctance to think for themselves. New undergraduates seem to expect to be told what to do at every stage. It is almost as though the spoon-feeding-and-teaching-to-the-test culture at school has drained them of independent thought.

Jonathan Kestenbaum, Chief Executive of the National Endowment for Science, Technology and the Arts, echoes this observation:

Students will need to take more responsibility for their own education and how it is delivered – to ensure that it equips them with the aptitudes they need for the future.

Inclusion of the following skills or aptitudes will mean the difference between success and failure for the majority of young people:

- Critical thinking and problem solving
- Collaboration and leadership
- Agility and adaptability
- Initiative and entrepreneurialism
- Effective oral and written communication
- Accessing and analysing information
- Curiosity and imagination

All skills are, of course, only really useful when they can be transferred to any context, even those yet unknown. My nephew, recently completing his PhD in chemical physics from University College London, graduated with certainty that he would slot easily into a top-ranking financial institution. Months later, with no success, the skill he has most drawn on to create his own future is entrepreneurialism and technical expertise: his own website, his ability to sell his skills, networking and, using his scientific skills, brewing his own beer on the side as another possible option! How times have changed, when a student's path in life could be laid in accordance with the choice of degree or apprenticeship. We must include the above skills and their application in our teaching to prepare students more appropriately for a new society, whether they are legislated or not. Much freedom still exists in what we cover beyond statutory requirements.

Why is formative assessment the answer? The evidence...

The most powerful educational tool for raising achievement and preparing children to be lifelong learners, in any context, is formative assessment. The research evidence for this is rigorous and comprehensive. Hattie (2009) has contributed significantly to the evidence about what works and doesn't work in his ground-breaking book *Visible Learning*. Over a period of 18 years, Hattie attempted to answer one simple question: what do we do in schools and how much impact does it have? He synthesised over 900 meta-analyses, involving over 50,000 studies and 240 million students, in order to answer his question. He established an 'effect-size' for the different elements of education and calculated that the midpoint effect-size is 0.4. Any 'influence on learning' below 0.4 needs to be reviewed and questioned, as its worth is suspect. Anything above 0.4 is worth doing, and the greater the effect-size, the more worthwhile it is. Once you reach an effect-size of 1.0, the progress, for a child, is the equivalent of being one year ahead of where he or she would have been. Hattie's 150 elements of education are rank-ordered, with the key aspects of formative assessment at the top of the list, as shown in Table 1.1.

Influence on learning	No. of studies	Effect-size
Assessment literate students (students who know what they are learning, have success criteria, can self-assess, etc.)	209	1.44
Providing formative evaluation	30	0.90
Lesson study	402	0.88
Classroom discussion	42	0.82
Feedback	1310	0.75
Teacher–student relationships	229	0.72
Meta-cognitive strategies	63	0.69

Table 1.1 *Data from* Visible Learning *(Hattie, 2009)*

Assessment literacy is the term used in many countries to describe pupils who have clear understanding of what and how they are learning and can self-assess and improve their learning – all the basic elements of formative assessment. **Classroom discussion** is central to formative assessment – talk partners discussing questions asked by the teacher and cooperatively discussing and improving their learning. **Feedback and providing formative evaluation** amount to the same thing and are key to formative assessment, because they are the means by which we progress – learning from teachers and peers. **Meta-cognitive strategies** form the foundation of formative assessment, as part of a growth mindset culture, where pupils know that their learning disposition at any one time is as important as the skill or knowledge in question. The two remaining aspects – **teacher–student relationships** and **lesson study**, important factors in their own right – are discussed in the following chapters.

The Sutton Trust *Toolkit of Strategies to Improve Learning* (2011), referencing the same studies, placed **effective feedback** at the top of their table, with a potential gain of 9 months and a summary of 'very high impact for low cost'. Next comes **meta-cognition and self-regulation** at a gain of 8 months and then **peer tutoring/ peer-assisted learning** at a gain of 6 months – some new words to mean the same key elements of formative assessment.

Hattie's 900 meta-analyses take account of all the rigorous studies in the literature, including the famous review in 1998 carried out by Paul Black and Dylan Wiliam

(1998a), itself one of 209 studies, so any other research I could mention will already have been subsumed in Hattie's work. The number of studies analysed each time, seen in Table 1.1, gives an indication of the scope of his work and its subsequent significance.

What *is* formative assessment?

In my many years in education I have never witnessed such confusion over a concept as I have with formative assessment – variously known as *assessment for learning, assessment is learning, balanced assessment* and who knows how many other definitions across the world. In the USA, formative assessment is defined by Stiggins (2005), a highly influential figure in assessment in the States, as frequent summative tasks, and assessment for learning as the continuous active learning described in this book. In the UK and many other parts of the world, however, *formative assessment* and *assessment for learning* are terms which usually describe the same thing.

Hargreaves (2005) found that there were many interpretations of *assessment for learning* in 2003, as follows:

- Monitoring pupils' performance against targets or objectives
- Assessment which informs next steps in teaching and learning
- Teachers giving feedback for improvement
- Teachers learning about children's learning
- Children taking control of their own learning and assessment
- Turning assessment into a learning event

Bullet points 3, 4 and 5 are explicitly correct in their interpretation, but where the word *assessment* appears, in points 2 and 6, it implies some kind of task or test was given from which information was gleaned. This is not formative assessment – it is summative, the end rather than the means. Deciding how much the learner knows and what they need next is a minute by minute necessity in the classroom, but the word *monitoring*, in the first point, seems to imply something more formal, such as work scrutiny. It is this detail which I believe causes the confusion – the words we use to imply different activities.

In the *Times Educational Supplement* on 13 July 2012, Dylan Wiliam, in an article about his disappointment over the interpretation of formative assessment in many schools, blamed the introduction of 'Assessing Pupil Progress' (APP) as contributory to the general confusion about the meaning of formative assessment. He complained:

❝The problem is that government told schools that it was all about monitoring pupil progress; it wasn't about pupils becoming owners of their own learning. The big mistake that Paul Black and I made was calling this stuff "assessment". Because when you use the word assessment, people think about tests and exams. For me, AfL is about better teaching.❞

Amen to that, although we need to include the word *learning* to fully imply the real meaning of assessment for learning, or formative assessment – which, as it was the first term used, is the one I have steadfastly stuck to, with the hope that my constancy paves a path of comprehension for teachers.

Formative assessment, as a concept, all started with a move away from summative assessment to what really makes children progress, which is being much more in control of their learning and its assessment. Various academics coined the phrase *formative assessment* to describe a set of learning processes with which pupils do better at tests and are more likely to become lifelong learners. Following Black and Wiliam's review of the literature (1998a), they laid out the elements of formative assessment, stated thus:

❝• clarifying and understanding learning intentions and criteria for success;
• engineering effective classroom discussions, questions and tasks that elicit evidence of learning;
• providing feedback that moves learners forward;
• activating students as teaching and learning resources for each other;
• activating students as owners of their own learning.❞

In Leahy et al (2005)

My own work – with over 13 years of action research teams across England, Scotland and Wales and recently the United States (altogether involving some 2000 teachers across the phases) – has led to another point: the inclusion of involving pupils at the planning stage to maximise motivation and pupil ownership. Most important of all in the success of formative assessment is the appropriate *learning culture* and the belief that all children can *succeed*, a condition firmly established by Black and Wiliam in their initial findings.

My own expansion of the ingredients of formative assessment, at this moment (and continually evolving), are as follows:

- A learning culture, where children and teachers have a growth mindset, self-belief, meta-cognitive skills and the belief that all can succeed;
- Involving pupils at the planning stage to enhance motivation and ownership;
- Talk partners and a 'no hands up' culture, where children are resources for one another and all can be included in class discussion;
- Mixed-ability learning, with differentiated choices, so that self-esteem is intact and expectations are high;
- Clear learning objectives shared with pupils, not necessarily at the beginning of a lesson, but sometimes after their interest has been captured;
- Co-constructed success criteria;
- Effective questioning, especially at beginnings of lessons, to establish current understanding and prior knowledge;
- A continual quest to find out how far children are understanding their learning, so that individual and class feedback and the direction of the lesson can be adjusted appropriately;

- Examples of excellence analysed and shared, before children produce their own 'product';
- Feedback from peers and teachers which focuses on successes, where the excellence is and where improvements are needed;
- Cooperative peer feedback in which examples of improvement are modelled via mid-lesson learning stops, so that feedback and improvement-making is immediate and part of a lesson;
- Effective ends to lessons, where learning is summarised and reflected upon.

Throughout this book these elements are discussed, detailed and exemplified using the many wonderful examples from teachers in my learning teams.

PART TWO
Lesson Culture and Structure

Laying the foundations

There are three main elements which I see as *conditions* for children to be able to function as active learners in the classroom: having **a learning culture** (Chapter 2), being **involved at the planning stage** (Chapter 3) and having frequently changing **talk partners** (Chapter 4), with continual opportunities for dialogue, classroom discussion, collaboration and a 'no hands up' rule. Once these things are established, we can effectively move on to pupil generation of success criteria. At that point self- and peer evaluation, continual review and improvement can be successfully controlled by the learner, because he or she has all the tools and emotional support and power to be able to function confidently as a learner.

The most important of the three is, of course, the appropriate learning culture....

2 The spirit of formative assessment in the learning culture of the school and classroom

Although the various aspects of formative assessment are reasonably well known (learning objectives, success criteria, feedback, and so on) the true 'spirit' of formative assessment is less familiar, mainly because it is harder to define. Without the appropriate learning culture, however, the strategies and techniques have limited impact and become nothing more than another thing to do. It would be possible to have a lesson where all the elements featured but were more or less cancelled out by the absence of a true learning culture. If, for instance, there are rewards given to some children and not to others for the same lesson, the subsequent loss of self-efficacy will create a sense of the purposelessness of keeping going or doing the best you can do. Those children who received them will be likely to learn to strive for the reward rather than the achievement. Similarly, if children have success criteria but are in ability groups, rather than differentiated choices sitting with a talk partner, we know that there will be lower expectations, on the part of both the teacher and the child. Another example: children feeling anxious about their work being randomly picked to be discussed at the visualiser is nearly always because the culture of cooperation and learning from one another has not been talked about and established in the classroom.

I believe there are three main aspects to the creation of the ideal learning culture in a school:

- **developing growth mindsets;**
- **integrating meta-cognition strategies;**
- **mixed-ability learning**.

To develop such a culture needs much honest discussion, reference to evidence, and cooperative planning and development between all staff. What applies to children must apply to teachers – we are all sensitive learners.

Developing a growth mindset – brain truths and myths

First of all, however, I want to look at what we know about the brain and how it 'works', as this is central to the notion of mindsets. People with a fixed mindset believe that they are born with a certain amount of intelligence and that it is fixed for the rest of their lives. People with a growth mindset, however, know that intelligence is not fixed and that you can, in effect, 'grow' your intelligence. Brain research has made this a reality.

Neurotruths

We now know that the brain can be developed like a muscle, changing and growing stronger the more it is used. The brain grows new cells when we are learning new information and skills. Even older people can develop their brains in an enriched environment.

Carol Dweck (2011), in her website article 'You can grow your intelligence', explains in simple terms how the brain works. Many teachers in my teams have used this article to introduce the workings of the brain to their pupils:

'Inside the cortex of the brain are billions of tiny nerve cells, called neurons. The nerve cells have branches connecting them to other cells in a complicated network. Communication between these brain cells is what allows us to think and solve problems.

When you learn new things, these tiny connections in the brain actually multiply and get stronger. The more that you challenge your mind to learn, the more your brain cells grow. Then, things that you once found very hard or even impossible to do — like speaking a foreign language or doing algebra — seem to become easy. The result is a stronger, smarter brain.'

Dweck (2011)

Intelligence tests used to be thought of as conferring a lifelong score, which we now know is wrong. The score is simply an indicator of one's achievement at that time, not a predictor of future achievement – the same with any test, unless there are severe learning impairments. I urge teachers to use the terms *lower achievers* and *higher achievers*, which implies 'at this moment', as opposed to *high ability* and *low ability* or *able* and *less able*, which imply permanence.

The route to developing a 'smarter' brain is practice and input. We are all born with different aptitudes for certain subjects or skills, based on our genetic heritage – a reason so many of us, at an early age, write off certain subjects when we compare ourselves to others who are more naturally adept. It is important to know that with varying amounts of **time, effort, practice and input** we could *all* reach a given level of proficiency. The less genetically predisposed we are, the more practice and effort will be required. Even those for whom a subject or skill comes naturally have to practise for hours a day to reach expert status or very high levels of proficiency (e.g. a ballet dancer, concert pianist, professional footballer). A crucial component of the learning culture in the classroom is to continually talk with pupils about how the brain grows, how you can grow your abilities through practice, the gift of being able to learn from one another – tapping all our different strengths, and the fact that we are all born with different strengths.

Research into London taxi drivers' brains (Woollett and Maguire, 2012) discovered that the huge amount of memory they had to use to learn 'The Knowledge' – every street in inner and outer London – resulted in a slightly enlarged area of the hippocampus. These drivers could also memorise other things easily as a result of this. Similarly, people who have for many years learnt a musical instrument which uses fingering find it easy to learn to type, because the connections made in the brain for the instrument are the same as those needed for typing. Once the neural connections have been made repeatedly, the pathways become more fixed. Making children aware of these facts, showing them *YouTube* clips of neurons connecting and so on leads to children being able to identify when they can feel their brain 'growing'. *'This is really making me think! I can feel my neurons connecting!'* is a commonly heard cry in such a learning culture.

Neuromyths

It is important to rethink some of the traps we have fallen into which have now been largely discredited – multiple intelligences and learning styles being the main offenders:

> ❝*"Multiple intelligences" is flawed as a model of human abilities. Evidence from brain localisation and idiot savants do not justify the proposition that a number of independent intelligences exist. A hierarchical model consisting of special abilities underpinned by a general intellectual processor offers by far the most plausible structure of human intelligence. School curriculum designs based on the theory of multiple intelligences are misguided.*❞
>
> Adey and Dillon (2012)

In other words, although there is no doubt that we can distinguish different sorts of abilities – such as spatial, numerical and so on – these special abilities are not independent from one another. The evidence shows that underlying a person's special abilities is one common general intelligence factor.

Although one person might put a great amount of effort into one thing (e.g. a footballer), eclipsing other skills, over the population as a whole, abilities in different areas are correlated.

Linked to the concept of multiple intelligences is the very popular idea that we all have a best 'learning style.' In Hattie's meta-analysis, 'matching learning styles' has a very low effect-size of 0.17, based on 244 studies. The problem here is that deciding the best learning style for a pupil, and channelling them in that direction only, restricts their opportunities to develop a wider skill set of styles. As John White (2005) says:

'Putting children into boxes that have not been proved to exist may end up restricting the education that they receive, leading teachers to overly rigid views of individual pupils' potentialities, and what is worse, a new type of stereotyping.'

Other neuromyths evidenced in Reid and Anderson (2012) include:

- We use only 10% of our brain;
- Some people are left-brain thinkers while others are right-brain thinkers and each needs a different form of learning instruction;
- There are critical periods in brain development during which learning can take place;
- Brain training can enhance learning.

Developing a growth mindset – what it means and how to get one

Definition

A growth mindset (Dweck, 2000) has become an accessible concept for the way learners need to feel about themselves and their abilities to be successful learners. Research over many years has highlighted that we all differ as learners, being somewhere on the continuum between a fixed and a growth mindset (Fig. 2.1).

Fixed mindset (*performance* orientation)	Growth mindset (*learning* orientation)
Intelligence is static. *I must look clever!*	Intelligence is expandable. *I want to learn more!*
Avoids challenges	Embraces challenges
Gives up easily	Persists in the face of setbacks
Sees effort as pointless	Sees effort as the way
Ignores useful criticism	Learns from criticism
⇩	⇩
Likely to plateau early and achieve less than full potential	*Reaches ever-higher levels of achievement*

Fig. 2.1 *Characteristics of the fixed and growth mindsets*

A fixed mindset is the result of a continual focus on your ability rather than your achievement and effort. Praise to young children reinforcing 'cleverness' or intelligence and exclaiming over speed of mastery gives a clear subliminal message: to get approval you need to master new things quickly, with little effort, both of which will earn you the 'clever' label. The more your ability, your speed and lack of effort are praised ('Well done! You hardly needed to think about/work at that at all! Clever girl!'), the more you don't want to lose that position of greatness, so the less you want to engage in tasks which require time or effort or might lead to some kind of failure. People with a fixed mindset avoid challenging tasks for fear of failure, thus missing many valuable learning opportunities.

Studies show that rewards – a concrete version of grades – given to a select few for their achievement, effort or behaviour, reinforce a fixed mindset, for both those who get the reward and those who don't. Children do not need rewards when the culture is focused around all children competing against themselves and their own previous achievement. When there is a growth mindset culture in which the learner's achievement is celebrated verbally and personally, and the goal is to strive for excellence, stickers and stars seem tokenistic and patronising. In one school, celebration assemblies were replaced with the drawing of three random lollysticks before the assembly and those children came to the front and described their achievements for that week. Teachers started this in their classrooms and helped children to be specific, referring to success criteria for school learning and giving details for personal or outside achievement.

VIDEOCLIP TASTER #1 Verbal celebration of achievement

As she dismisses her class of 5 year olds, the teacher's comments show the children that even their smallest achievements can be celebrated. http://bit.ly/1mQ5gRx

Table 2.1 was included in 'Mindsetworks', an invaluable online resource linked with Carol Dweck's research, and shows how the mindsets affect the effort a learner applies to a task. We are all somewhere on the continuum between having a fixed or growth mindset, so the addition of the 'mixed' column helps to identify some of the features and therefore needs of those pupils in-between the two mindsets. This would be especially useful when establishing a rough baseline of pupils' current mindsets.

	Fixed	Mixed	Growth
Taking on challenges	You don't really take on challenges on your own. You feel that challenges are to be avoided.	You might take on challenges when you have some previous experience with success in a related challenge.	You look forward to the next challenge and have long-range plans for new challenges.
Learning from mistakes	You see mistakes as failures, as proof that the task is beyond your reach. You may hide mistakes or lie about them.	You may accept mistakes as temporary setbacks, but lack strategies to apply what you learned from the mistakes in order to succeed.	You see mistakes as temporary setbacks, something to be overcome. You reflect about what you learned and apply that learning when revisiting the task.
Accepting feedback and criticism	You feel threatened by feedback and may avoid it altogether. Criticism and constructive feedback are seen as a reason to quit.	You may be motivated by feedback if it is not overly critical or threatening. Who is giving the feedback, the level of difficulty of the task, or their personal feelings might all be factors in your motivation.	You invite and are motivated by feedback and criticism. You apply new strategies as a result of feedback. You think of feedback as being a supportive element in the learning process.
Practise and applying strategies	You do not practise and avoid practising when you can. You do not have any strategies for accomplishing the learning goals or tasks, or you apply ineffective strategies.	You practise, but a big setback can make you want to quit. You are more willing to practise things you are already considered good at. You are open to being given a strategy to meet a challenge, but you rarely apply your own strategies unless it is something you are already good at.	You enjoy the process of practising and see it as part of the process of getting good at something. You may create your own practice or study plans. You fluidly use many strategies, think of some of your own strategies and ask others about their strategies.
Perseverance and focus	You have little persistence on learning goals and tasks. You give up at the first sign of a struggle.	You may persevere with prompting and support. Unless you are provided with strategies for overcoming obstacles, you will stop or give up.	You 'stick to it' and have stamina for the task(s). You keep working confidently until the task is complete.
Asking questions	You do not ask questions or do not know which questions to ask, but you can usually say you 'don't get it' if asked.	You might ask questions about a portion of the task that you feel you can do. If you perceive it to be out of your ability, you probably won't ask questions.	You ask specific questions, ask questions about your own thinking and challenge the text, the task and the teacher.
Taking risks	You do not take risks, and if something is too hard you give in blank or copied work, if anything at all. You are not engaged in the process/task.	You will take risks if the task is already fairly familiar to you. If not, you will resort to copying or giving in partially completed work.	You begin tasks confidently, risk making errors and openly share the work you produce.

Table 2.1 *The mindsets continuum (copyright © Mindsetworks Inc. www.mindsetworks.com: used with permission)*

Strategies for developing a growth mindset culture

Intelligence

As the belief that your intelligence is limited is a critical barrier to having a growth mindset, it is useful to engage children and adults in a discussion about the nature of intelligence. Many teachers have found the following task very successful:

Arrange these famous people in order of intelligence:

Albert Einstein, J.K. Rowling, David Cameron, David Beckham, Justin Bieber (or similar!)

VIDEOCLIP TASTER #2 Ordering celebrities for intelligence

An insight into 8 and 9 year old children's perceptions of intelligence…. http://bit.ly/1fnYWRa

It is interesting to see how many different definitions of intelligence emerge and the different ways the famous people can be ordered according to those definitions. Common criteria given include academic achievement, making money, getting a long way from where you started, a subject excellence, social skills, and impact on society. Children gradually realise that intelligence can mean many things. The book *All Kinds of Ways to be Smart*, by Judy Lalli, is a popular follow-up to this activity. Of course, we need to beware of children pigeonholing themselves into only one way of being 'smart'. The emphasis needs to be the fact that intelligence is not just academic.

A teacher from a Kentucky elementary school described what happened when she presented the task to a class of 8 year olds:

Students worked in groups of four. I showed the whole class pictures of the famous people and explained who each person was: Tiger Woods, George Washington, Aly Raisman, Walt Disney, Barack Obama, Thomas Edison, Christopher Columbus, J.K. Rowling, Michael Jordan, Taylor Swift.

They were instructed to put these pictures in order of intelligence. Some comments I overheard:

- 'I don't think a president should go at the end.'
- 'But she won a gold medal!'
- 'You don't have to be really smart to play basketball.'
- 'She was poor and then she became famous.'
- 'The presidents should be together.'
- 'But she's the most famous!'
- 'The paparazzi would like her more.'

Behaviour I noticed:

- Students who were normally 'pushovers' were adamant about their opinions and would back up their beliefs.
- They naturally compromised to determine the order.
- The most popular people for this generation were not necessarily at the top.
- They were really thinking about their justifications.

I then read a book called *All Kinds of Ways to be Smart*, by Judy Lalli. We discussed 'smartness' in different areas: word, logic, picture, music, nature, body, self, people. There is not just one way to be smart. We also discussed what each of the people had to do to accomplish what they have and also how they had to excel in different areas.

I learned:

- I need to give more opportunities to work in this manner – compromise, negotiation, open-ended activities, not necessarily math content with right or wrong answers.
- Kids can really handle this and can learn from it.
- I need to *LISTEN* to them more. They have a lot to say and need to be heard.

Lori Riney, Washington County Elementary School, Springfield, Kentucky.

Current mindsets

Carol Dweck's book *Self-Theories* (2000) contains some useful questionnaires in the appendix which can be given to children to try to gauge their current mindset. Her website also contains surveys for children. The following list is particularly pertinent, although probably appropriate only for older children. Children agree or disagree with the statements:

❝1.   *I like school work that I'll learn from, even if I make a lot of mistakes.*

2.   *I would feel really good if I were the only one who could answer the teacher's questions.*

3.   *An important reason for doing my school work is because I like to learn new things.*

4.   *It's very important to me that I don't look stupid in class.*

5.   *I like school work best when it really makes me think.*

6.   *It's important to me that the other children in my class think that I'm good at my work.*

7.   *An important reason why I do my work at school is because I want to get better at it.*

8.   *An important reason for doing my school work is so that I don't embarrass myself.*

9.   *I do my school work because I'm interested in it.*

10.   *I want to do better than other children in my class.*❞

For young children, differentiated mazes (downloadable from the internet) or different jigsaws have proved useful in finding out what children feel about their abilities. Children who head towards the hard jigsaw or the complicated maze are more likely to have a growth mindset.

Making mindsets accessible

Once the baseline is roughly cast, the next step in creating a class or school-wide growth mindset culture is to give children the facts about the brain and the mindsets, in whichever way suits the age the best. I have seen fake brains, displays of neurons connecting, characters and puppets, white mice and any number of devices to get the information over to the children. The children's book *Your Fantastic Elastic Brain*, by JoAnn Deak, is a great resource for explaining the workings and potential of the brain.

A commonly used *YouTube* clip, 'Famous Failures', gives a very clear message that you can grow your intelligence. Some excerpts:

➤ *He wasn't able to speak until he was 4 years old and his teachers said he would 'never amount to much'* (Albert Einstein, theoretical physicist and Nobel Prize winner)

➤ *Was demoted from her job as a news anchor because she 'wasn't fit for television'* (Oprah Winfrey, host of a multi-award-winning talk-show and the most influential woman in the world)

➤ *Fired from a newspaper for 'lacking imagination' and 'having no original ideas'* (Walt Disney, creator of Mickey Mouse and winner of 30 Academy Awards)

One teacher, Paula Hill from Milby Primary School in Nuneaton, tells her story of introducing the growth mindset with her 6 year olds:

I started my session sitting in a talking circle reading *Giraffes Can't Dance*, by Giles Andrae and Guy Parker-Rees. I had also copied onto large paper pictures of Gerald – one where he says he is useless and one where he can dance.

I read the book, drawing attention to the fact that he couldn't dance but he wanted to. I stopped reading at the part where Gerald says he is useless and asked the children to talk to their talk partner about how he might be feeling. They said:
'sad, unhappy, lonely, worried, shocked, left out, jealous and cross'.

We discussed why he was feeling like that but then moved on to how he could help himself:

'Practise, try, think you can, smile, make it easier, join in and have a go, try try and try again, keep going.'

I continued the story, putting in their ideas as the story continued – *'Look he's having a go!'* Once Gerald had learnt to dance, the children talked again then said he felt:

'Amazed, good, enjoying it, happy, joy, delighted, much better, excited, overjoyed.'

I then talked about how this story relates to us all. The children talked about Gerald for the rest of the day:

'It was fun.'

'Fantastic you got to think about yourself.'

'I enjoyed it when he said he could do it.'

'I didn't like it when he was a fixed learner – better when he opened his mind.'

The impact was that the children started to talk about themselves as learners. I now have a 'stuck learner' wall with ideas.

Giraffes Can't Dance is one of many recommended books which encourage growth mindset thinking and can be used for classroom discussion. Some favourites listed on the Growth Mindset blog from the Mindworks website are:

- *The Dot*, by Peter Reynolds, tells of a child who believes she can't draw, but her teacher tells her to 'make a mark and see where it goes'.
- *Rosie Revere Engineer*, by Andrea Beaty, tells of a child who invents something that fails.
- *Ryan the Spy and : the SuperHero Secret*, by Jason Rago, talks about hard work and practice being the keys to success.
- *Cindersilly*, by Diana B. Thompson, is a non-traditional take on Cinderella in which she problem-solves her life.

Another teacher, Katie Walton from St Michael's C of E Primary School, wrote her own book, *I Can't Do This*, and self-published it. In her story the main character gets the better of his negative fixed mindset by adding the word '*YET*' to his thought '*I can't do this*'. The book is beautiful and can be obtained via her useful website www.growthmindset.org. I now see many teachers using the addition of **YET**, on posters and in what they expect children to say in response to something they don't know or can't do. In one classroom I visited, it was inspiring to hear children saying '*I don't know yet*' in response to a question, and having that response backed up by the teacher.

A Kentucky high school teacher asked her 17 year olds what 'yet 'meant to them in the context of their learning:

> ➤ 'To me "yet" means I don't have the skills and knowledge right now to accomplish what I want to, but if I stay focused I can gain these skills.'
>
> ➤ 'As a learner there are always concepts you have yet to come across and experiences you have yet to come. These "yets" are the border between the present and future and they are what will shape not only your knowledge but the person you will be.'
>
> Stephanie Harmon, Rockcastle County High School, Mt Vernon, Kentucky

Two teachers from Windhill Primary School in Hertfordshire, Phillipa Hampton and Kate Smith, created a videoclip of themselves in role as 'Madge (fixed) and Mildred (growth)' trying to build a Lego model, doing difficult versus easy sums and shooting in netball. The video is hilarious and very powerful in demonstrating the differences in approaches to the two mindsets. The teachers found this a very effective way of helping their children understand the mindsets.

One teacher of 10 year olds had introduced a 'learning journal' for the children to write their thoughts at the ends of lessons as they related to the mindsets. By looking at their comments, we have a real insight into what causes distress, how resilient they are, any patterns in their thinking and whether confidence develops over time. Figs 2.2 and 2.3 show excerpts from two children's journals.

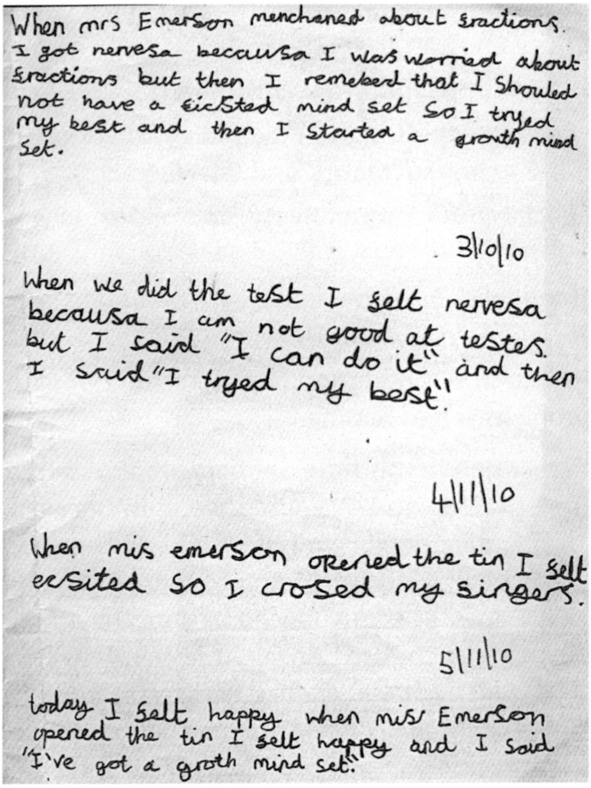

When mrs Emerson menchaned about sractions. I got nervesa becausa I was worried about sractions but then I remeberd that I shouled not have a eicsted mind set So I tryed my best and then I started a growth mind set.

3/10/10

When we did the test I selt nervesa becausa I am not good at testes. but I said "I can do it" and then I said "I tryed my best!"

4/11/10

When mis emerson opened the tin I selt ecsited so I crosed my singers.

5/11/10

today I selt happy when miss Emerson opened the tin I selt happy and I said "I've got a groth mind set."

Fig. 2.2 *Excerpt from a 10 year old's learning journal*

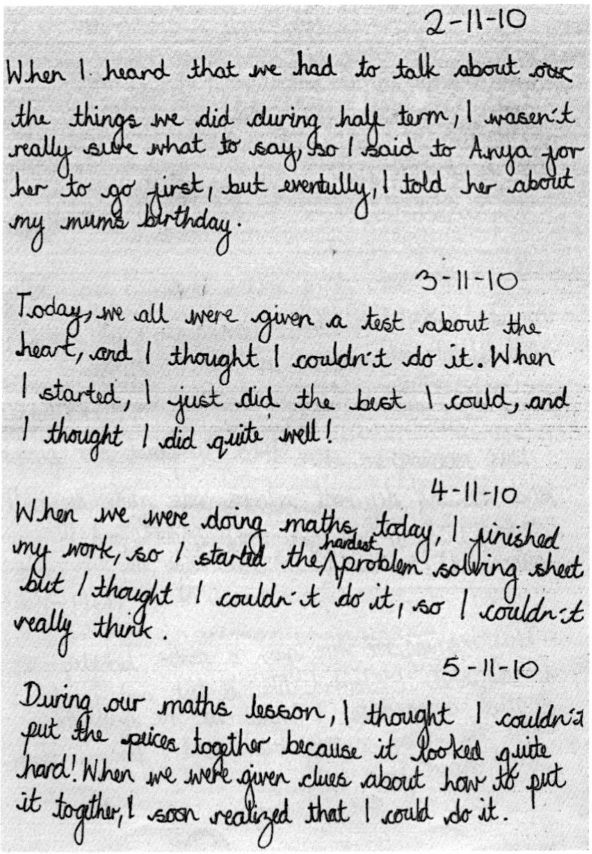

2-11-10

When I heard that we had to talk about our the things we did during half term, I wasen't really sure what to say, so I said to Anya for her to go first, but evertully, I told her about my mums birthday.

3-11-10

Today, we all were given a test about the heart, and I thought I couldn't do it. When I started, I just did the best I could, and I thought I did quite well!

4-11-10

When we were doing maths today, I sinished my work, so I started the hardest problem solving sheet but I thought I couldn't do it, so I couldn't really think.

5-11-10

During our maths lesson, I thought I couldn't put the peices together because it looked quite hard! When we were given clues about how to put it together, I soon realized that I could do it.

Fig. 2.3 *Excerpt from a 10 year old's learning journal*

The same teacher sent home a single sheet with a brief explanation about the mindsets and a comment box. Fig. 2.4 shows two examples of parent responses.

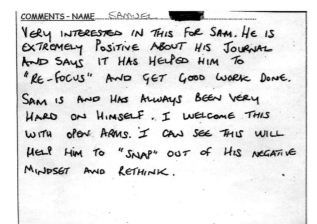
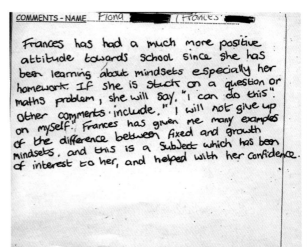

Fig. 2.4 *Parent views on the mindsets*

A high school teacher from Kentucky described how she kept the focus on the growth mindset after initial activities:

> After introducing the growth mindset over several activities (fixed vs growth statement cards to sort, ordering people for smartness, etc.), I was concerned about how to continuously incorporate the growth mindset in a content-based class without having mini-lessons daily. Each week I displayed a growth mindset quote from www.practicalsavvy.com (inspiring quotes reflecting the growth mindset), such as:
>
> *'Great works are performed, not by strength, but by perseverance.'* Samuel Johnson
>
> *'Anyone who has never made a mistake has never tried anything new.'* Albert Einstein
>
> *'Most of the important things in the world have been accomplished by people who have kept on trying when there seemed no hope at all.'* Dale Carnegie
>
> I asked them to discuss why the quote exhibited a growth mindset. At first there was minimal discussion so I underlined some key words then brought them altogether for a whole-class discussion. As the math lesson started and students were expected to be doing the practice, if any student wasn't working I would engage them in a conversation and refer to the quote to persuade them to make attempts. Students actually reminded me if I forgot to change the quote and looked forward to the new quote. They began to ask if they could get out cell phones and put quotes on social media.
>
> Holly Medley
> Washington County High School, Kentucky

Excellent 'growth mindset' posters can also be purchased through www.zazzle.com.

Children's voice

Children's comments give us great insight into the impact of our focus on growth mindsets:

➤ *'Fixed mindsets can keep you in your comfort zone – a growth mindset helps you to challenge yourself.'* Toby, aged 11

➤ *'I think the brain has grown allot since September, Because I've cracked my times tables!'* Hannah, aged 8

➤ *'I like lerning new things and lear form my mistacs.'* Bethan, aged 5

➤ *'I have learnt that I can achieve to the best of my ability, not focusing on what other people are doing, just what's best for me.'* Giorgia, aged 11

➤ *'Before I found out about growth mindset I used to think that I couldn't ever learn to read well but when my teacher told me that I could make my brain grow and learn more I had a go and it worked!'* Marcel, aged 11

➤ *'Sometimes I think it's the fixed mind people who are too bossy and always have to get their way.'* Girl aged 10

➤ *'I thought I'd be terrible at fractions but I persevered and practiced a lot and I've got so much better. I found out that I could do it if I asked for help, if I tried and believed that I could do it.'* Harvey, aged 11

Praise language

Perhaps the most significant aspect for the teacher in developing a growth mindset culture is to use praise language which focuses on achievement and effort, and to use encouraging growth mindset mantras which reinforce the message. Some examples of appropriate praise and encouragement language used successfully by teachers:

➤ *Well done! You're learning to… (do your buttons up/put in capital letters and full stops/ write persuasively…)*

➤ *Good – it's making you think – that's how you know your brain is growing!*

➤ *Every time you practise, you're making the connections in your brain stronger.*

➤ *You're good at things you like because you spend a lot of time doing them.*

➤ *If you could already do it or it was easy, you wouldn't be learning anything.*

➤ *Your skills have really improved. Do you remember how much harder this was last week/ last year?*

➤ *You kept going – well done!*

➤ *Don't say no – have a go!*

➤ *You mean you don't know YET!*

The first example, including the words *'You're learning to…'* is particularly important, because it implies that learning is a continuum rather than a job to be done and finished with. With closed skills you could argue that, once learnt, they are finally attained, but with open skills, such as those used in writing, information retrieval, reading, etc., to use the words *'I can…'* imposes a false ceiling for a skill which continually develops. Because of this, many schools have changed their *'I can…'* statements into *'I am learning to…'* or even *'I am beginning to…'* statements.

Parents

A common worry amongst teachers is that parents can all too often undermine the growth mindset thinking in what they say to children at home. Citing 'genetic' weaknesses in various subjects or being fixed mindset role models is inevitable. Where the growth mindset is truly embedded in a school and a constant feature of classrooms, children take it on regardless of their parents' attitudes. In fact I hear many stories of children correcting their parents and accusing them of having fixed mindsets. It is usually the case that each successive generation in some way educates the previous generation. Of course we should do what we can to convey an understanding of the mindsets to parents, but, in the end, it is the children who will encourage their parents to have growth mindsets because of their own convictions.

Teacher–student relationships

Remembering Hattie's effect-sizes, there is another element of education with a very high effect-size which, although not explicitly linked to the growth mindset, will make or break the impact of any development: teacher–student relationships (effect-size 0.72). This strikes a deep chord with me, as I'm sure it does with everyone who looks back on their secondary school experience. Children are highly tuned to the subtlest body language, tone or voice or words used by their teachers in decoding what their teacher thinks about them. Knowing whether your teacher appears to like you or not is a key factor in pupil achievement, let alone whether the teacher rates you as a learner. How many of us can remember, as if it were yesterday, those teachers who held eye contact, used our name and smiled when communicating with us? Those will be the teachers of the subjects you, unsurprisingly, did best at. So, along with a growth mindset, we should never forget that children are also at the mercy of our attitude towards them, not only as learners, but also as young people.

Creating a whole-school growth mindset culture

The ultimate goal, to create a school-wide growth mindset culture, has been achieved in many schools. We need to model our own growth mindsets both with children and as senior managers in schools. The growth mindset is often launched via a whole-school assembly. In one, the headteacher told the children he wanted to get into the Guinness Book of Records for peeling an apple, and sat at the front doing just that. When the peel broke off he asked if he should give up and the children all shouted out *'No! Keep trying!'* The strong message resulted in children across the school constantly referring back to the assembly when they faced a difficult task. Another headteacher starts every year by announcing which musical instrument he is learning to play this year and periodically demonstrates his progress, illustrating that he is setting himself a personal, difficult challenge each time. These are powerful examples of helping children to understand that the vision for everyone in a school is the same.

Setting up structures to support the growth mindset at the beginning of the year – such as revisiting the concepts, providing posters, checking praise language and so on – creates a school-wide approach. One idea is to have a letter for each child at the beginning of the year, along the following lines:

Dear.............

Welcome to Year 4! I am so excited to share the journey of this coming school year with you.

This year brings us all so many opportunities to grow and learn. We are all being challenged to have high expectations for ourselves. As your teacher, I will expect you to have high expectations for yourself and work as hard as you can to be the best you can be. I promise to have some goals for myself to reach too, so I can be the best teacher I can be.

Reaching your goals can be scary and sometimes frustrating, especially when you get stuck at something. It takes a very long time to become an expert and something that you are not yet so good at. In fact, scientists have proved that the only way to learn and become more intelligent is to try something new and work really really hard at it... even if you make a lot of mistakes.

Yes – I want you to make a lot of mistakes! In order to be successful you need to try something tricky, make mistakes, get feedback and then learn from that.

Remember – the worst mistake anyone can make is to be too afraid to make one...

I look forward to learning with you this year!

Three accounts of how a whole-school approach was achieved now follow: at an infant school, a primary school and a secondary school.

Case study 1: Growth mindset at Wescott Infant School

1. Assessment for Learning strategies, such as talking partners, the generation of success criteria, higher level questioning, self-assessment strategies, and *'tickled pink and green for growth'* marking, had been fully embedded across the school following staff training.

2. Stakeholders had recently reviewed the school vision, including the belief that 'Anything's Possible'.

3. Deputy Headteacher was inspired by Shirley Clarke's conference and felt Growth Mindset resonated with the new vision.

4. Growth Mindset made a priority on the School Development Plan.

5. Deputy Headteacher conducted further reading and research regarding Growth Mindset (Carol Dweck, Shirley Clarke, Matthew Syed and others).

6. Deputy Headteacher delivered training to staff (teachers and teaching assistants) to enable them to understand the concept of Growth Mindset and to develop a Growth Mindset in themselves.

7. Staff (teachers and teaching assistants) worked with a 'talking partner' to develop one performance management target to bring to their September performance management meeting.

8. Deputy Headteacher delivered training to staff (teachers and teaching assistants) to develop a Growth Mindset in children. Referred to Sutton Trust: *'The greatest strategy to improve performance is feedback'*.

9. Teachers analysed the mindsets of the children in their class using their own knowledge as well as suggested scenarios to identify children with Fixed Mindsets and Growth Mindsets.

10. Teachers able to target Fixed Mindset children using Growth Mindset children as role models. Staff discovered that Able, Gifted and Talented children often held a Fixed Mindset.

11. Staff created classroom displays and videos were shown to the children of incremental learners in other schools.

12. Staff experimented daily with praising for effort rather than achievement, and using the language of being brave, learning, challenge and valuing mistakes.

13. Staff encouraged children to be more independent and develop resilience when approaching tasks (see classroom poster displays – Figs 2.5 and 2.6).

14. Using the Growth Mindset checklist (see below), staff analysed how well a Growth Mindset culture had been established in their class and the impact on the children and their learning.

15. Growth Mindset culture extended to celebration assemblies where children shared new learning and a learning wall was developed.

16. Parent Information session delivered to develop parental understanding of how Wescott promotes a Growth Mindset and guidance as to how they can nurture this ethos at home through 'effort praise' and role modelling.

17. Fixed Mindset children recognised as a vulnerable group in whole-school tracking and discussed at half-termly pupil progress meetings.

18. Training session delivered to Governors to inform them of the impact of Growth Mindset on the children at school.

19. Growth Mindset culture embedded at Wescott and checklist used annually for reflection and review.

20. Next Step: support children to develop self-talk strategies when faced with challenging situations, such as assessments, new situations.

Celia Thatcher, Deputy Headteacher says: 'The growth mindset culture truly encapsulates our "Anything's Possible" motto for Wescott Infant School and has helped both staff and children consider learning in a different way. The children understand that in order to learn they must be brave and make mistakes and this allows them to tackle challenges they wouldn't have attempted before.

We truly believe a fixed mindset is a huge barrier to learning. A mindset can be changed whatever the age of a person, but the younger the child is when a growth mindset is fostered, the better the child's chance of success now and in later life.

The success of this culture is seen through the buzz in every classroom at our school, where both children and adults challenge themselves daily to progress and learn. Glass ceilings have been well and truly smashed...and anything really is possible!'

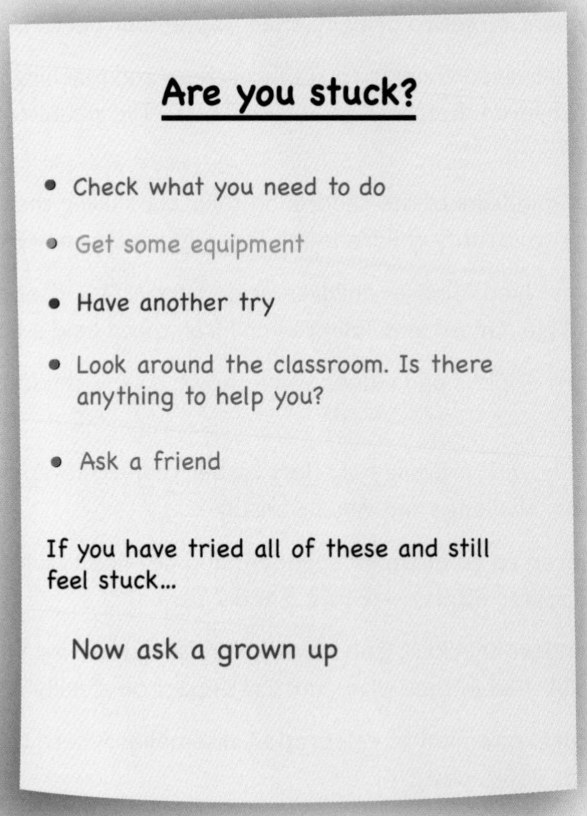

Are you stuck?

- Check what you need to do

- Get some equipment

- Have another try

- Look around the classroom. Is there anything to help you?

- Ask a friend

If you have tried all of these and still feel stuck...

Now ask a grown up

Fig. 2.5 'Are you stuck?' poster

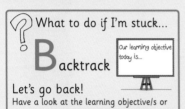

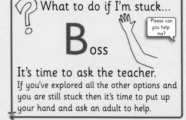

Fig. 2.6 *Six Bs, from Teacher's Pet website* www.tpet.co.uk: *reproduced with permission*

Suggested scenarios to use with younger children to establish whether they have a Growth Mindset or a Fixed Mindset

- Your teacher gives you some really hard work. What do you do?
- You find it difficult to throw and catch a ball in P.E., but your partner is really good. What do you do?
- You go to try out for a football team and the coach tells you that you are not good enough yet. What do you do?
- You paint a picture but it doesn't really look how you hoped it would. What do you do?
- Your mum tells you that you are moving house and will have to go to a different school. What would you do?
- You haven't learnt to read yet but your best friend is on books with words. What do you do?

Growth Mindset Checklist for teachers

Classroom:

This year.....

- Have you displayed your Growth Mindset display?
- Have you taught your children what is meant by an 'incremental learner' using Growth Mindset strategies captured on display?
- Do you regularly celebrate:
  - learning
  - challenge
  - brave choices
  - mistakes – and learning from them, e.g. 'Mistake of the week'?
- Do you regularly remind children of their targets or next steps? Do they know where to find them?
- Do you review the children's questions at the end of a topic to check they have covered all the learning (by use of a Question Wall or similar)?

Questions to ask your children:

What does 'learning' mean?

What does your teacher do to help you learn?

What has your teacher told you about incremental learners?

When does your teacher talk about challenge?

When do you work together to solve problems?

What does your teacher do to help you know what your targets/next steps are?

Fig. 2.7 *Some strategies for developing growth mindsets*

Case study 2: Implementing the teaching of growth mindsets at Ludworth Primary School

After being inspired, listening to Shirley Clarke describe Dweck's concept of mindset, I was eager to develop this with younger children. I wanted to develop a way of turning an abstract concept into something that was tangible and engaging.

Aims

To implement the direct teaching of growth mindsets across the whole school and develop a culture that supports and enhances learning.

Strategies used

Stages	Method
Stage 1	Initially, we piloted the teaching of growth mindset in Year 2: we were fortunate to receive funding for a small-scale research project that examined the impact of teaching the concept of growth mindsets to children who had been identified as gifted and talented. The study focused on six children and looked at their academic progress and attitudes to learning. The pilot created a buzz in school, with other teachers asking about it and noticing the difference in the children's attitudes.
Stage 2	The following year, we introduced the concept to the whole school in a staff meeting. The pilot enabled us to learn from our mistakes and create resources to use in staff meetings such as videoclips that were a powerful tool.
Stage 3	The initial staff meeting began by staff looking at Dweck's (2000) questionnaire *Implicit Theories of Intelligence Scale for Children*. Staff were asked to complete them independently and were then shown how to score them. The concept of growth and fixed mindsets was then introduced and the key features shared. The presentation was interspersed with videoclips of our children discussing the effects mindsets had on their learning. Following the staff meeting, the teachers then used Dweck's questionnaire with the older children and a modified version with the younger children. This data was then collated and tracked through the year alongside academic progress.
Stage 4	A follow-up staff meeting then focused on introducing the scheme of work to the staff and looking at clips of lessons. We placed emphasis on developing the teacher's role as a facilitator in learning.
Stage 5	Time was set aside for me to work alongside class teachers to team-teach and to support the implementation.
Stage 6	Our performance management objectives were linked to the implementation of the growth mindset work and lesson observations focused on how the children discussed their learning, challenged themselves and how teachers gave feedback which reinforced the concept.
Stage 7	All of the teaching assistants also received training about growth mindsets: this focused on how to give effective feedback and how they could effectively deliver this.
Stage 8	We ran an information evening for parents, which explained the concepts and how they could support their child at home.
Stage 9	Children were asked to complete the mindset questionnaire again and a selection of children from every year group were filmed being interviewed. We used a group of Year 6 children to interview others to enable the children to answer questions more openly.
Stage 10	Final staff meeting — an informal session, where the teachers shared what worked well for them and areas that they found more challenging or wanted to develop further. We shared ideas and supported each other. This information then fed back in to the scheme of work and how we would next develop the teaching of mindsets.

Resources used

- Videos of our children talking about mindsets and in lessons that we filmed.
- Carol Dweck's questionnaire *Implicit Theories of Intelligence Scale for Children*.
- Videoclips of Carol Dweck talking about mindsets.
- Data and evidence from our research project.
- Time to team teach and work in conjunction with colleagues.

Impact/Outcomes

- The mindsets of the children changed considerably and this had a very positive effect on their learning. *'I am going to develop my brain by thinking it is ok to make mistakes, you need to not cry and think of the work you did when you were younger and see what progress you have made.'* (Anne, aged 6)
- *'The school's strong focus on developing pupils' personal skills and independence through the "growth mindset" lessons has been significant in developing in pupils a real enjoyment of learning and a confidence to tackle any challenge that they encounter. These skills make a significant contribution to their outstanding achievement.'* (OFSTED Report 2013)
- Children choose to challenge themselves and each other rather than relying on the teacher. Children can be heard discussing how to challenge themselves – for instance, Nina (aged 6): *'I love a challenge in maths, I am going to try the tricky one next? Have you challenged yourself today, Sam?'*
- Children who had been identified as underperforming in school engaged more in learning and made greater progress. Generally children achieved 0.2 (in fine grades, which is almost a sub-level) more than their expected progress, but in some year groups this was greater.
- Staff worked as a team and went on the journey together, embracing the concept as they saw the effects on the children's learning.
- *'Working together as a staff enabled us to embed the concepts of mindsets across the whole school. Teaching mindsets opens a gateway for children to challenge themselves and learn from mistakes.'* (Denise Storey, Year 2 teacher)
- *'Embedding the concept of mindsets in the school culture allows everyone (staff and pupils) to become more effective at challenging themselves and embracing change.'* (Frank Earp, Year 5/6 teacher)

Plan for the future

- To continue to develop ways of embedding the concept further, focusing on the personalisation of effort.

Evaluation/Recommendations

- To pilot the teaching of mindsets in part of the school to provide evidence and videos about the effectiveness of the concept with children in your own school.
- To model your own growth mindset and make mistakes on a daily basis.
- To implement the concept slowly over time.
- To link it to your performance management/appraisal system and have it as a whole-school focus.

Developing Growth Mindset
Year 1 – one example from the scheme of work

Objective	Lesson	Resources	Evaluation

To identify characteristics of the different mindsets.
 	
To suggest ideas on how a character can develop a growth mindset
	Children to then watch a clip of Charlie and Lola 'Too many big words', available at www.bbc.co.uk/iplayer/episode/b00793rc/ Charlie_and_Lola_Series_2_Too_Many_Big_Words Watch up to 4:43mins.
	Ask the children to think and then talk to their talk partner to answer the following questions:-
	    – *How is Lola feeling?*
	    – *Have you ever felt like that?*
	Then in small groups ask the children to discuss:
	What they would say to Lola if they were Charlie?
	
	Plenary: Children to then feed back their ideas and discuss what would be the best thing to do. Teacher to scribe ideas for a display.
	Children to watch the end of the story and discuss if their ideas were similar.
		Charlie and Lola clip 'Too many big words'
		Growth mindset flipchart	

Katherine Muncaster www.feedyourbrainlearning.co.uk

Case study 3: Growth mindsets at Wickersley School and Sports College

What we did as a school

As a school we were interested in the idea of developing a growth mindset in our students. As a staff and as a leadership team, we were concerned that there is a growing tendency to 'spoon feed' our students. We want our students to be:

- Original thinkers
- Risk-takers
- Confident enough to make mistakes
- Willing to embrace challenge

We kept returning to a recent quote by author Philip Roth when he said:

'Your mistakes propel you forward'

To gather a picture of the current position, we conducted student voice activities across all year groups. To maximise the impact of what we wanted to achieve, we decided to use both pastoral and curriculum routes. The main strategies we introduced were:

Pastoral

- Launch-assemblies to all year groups on the idea of a 'growth mindset' – use of *YouTube* video on 'Taxi drivers' brains' to illustrate the point.
- Developed a programme of activities for use in form period time to build awareness and other practical strategies for students and teachers.
- Training of all form tutors.

Curriculum

- Curriculum change: growth mindset introduced into the Year 7 Integrated Studies course to specifically address the concept and build on the work completed in form period time.
- January–February 2012: curriculum audit planned to assess the extent to which teaching and learning provides challenge and encourages self-engagement.

Impact on learning as a result

The work on growth mindsets is still a work in progress, but we feel we are now making real progress. To have a full impact we feel it is advisable to address this in both pastoral and curriculum spheres. Measurable impacts at this stage:

- A recent survey indicated that a significant number of students (54%) know what is meant by a growth mindset and could give examples of how they could develop this.
- In a form period Monitoring, evaluation and review, one class was observed in a discussion about what they had done recently to demonstrate their own examples of how they are working towards a growth mindset.

Integrating meta-cognition

Learning 'powers'

Meta-cognition is the term used to describe learning about learning, or what learning consists of. The Sutton Trust research gives its use a potential gain of 8 months and 'high impact for low cost' as the verdict.

Hattie (2009) looked at 63 studies and deduced an effect-size of 0.69 for meta-cognition, making it extremely worthwhile. Hattie makes some interesting points about the nature of learning: that it is not as simple as surface learning, requiring more specific goals and deep learning necessitating more investigative learning. Sometimes the reverse might be true, depending on the learning involved, but his main point is that we should be developing 'overlearning', whatever the skill – such as happens when we learn to walk, master a language or a musical instrument – to help pupils achieve fluency in their learning. Hattie goes on to say:

❛When tasks are more complex for a pupil, the quality of meta-cognitive skills rather than intellectual ability is the main determinant of learning outcomes.❜

Another significant aspect, as always, is the language we choose to use with children and the values that are implied by that choice. Using the word *learning* instead of *work* is one example of this, changing the nature of the task in hand to something exciting and developing rather than tedious and difficult.

Over some years, teachers in my learning teams have found ways of helping children identify different learning 'muscles' or 'powers' so that the learning skills we are using can be discussed and developed in the same way that we would develop an academic skill. The growth mindset gives children the appropriate attitude and self-belief, but meta-cognition gives them the tools to be able to talk about and understand their learning, giving them a shared language and understanding. It is not enough to talk to children about effort, for example, without making it clear what it *means* to put effort into a task.

I have taken three well-known educationists whose individual lists of learning dispositions together seem to make a comprehensive whole, and synthesised these into one 'ideal' list of learning powers. The sources are Guy Claxton's learning dispositions, Art Costa's *Habits of Mind* and Chris Quigley's *Secrets of Success*. My final list is shown in Fig. 2.8, but could be added to as appropriate.

Teachers have used these categories in different ways, but always aiming for a 'split screen' approach, where the focused learning power has *equal status* to the knowledge or skill learning objective of the lesson. One of the most successful strategies has been to attach a 'character' to each of the eight categories, write a story for the character in which the various elements are explored, then use this story to introduce the particular learning power to the class. Teachers usually focus on one story a week, displaying the characters and their breakdown of skills, until all the categories are known. At that point the 'split screen' effect becomes meaningful, such as in Fig. 2.9.

Successful learning means...

Concentrate	Manage distractions Get lost in the task Do one thing at a time Break things down Plan and think it through Draw diagrams, jot down thoughts or things which help you think
Don't give up	Work hard Practise lots Keep going Try new strategies Ask for help Start again Take a brain break
Be cooperative	Listen to others Say when you don't understand Be kind when you disagree Explain things to help others Be tolerant
Be curious	Ask questions Notice things Look for patterns and connections Think of possible reasons Research Ask 'What if...?'
Have a go	Have a growth mindset Don't worry if it goes wrong Learn from mistakes Be excited to try new things
Use your imagination	Be creative Let your imagination go Think up new ideas and questions
Keep improving	Keep reviewing your work Identify your best bits Improve one thing first Try to be better than last time Don't compare yourself to others, only yourself! Take small steps
Enjoy learning	Feel proud of all your achievements Feel your neurons connecting! Imagine your intelligence growing by the minute! Use what you have learnt in real life Know you can do it if you have input and you practise

Fig. 2.8 *A breakdown of learning powers*

We are learning to:	We will use these learning powers:
• Arrange objects • Think about composition • Create 3D patterns	**Like Doris,** • Imagine what it will look like • Use lots of different resources **Like Krishna,** • Make plans • Change plans • Talk about ideas

Fig. 2.9 *Split-screen example*

Some approaches to introducing meta-cognition

Thameside Primary School teachers describe how they introduced meta-cognition to the whole school, linked with the growth mindset. Three of the character stories written for 4 and 5 year olds are included.

Foundation Stage

In Foundation Stage I developed eight characters which represent each of the different elements of being a successful learner. Each of these characters is introduced to the children through a simple story (three of which are seen below), designed to fit in with things relevant to the children (for example, a story about Deema the duck, as we are very close to the River Thames). I was also careful to give these characters multicultural names, as we have a range of children from different cultures and countries at school (the little Polish girl in my class really lit up when she realised one character had a Polish name!).

The children then had opportunities to learn about these animals through the week and colour in or draw their own pictures of the characters. We would discuss with the children different ways they could use each character to help them in school – for example, how they could have a go around the setting. The children would then be praised for the focus aspect of the week all week by all adults in the classroom and encouraged to use the words with each other. Once the children had learnt all eight elements of being a successful learner, for each lesson taking place, the adults and children would choose the characters they would particularly need to use in that lesson to help them learn. These characters would then be stuck to the board underneath the learning objective and success criteria to remind the children.

The children have really taken to these characters, with the children being very concerned when I borrowed two for a day! Comments from Foundation Stage pupils include:

• *'Kuba helps us to learn nicely.'* (Joshua, age 4)

• *'When Kuba's friends say does he want to play he says no because he's busy. He's concentrating.'* (Eva, age 5)

• *'The caterpillar works hard. He's ignoring the children playing.'* (Henry, age 4)

Key Stage 1

In Key Stage 1, I created an octopus with the children, and as we introduced each aspect on a Monday morning it would be written up onto one of the legs. In a similar way to Foundation Stage, the children would be encouraged to think of ways they could demonstrate this characteristic in school. Again these characteristics of effective learning would be emphasised over the course of a week, with every child being given praise at home time for a time in the day when they had demonstrated it successfully.

Once all eight aspects had been covered, the children then thought which aspects would be most useful to them in individual lessons and these were written on the board along with the learning objective and success criteria. At the end of each day the children were all given praise for something they had done well that day, and this would always be linked to the aspect of effective learning. For example: *'Well done, Isabella, you didn't give up in maths today, you are becoming a good learner.'* The praise always told the children what they had done well, made the children feel valued and at the same time reinforced that they need to continue doing these things.

Some comments from Key Stage 1 children include:

- *'If we don't have a go, how will we achieve things?'* (Orlando, age 7)
- *'It's the growth mindset octopus. You mustn't give up! If you give up you won't learn.'* (Mohammed, age 7)
- *'If you try something and get it wrong, you've still learnt something. You know what to do next time. Every class should have an octopus because it helps you know how to learn.'* (Eloise, age 7)

Key Stage 2

In Key Stage 2 the children first did a quiz to find out whether they had a fixed or growth mindset. The children then watched the video on *YouTube* about taxi drivers growing their brains and had a detailed explanation of fixed and growth mindset. The eight characteristics of effective learning were then introduced, one each week through a PowerPoint presentation, and the children were encouraged to link these to learning in lessons, as children did lower down in the school.

Whole School

At Thameside, as a SLT, staff and school we have been currently re-writing our school values and vision. We came up with a new motto of 'Use your brain' where **b** = *belonging*, **r** = *resilience*, **a** = *assurance*, **i** = *independence and integrity*, and **n** = *no limits*, following discussions about the skills we wanted children to leave Thameside with. Staff, parents, children and governors then thought about associated behaviours linked to these. Alongside Iain Gunn and the Headteacher, Helen Wallace, we then linked each of the eight aspects of effective learning into this vision, and we are now introducing a cohesive vision and learning culture at school.

Charlotte Rollinson
Foundation Stage Team Leader, Thameside Primary School

Learning characters

1. Concentrate, Kuba, caterpillar

Once upon a time there was a family of caterpillars – Mummy caterpillar, Daddy caterpillar and their son, Kuba the caterpillar. One day, Mummy caterpillar asked Kuba to go out and collect some leaves for dinner. As he set off he met his friend Tom, who wanted to go and play football. But Kuba said 'No, I need to collect my leaves'. A bit later, he met his cousin Kacper, who asked him to go to his house for lemonade, but again, Kuba said 'No, I have to collect leaves. I need to concentrate on what Mummy asked me to do.' When he had finished collecting leaves, he went home and told his Mummy what his friends had said. 'Well done Kuba for concentrating on what I asked you to do, now you have finished, you can go and play!'

2. Don't give up, Deema, duck

One sunny morning, Deema the duck was happily swimming along the river where she lived. The river was flowing very fast and her legs had to paddle very quickly under the water so she didn't get washed down the river! That morning, some children went with their teacher down to throw some bread to feed the ducks. All the other ducks were swimming nearer to the edge than Deema, and quickly gobbled up most of the bread before swimming away. Deema could see the children throwing bread, but the river was too fast for her to swim over. She tried to swim over three times, but each time she nearly got washed underneath the water! After that, she saw a rock nearby. She used all her energy to swim to the rock, then jumped over the fast flowing water to where the children were, and because they had seen how Deema hadn't given up they threw her some extra bread!

3. Be co-operative, Tim and Tina, tortoises

It was a stormy night, when Tim the tortoise went to visit his friend Tina. She was huddled up inside her shell on the seashore, shaking in the cold and rain. Tim was very upset when he saw his friend so sad. 'Why don't we build a hut before the thunder comes and we can shelter there together?' Tim said to Tina. 'I've already tried, and I can't manage,' Tina cried. But Tim ignored her and started to gather together some sticks. 'Please come and hold these together while I tie them', asked Tim, because he couldn't do it by himself, so Tina crawled over. Together they worked hard to build the hut and stayed there together in the warm while the thunderstorm went through the sky above them.

Using characters or creatures to embody the various learning dispositions without a story is another common strategy, seen in the posters in Figs 2.10 and 2.11.

Resourcefulness

Sensible Squirrel is a resourceful questioner.

Hello, I'm Sensible Squirrel.

I am very resourceful. I try to find things out for myself and make good use of resources to support my learning.

I make connections with prior learning and this helps me to learn new things. I have a step by step approach to my learning.

- I use pictures in my head to support my thinking.
- I am confident to ask questions.
- I like to go exploring for the answers and love using the computer and books to increase my knowledge and understanding.

Fig. 2.10 *Resourcefulness character*

Reciprocity

Hi – We are Team Ant.

We can work independently and we are also good team players.
We can put ourselves in someone else's shoes and show empathy.
We like to congratulate others on their ideas and we are good listeners.

Team Ant are team players.

- I'm a good listener.
- I like working in a team.
- I can work independently.

Fig. 2.11 *Reciprocity character*

Some schools focus on the learning powers or 'muscles' without the characters, so posters with captions such as *'I'm using my questioning muscle'* or *'I'm using my perseverance muscle'* are common features in the classroom.

Once the dispositions are known, teachers usually take one of the posters/ characters/lists displayed to place on the whiteboard alongside the learning objectives of the lesson, day or week and that is referred to during the lesson. Some teachers ask children which learning power they think best fits the skill they are focusing on for that lesson.

A high school teacher from Kentucky described her approach:

> I gave the students a copy of the Successful Learning sheet with the eight learning powers. We discussed each and how they relate to learning. Students nominated characters to represent each, mainly Disney characters, which seem to fit every category! We then had an election to choose the representative for each. Next, we chose one power to focus on for the remainder of the year. Because of our continuing work with talk partners, we chose to focus on being cooperative. Each time students work with partners, in groups or sharing of any kind, I reminded them of the success criteria for being cooperative. I would hear them sometimes reminding each other when necessary. I noticed students made progress in the area of communicating with

> their partners. They also got better at explaining to one another, using vocabulary and diagrams, etc. Many students who did not normally speak were much more comfortable talking to a partner. Some were more confident in their explanations and ability.
>
> Rita Messer, Washington County High School, Kentucky

Another high school teacher asked students to reflect on the focused learning power of the day in a journal:

> **How does the Learning Power 'keep improving' relate to the work you have completed today?**
>
> ➤ *'I didn't judge my answer off someone else's. I worked by myself and took it one step at a time.'*
>
> ➤ *'It reminds you to keep reviewing your work and to identify the best bits and to improve only one thing and to not compare yourself to others.'*
>
> Stephanie Harmon, Rockcastle County High School, Mt Vernon, Kentucky

Mixed-ability learning

The evidence

For many years studies have concluded that ability grouping, still very common in the UK, is detrimental to the progress of most pupils and has a direct impact, usually negatively, on their mindset. When children are grouped by ability, expectations placed upon them tend to be fixed and children's achievement is matched to those expectations. Given the opportunity to explore higher-level learning, children often surprise their teachers by surpassing previous expectations. Being on a 'lower-ability table' results in negative self-belief. Being on a higher-ability table is more likely to result in complacency and a fixed mindset, with a fear of failure.

Hattie's meta-analysis looked at 500 studies on ability grouping and resulted in an effect-size of 0.12 – a very low impact on pupil achievement. The Sutton Trust (2011) stated:

The evidence is consistent that though there may be some benefits for higher attaining pupils in some circumstances, these are largely outweighed by the negative effects on attitudes for middle and lower performing learners.... the evidence is robust and has accumulated over at least 30 years of research.... If schools adopt mixed ability, they are more likely to use inclusive teaching strategies and to promote higher aspirations for their pupils.

Advice by Ed Baines (2012) was that:

> *Greater use should be made of peer co-learning, since these approaches can enhance the learning of all pupils.*

Stigler and Hiebert, in their inspirational book *The Teaching Gap* (1999), outline the differences between high-achieving Japanese classes and comparatively lower-achieving American classes. One of the key differences was that US teachers (and many UK teachers) see mixed ability as a problem, whereas Japanese teachers see mixed ability as a gift. Individual differences are seen as beneficial for the class because they produce a range of ideas, methods and solutions that provide the material for pupils' discussion and reflection.

Mixed-ability seating

The standard configuration of classroom furniture in UK and US primary schools has been, for many years, groups of four or six children sitting around a table. This, in itself, has encouraged teachers to group children according to ability, for literacy and numeracy lessons especially. Some teachers, however, have their classroom arranged with a U-shape of tables around the perimeter of the room, then rows of tables across the middle (see Fig. 2.12a). This means that all children can face the front but also have a talk partner beside them. Another model is lots of two single-metre tables making an arrow shape (see Fig. 2.12b), with two children at each table, so that the children can talk as pairs or a four and the teacher can talk to any child face to face in the space between the tables. More space is needed for this arrangement.

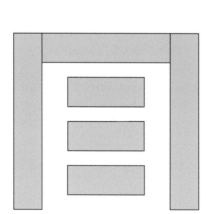

Fig. 2.12a *U-shape with rows*

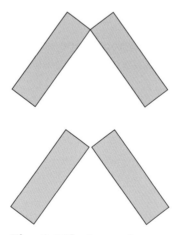

Fig. 2.12b *Arrow shapes*

Talk/learning partners

Talk partners make mixed-ability teaching and learning fall into place. By changing talk partners randomly once a week, or every two or three lessons in secondary, over the course of a year children have a rich experience of different learning partners, all learning from one another in different ways (see Chapter 4 for more detail about mixed-ability talk partners). Literacy is mainly differentiated by outcome, meaning that children can all work at the same task or be drawn off for 'mini-lessons' whereas *mathematics* has been the main area of concern when teachers consider moving to mixed ability.

Mixed ability and mathematics

There are various pieces to the jigsaw of what seems to be the answer to mixed-ability mathematics teaching, all of which are outlined throughout this book, but, in summary, they consist of:

- A growth mindset culture, in which learning from one another is seen as a privilege and a valuable asset;
- A starting-point task to judge current competence and understanding;
- A basic maths skill taught to the whole class and the success criteria gathered;
- Practice of the skill with differentiated challenges (mild, spicy, hot, for instance – see Fig. 2.13) which children can choose from, moving up or down if the fit is not appropriate;
- Much discussion, both as a class and with individuals as they are involved in their learning, about the processes involved;
- In some lessons, pupils writing their own individual success criteria then one or two randomly discussed at the visualiser for 'best bits' and 'even better if…'. This probes the clarity of children's understanding by looking at how well they can explain the steps involved. A 'why' column is often added to the success criteria at this stage, so that children have to say *why* the step is made (e.g. first step in finding percentages is to divide the whole number by 100: this is because we are finding what 1% is). More detail is included in Chapter 6, on success criteria.

One teacher wrote to me about her Year 6 (11-year-old) pupils after changing to mixed ability in mathematics:

> *'In January only 50% of the children were on target to make satisfactory progress. By May, after mixed-ability learning, with three differentiated challenges given each lesson, the picture had very much changed: 36% of the children were Level 5+, with 15% of the children attaining Level 6.'*
>
> Liza Craggs, Tannerswood School, Herts

Level 4 is the government expectation for most 11 year olds, so this meant that Liza's pupils were attaining at the average level of a 13 or 14 year old. I know that test results are not the most important aspect of formative assessment, just a by-product of it, but it is useful to have some measurement which can indicate progress. The key to mixed ability appears to be *(a)* children operating as resources for one another, *(b)* having an established growth mindset culture, and *(c)* the skill of the teacher in making sure all are appropriately challenged.

Seamus Gibbons detailed for me exactly how he teaches mixed-ability maths lessons:

> '*I don't decide before the lesson who will do what and what they will achieve. I always spend some time trying to find out where they already are in their understanding, in terms of John Hattie's "phases of how we learn" – from novice to capable to proficient. Once I have that, I look one level above and think what the children could do so they can all move up a level from their own starting point. For example, in chunking for division, it would be very easy for me to think "OK, my Level 1s and 2s can sit in a group and share some cubes, Level 3s can do some arrays and circle them, and my Level 4s can do some chunking." Little learning happening. Instead we all did chunking. I found out what they could all do first by giving them a task. I walked around and found that Level 2s could subtract really well but were getting stuck with 6, 7 and 8 times tables. So I differentiated their task to support them with this. I realised that Level 3s had no understanding of what a remainder was, so this was supported. Level 4s used chunking with decimals. By the end of the week they had all learnt chunking and had all moved on in their learning.*'

Seamus's differentiated challenges for a percentages lesson for 11 year olds can be seen in Fig. 2.13. Notice the first level is practising the skill, the next level involves more calculations, and the highest level involves application of the skill in some problems. Many teachers are designing challenges like these and then working with children to see what they need to have developed. Rather than deciding in advance what the children should do, decisions are made as a result of continually finding out how they currently understand the skill or concept.

VIDEOCLIP TASTER #3 Introducing challenge choices for mathematics

After practice and discussion about finding percentages, Seamus introduces the three differentiated challenges.
http://bit.ly/1mQ5jgh

Mild!

Find percentages of these numbers:

a) 4% of 400
b) 9% of 500
c) 8% of 800
d) 23% of 500
e) 37% of £900
f) 64% of £300
g) 39% of £1,300
h) 53% of 5,200
i) 18% of 540

Spicy!

Find these percentages:

a) 22% of 700
b) 69% of 1,400
c) 57% of 520
d) 18% of 66
e) 46% of £70
f) 78% of £64
g) 49% of 1.2kg

Which is greater? How do you know?

a) 34% of 500 or 41% of 600?
b) 67% of 210 or 72% of 220?
c) 92% of 640 or 84% of 790?
d) 95% of 570m or 81% of 610m?

HOT!

Are the following statements true or false? How do you know?

a) 34% of 500 is greater than 42% of 600.
b) 69% of 390 is less than 71% of 450.
c) 93% of £2,400 is more than 87% of £2,900.
d) 79% of 39 is less than 69% of 46.
e) 49% of 46 is the same at 51% of 48.

Answer the following:

1. A coat is on sale. The original price of the coat is £450. It has a 34% reduction. What is the new cost?
2. A puppy costs £220. The owner has said if you buy 2, you can have a 28% discount. How much will 2 puppies cost?
3. Entrance to Chessington is £22. Masum has a voucher which will get him a 61% discount. How much does Masum pay?
4. Year 6 go to a restaurant for a meal. The meal costs £162. The waiter adds a 17.5% service charge to a bill. How much is the service charge? How much does the bill now cost?

Fig. 2.13 *Differentiated challenge choices*

Children's thoughts

The last word from some 11 year old children, articulate enough to say what they are feeling, but expressing sentiments felt by many children of all ages about ability grouping:

➤ *'I like choosing which level of work to do because you can make it harder for your brain or start off easier to get more confident first.'*

➤ *'I feel happier with no groups. Some people were unhappy because they were in the bottom group and they felt that they were labelled and couldn't choose what to do.'*

➤ *'I like not being in a group, because when you're in a lower group you think you're not clever enough.'*

➤ *'In groups you can't learn anything new, because you sit with the people that know as much as you know.'*

Postscript

Seamus found that, after a while, the growth mindset was so embedded that children were all trying to do the 'hot' challenge because they didn't want to be seen to be not pushing themselves. He is currently experimenting with a slightly different approach: the three challenges are called 'The Amazing Challenge', 'The Incredible Challenge' and 'The Fantastic Challenge' or similar. The challenges are still differentiated, but they change their position, so one day the amazing challenge might be the hardest one, the next it might be the easiest one. So far, this has led to the children having to carefully look at the maths to decide which challenge to choose....

Summary

As the basis of the ideal learning culture, therefore, we need to consider:

- **Developing a growth mindset for all**
  - Successful learners have a growth mindset
  - Comparative rewards reinforce a fixed mindset
  - Praise needs to focus on effort and achievement, not ability
  - Student/teacher relationships are key to pupil success
- **Integrating meta-cognition, or 'learning powers' which give children the tools to identify and extend their learning skills**
  - Characters for each power, especially those chosen by children, make the concepts more accessible
- **Organising mixed-ability learning**
  - Mixed-ability learning is more inclusive
  - The seating arragement in classrooms can obstruct collaborative learning
  - Random talk partners which change weekly make mixed ability work
  - Many teachers offer children a range of differentiated challenges in mathematics

This forms the foundation upon which the bricks of formative assessment are built – an empowering, dynamic learning environment in which pupil self-belief is maximised and pupils know how to use their learning skills.

3 Involving children at the planning stage

Formative assessment is essentially about pupils being actively involved in their learning, so their input into it needs to start before lessons begin, at the planning stage. The convention has been to exclude pupils from any real thinking about the context for their learning, even though the context is what tends to be the main source of motivation. Teachers in many countries are statutorily bound to aim for coverage of certain skills, but contexts for those skills are mainly very broad. Knowledge content might be dictated here and there, but exactly how this would be taught and learnt has always been up to teachers.

Over some years, teachers in my teams have experimented with ways in which pupils can be involved in planning, and this continues to evolve. What is clear, however, is that structured involvement increases their motivation and leads to higher achievement.

There appear to be five main ingredients in maximising the impact:

1. **Finding out what they already know or can do**
2. **For most subjects, some kind of immersion in the subject matter**
3. **Presenting the main skills to be covered**
4. **Asking for their ideas about how to learn those skills**
5. **Involving parents**

As always, the strategies to fulfil these principles vary according to the age of the children, so this chapter is very practical, with many examples of successful inclusion at the planning stage.

1 Finding out what they already know or can do

Establishing current understanding is a running theme with formative assessment, not just at the planning stage, but at the beginning of every lesson and as a permanent quest throughout lessons. As Ausubel et al (1978) said:

The most important single factor influencing learning is what the learner already knows. Ascertain this and teach him accordingly.

A number of strategies have emerged, as follows, all of which go far beyond simply asking children *'What do you already know about…?'* – a question which inevitably produces many random thoughts and no clear idea of what is really understood.

Breaking down the subject (good for history, geography and science topics) involves creating a list of elements of the topic then systematically asking what children already know about each. Talk partner discussions followed by whole-class feedback yield enough information to give teachers a feel for the appropriate pitch they will need to take. Most feedback from teachers indicates that, by asking the right kind of questions, they have realised that children often know more than they had expected, requiring a rethink of the level to aim at.

Example: For a topic on a period in history, list about six major aspects – the elements you would probably have covered, including key people, events, inventions or discoveries, home life, transport, etc. Ask what they already know about each of these.

VIDEOCLIP TASTER #4 Prior knowledge discussion

Alice splits the theme of ladybirds into four aspects for her class of 6 year olds to show what they already know. http://bit.ly/1hHoC5V

Breaking down the subject via learning objectives (good for all subjects, but especially mathematics) involves listing the learning objectives to be covered, in an accessible form, and asking what they already know about each of these. Don't assume anything, even with new vocabulary, as there are often surprises. One teacher of 8 and 9 year olds listed five fractions objectives in the order she would have taught them, but discovered that the children knew more about some of the supposedly higher-order objectives than the lower.

Listing the vocabulary (good for all subjects) involves making a list of key vocabulary and finding out children's understanding of their meanings. The words can be made into cards and given out for paired and group discussion. One teacher gave the class 36 words about World War 2 (e.g. Nazi, Luftwaffe, etc.) and asked the children how the words could be grouped. They discussed these and explained each word according to their current understanding.

Exploring the resources (good for maths and especially science) involves giving children the resources and either asking what they can discover or do with them or setting a specific *'Can you …'* task. Watching and listening reveals much of their current understanding. One teacher gave children magnets and metals and discovered that they already knew words such as *repel* and *attract*. Another teacher gave out circuit resources and saw again how far they appeared to understand electricity.

Giving a question to answer or a problem to solve (good for maths, science and literacy) involves giving a question which will get the children thinking and discussing (e.g. *True or false? – electricity buzzes around us/you can see electricity/electricity flows through wires*) or demonstrating a skill (e.g. *The average of 5, 6 and 7 is a prime number. Do you agree or disagree?*).

Starting with a picture, object, video, visit, etc. (good for all subjects) involves inviting discussion about what it is, what they see, what they want to find out, etc. A picture with a statement is particularly useful with younger children (e.g. a picture of an insect with the statement *'This is a bird – agree or disagree?'*)

2 For most subjects, some kind of immersion in the subject matter

Asking children what they would like to learn is very difficult when they have very limited knowledge of the subject in hand. Many schools now have 'immersion' afternoons or sessions in which children are given multi-sensory experience of the subject in a short time, so that they have a basis from which to draw their questions and interests. A topic on India, for instance, began with various stalls set out in the hall for children to experience tasting food, listening to music, looking at photographs, watching video, trying on saris and henna hand-painting. A topic on World War 2 began with a visit to a museum, and a focus on poetry began with hearing and reading all styles of poetry and a recital.

3 Presenting the main skills to be covered

This had been the missing piece of the jigsaw for some time, as there was still a problem with children coming up with two years' worth of ideas for a topic and too many ideas focusing on art or literacy. Everything changed when teachers started to present children with the key skills to be covered for the theme, as children's ideas now had to be restricted to specific skills. Examples 1 to 9, on pages 50–55, show how pupils have been involved in planning their learning.

4 Asking for children's ideas

Feedback from teachers shows that children often come up with ideas which are more interesting and meaningful to them than ideas from teachers. It is also advisable to remain flexible throughout a unit of work, as children's interests develop as the subject is explored. As long as the skills are covered, the content can be manipulated, with more time spent on one thing than another, for instance.

5 Involving parents

Parents represent an often untapped body of knowledge, expertise and contacts. One school became fully aware of this when they took part in the National Gallery 'Take a picture' project. A letter was sent home to parents with the picture asking for their ideas for activities. Their responses exceeded expectations (see Fig. 3.1), with a wealth of suggestions, offers of help and many experts offering to give demonstrations, donate materials or give contacts of friends who were artists. Simply informing parents of the coverage for a half-term is not the same as asking for their ideas.

'Take a Picture' Fortnight, Summer Term

Picture of 'On the Beach' by Degas

As we are involving our pupils more in planning their learning, we would also like to involve our parents more in suggesting ideas. We will be linking our work to a painting by Degas entitled 'On the Beach'. Any part of the picture can be used for inspiration. I would particularly like to focus on different Art/ DT skills as well as English and Science. We are very keen to build on the children's interests and develop their skills through what they would like to really learn about, across a range of subjects. The children have already given me some fantastic ideas. If you feel that you have any interesting ideas/ artifacts/contacts, etc., please note them below and return it into class if possible by May 13th.

Don't be afraid to 'think outside the box'.

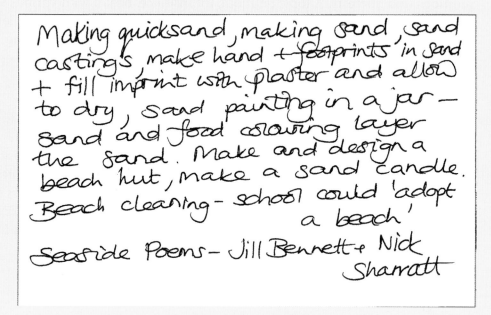

Making quicksand, making sand, sand castings, make hand + footprints in sand + fill imprint with plaster and allow to dry, sand painting in a jar – sand and food colouring layer the sand. Make and design a beach hut, make a sand candle. Beach cleaning – school could 'adopt a beach'

Seaside Poems – Jill Bennett + Nick Sharratt

Many thanks, Mrs Wells

Fig. 3.1 *Parent planning suggestions*

Examples of practice

The following examples illustrate the practice and impact of involving pupils at the planning stage.

Example 1

The summer half-term topic for our whole school was the Olympics. Immersion consisted of whole-school interactive assemblies, visits from Olympians and videoclips.

In Foundation Stage we made an A2 grid with visual images of the areas around our classrooms: construction, graphics, maths, role play, outside, painting, malleable and discovery, and discussed our learning targets for those areas. The children then discussed their ideas with talk partners for the different areas.

The children came up with fantastic, creative ideas, many of which were similar to ours, but they had far more (see Fig. 3.2). We had spent 3 hours as teachers preparing ideas, whereas the children had suggested all these within 20 minutes!

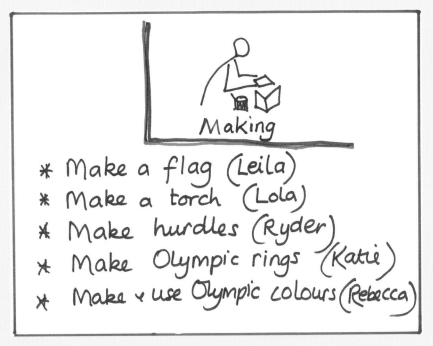

Making

* Make a flag (Leila)
* Make a torch (Lola)
* Make hurdles (Ryder)
* Make Olympic rings (Katie)
* Make & use Olympic colours (Rebecca)

Fig. 3.2 *Five-year-old children's ideas for Olympics topic*

The impact:

- Children are more focused and on task when using the provision areas
- All activities are attempted because they were their ideas, especially boys in the creative areas
- The quality of work is of a higher standard
- Behaviours and attitudes are improved

Charis Fletcher, St Nicholas Primary School

Example 2

At the end of the spring term I asked children to write their thoughts or questions on a class whiteboard about castles, our learning journey for the summer term.

At the start of the summer term we had a 'real knight' (www.thehistoryman.org.uk) visit for the day. He brought a cannon and a huge variety of artifacts, etc., for children to experience.

The following day I asked the children to say what they now wanted to learn about castles. They suddenly had a mass of 'deep' questions which showed real thought and interest.

> **Questions before immersion day:**
>
> *Why did they have castles?*
>
> *What were the names of the parts of the castle?*
>
> **After immersion day:**
>
> *How dark were the dungeons?*
>
> *How does gunpowder work?*
>
> *What happens if it rains and the gunpowder gets wet?*
>
> *Why is there no roof over the castle?*

Example 3

A class of 7 year olds explored toys, tried to make one of their own, then, given the skills coverage, co-constructed the plan shown in Fig. 3.3.

Skills	What would **you** like to learn?
• Write a character description	Batman　　　Spiderman Buzz Lightyear　　Jessie
• Write a letter	To Tom the class puppet To a character from a film or story To Father Christmas
• Make a graph	Favourite superheroes Toys we like
Find out about • You and your family' history • Children long ago	Did children play with cars? What puzzles and games did they play? What did children play with in 1666?
• Sketch by looking carefully	Draw cars and helicopters Draw teddies and transformers
• Make something with parts that move	Make a car Make a Dogger with parts that move Make small toys for our big toys

Fig. 3.3 *Skills linked with ideas planned by 7 year olds*

Example 4

Another teacher of 7 year olds described how the World Cup theme had initially focused on geographical aspects of the countries involved, but the children wanted to find out about their flags and the stories behind them. This led to exploration of the George and the Dragon myth. By following children's interests, they had asked more questions than ever before, there were more interesting discussions, boys were more involved and children were more engaged, bringing in things from home and doing homework.

Example 5

A teacher of 7 year olds involved the children in an art topic:

What did I do?

Our class theme for the term was 'Food, Glorious Food'. I wanted the children to plan their own art activities for this unit, based on their own interests and by choosing examples of famous 'food art' that could inspire their own work. The first lesson of the unit involved sharing with the class several images of food-inspired art from different periods. We discussed each in turn and shared our opinions. I then shared the key skills with the class and told them that these were the things that they needed to practise and learn over the next few weeks in art lessons. Talk partners were asked to share ideas, using their favourite food-art images, of what they would like to do and make. The children came up with many ideas, which we linked to the skills as we talked. The most popular idea was to make their own versions of 'food faces' in the style of Giuseppe Arcimboldo. This covered several of the skills that the children would need to learn. The second most popular idea was an Andy Warhol-style food packaging picture, with four colourful images of their favourite foods. The children's ideas collected in this session were organised into a unit of work for them to begin the following week. They were also given homework, related to their ideas, which would prepare them for the sessions ahead.

Fig. 3.4 *Food-art examples*

What was the impact?

- Children were excited and enthusiastic about all the activities
- Excellent standard of art work (see Fig. 3.4)

- Children felt ownership of the lessons
- A good understanding of the skills as starting point
- Child-led learning
- Building confidence

How do I know?

- The children's engagement in lessons is evident in the quality of the art they produced.
- The processes that we used (for the Warhol pictures, in particular) are something that I had only previously attempted with Year 4 children, but the Year 2 class really enjoyed the challenge, confidently approaching new skills in the context of their own activities.
- The children could make links between themselves as artists and the famous artists we viewed in the first session, which had a visible impact on their confidence. The children began to see themselves as 'artists' through knowing that their imaginative ideas were used.
- The children were able to talk about their activities in detail and relate back to key skills.
- The confidence of the more hesitant artists improved as they approached activities and ideas that they already knew about because they had a part in their invention.

Example 6

The class of 8 year olds, who had been involved in an 'India' immersion session, followed this up by co-constructing a class chart (Fig. 3.5). The teachers first made sure children understood the key skills, then spent a morning getting children to discuss with talk partners, then in fours, then whole-class, ways in which these skills could be developed.

Key skills	What do you want to learn?	How do you want to learn it?
To compare	➤ Spices	Cooking and food tasting
	➤ Sports	Playing Indian and English sports
To describe	➤ Landscapes	Painting landscapes
	➤ Clothes	Dressing up and fashion show
To use sources of information	➤ Places	Watching the clips of different places and using the internet
	➤ Religion	Researching and making things to do with festivals
To empathise	➤ Poor children	Acting and write a diary
	➤ Lifestyle	Interviews and debates
To explain why things happen	➤ Henna	Find out why people use henna and design and make our own
	➤ Weather	Weather and news report

Fig. 3.5 *Pupil planning for an 'India' topic*

Example 7

Remembering the teacher of 11 year olds who gave 36 words about World War 2 for them to discuss, the children were then asked to write a question each that they would like answered during the topic. This was whittled down to five class questions:

- Who was Hitler and why was he so mean?
- What was it like inside an Anderson shelter?
- How were children treated differently? (Evacuation, Hitler Youth, Jewish children)
- What military equipment was used in Britain?
- Who was involved in WW2 and why?

Children controlled the direction of the topic, giving them more ownership and therefore more motivation and enthusiasm.

Example 8

A languages teacher gave 14 year olds, in threes, the scheme of work she used, with three columns: *key knowledge/key skills/activities.* Students came up with activity ideas, and a visual display was produced by each group. The impact was that more students were on task, more focused, more cooperative, doing more homework and getting higher grades. This work led to students asking to lead lessons, another popular way of involving students in the planning and teaching.

Example 9

Some teachers involved students in planning for their final GCSE modules, asking them what they wanted to cover in the remaining four weeks. Teachers asked, *'Where do you feel less confident? What do you want to improve? What do you want to know or find out? How will we do this?'* The impact was a huge increase in confidence, independence and ownership.

Finally, some children's comments illustrate the impact of their involvement:

➤ *'When we choose our own topic we are really interested in it.'* 6 year old
➤ *'Sometimes Mrs. Brown doesn't know the answer so we find things out together.'* 6 year old
➤ *'It makes me think of good questions to ask.'* 7 year old
➤ *'I felt so proud when we did my idea.'* 7 year old
➤ *'You are helping us to learn what we want to learn.'* 8 year old
➤ *'It's brilliant to decide our curriculum, which makes us happy with our work because of having a choice.'* 10 year old

Summary

In order to fully involve children as active learners, we need to enable them to co-construct the planning of units. This enhances their motivation, their independence and their confidence in tackling new learning.

The elements are:

• Finding out what they already know or can do

• For most subjects, some kind of immersion in the subject matter

• Presenting the main skills to be covered

• Asking for their ideas about how to learn those skills

• Involving parents

4 Talk and talk partners

So far the foundations of the appropriate **learning culture** and **involving pupils in planning** have been outlined, with now only one more component left in setting the scene for effective learning and formative assessment: talk partners. The traditional classrooms where children only spoke when their hand was up and carried out all their learning in silence have hopefully long gone. We know the importance of discussion and learning from others, in a world where knowledge and excellence are increasingly shared rather than kept to oneself as evidence of one's own personal achievement. *Talk partners, response partners, learning partners* and *snowballing* are some of the terms which describe pupils discussing together, planning together, cooperatively improving each other's learning together.

The evidence

Classroom discussion is ranked seventh in John Hattie's list of influences on learning, with an effect-size of 0.82 calculated as the result of analysis of 42 studies. Pie Corbett's work on children's writing has 'Talk for Writing' as its description, illustrating the central position of talk in the construction of written language. Working in mixed-ability pairs which change often is a key ingredient of the process of writing – cooperatively discussing and improving each other's writing, looking at one book at a time. Robin Alexander carried out various projects throughout the UK focused around 'dialogic talk', culminating in his publication *Towards Dialogic Teaching* (2004). In this, he described talk in its many forms – not only talk between pupils but also, critically, the quality of our responses to what children say.

The emergence of talk partners was a direct result of the studies which showed that not enough 'wait time' (Rowe, 1974) was given for children to answer questions. The 'hands up' culture also excluded many children from thinking and was reinforcing fixed mindsets. Talk partners allow children not only time to think after a question is asked, but a chance to articulate their thinking (e.g. *'You have 30 seconds to talk to your talk partner about that question'*). A common consequence is that children, not surprisingly, write more after having more time to rehearse their thinking out loud. Although the social impact of talk partners is significant, the learning impact, although more subtle, is greater. If the partners are chosen randomly and they change every week (or every two or three lessons in secondary), children have a rich diet of different learning partners over the course of a year. If paired with a lower achiever, children are often *explainers*, a higher-order skill which deepens their own learning, and are often surprised by the quality of the verbal contributions a lower achiever might make:

> 'The impact has been that children now recognise that all children have ideas and talents. One boy never spoke in front of others and now he can't be stopped! The others used to think he was a lower achiever and were patronising to him at first when he got a question right – they all clapped. Now they respect his ideas and are all so supportive of each other.'
>
> Teacher of 6 year olds

> 'Two talk partners were working on counting-in-5s questions that they had generated. One boy noticed that his partner had made some mistakes, so he pointed out that he thought she might have missed a part of the success criteria. He then talked her through the process, which enabled her to complete the task and he also noticed a mistake of his own during the process.'
>
> Teacher of 6 year olds

If paired with a higher achiever, children have opportunities to learn which they might never have had if placed with a 'matched' partner. The random pairing has further benefits: apart from the much appreciated fairness, children are often paired with someone the teacher would not believe would be a best fit. This takes children out of their comfort zone and challenges them to work on their weaknesses. Two shy children, for instance, have to start to talk and two talkative children have to learn to listen. Children learn tolerance, negotiation and cooperation skills – all vital life skills. Children for whom English is a second language are superbly supported when placed in a three, and children with speech and language difficulties can have their first breakthroughs as a result of talk partners:

> 'After 3 weeks of talk partners in Year 2 a child who had been an elective mute for two years turned to her partner and said, 'Well actually, I think…' This year, through being a talk partner, she has found her voice and made valuable contributions to class discussions. Seeing her grow in confidence has been fantastic!'
>
> Teacher of 7 year olds

> 'One autistic boy has gone from barely being able to tolerate one person, to really enjoying being included in changing partners and meeting his social targets.'
>
> Special school teacher

Practical strategies

More detail about talk partners across the age groups can be found in my previous book, *Active Learning through Formative Assessment*.

Although many teachers ask children to 'turn to the person next to them' for discussion, feedback from my teams over 13 years has reinforced the fact that there need to be set talk partners, changing regularly, in order to ensure the success of the system. Changing partners is one important element, but also setting partners avoids the inevitability of children not wanting to talk to certain children, boys avoiding girls, and so on, if they are asked to simply turn to the person next to them, where there might be a choice.

> '*I introduced random talk partners changing weekly and one girl said that she really enjoyed talking to her partner because she hadn't ever spoken to him before. This was a Year 4 class (9 year olds), so they had been together for many years! Every week the children really look forward to talk partner change and review.*'
>
> '*My school has an intake from both a council estate and a more traditionally middle-class area. Using random weekly partners has broken down social barriers as well as learning barriers. The reaction to this has been overwhelmingly positive.*'

Choosing the pairs

Random pairing is usually carried out, quickly, at the end or the beginning of the week. Devices used to make the pairings include: named lollysticks in a pot or bag, photographs stuck on a wall display or a computer randomiser, like ''The Hat' from www.harmonyhollow.net. To avoid the same children being paired too often, some people create two sliding scales which ensure that all combinations take place before the pairings start again. Children then sit in their pairs for the week, usually placed by the teacher. With young children, talk partners are more effective if they sit knee to knee, facing each other, often on the carpet. One teacher of 4 and 5 year olds says '*Link eyes, link hands, link brains!*' Another teacher uses picture cards of children facing each other or the front, to cue the children every time she wants them to face each other or her.

As with everything in education, flexibility is necessary. Some teachers like to change partners more often, sometimes twos can snowball to make fours, and sometimes a three must be made because of absences. Children can still be drawn off for a guided reading, a writing session or a mini-lesson, while the remaining children pair up. Young children can have a 'magic spot' on the carpet with their partner.

Choosing who answers

Teachers usually have a number of ways of deciding who will answer a class question, whether by lollysticks in a pot, name generators on the computer or names on the backs of chairs, to name but a few. This avoids the damaging 'hands up' culture (see Fig. 4.1) – where the same children tend to be first with their hands up, distracting and stopping others from thinking – and makes a more inclusive learning environment. Once children have had a chance to discuss their thinking, it is more logical that anyone should then be able to answer. This also keeps children focused and alert, in case they are called on. I should emphasise at this point that choosing children randomly to answer without first giving them a short time to discuss with their talk partner is not productive and can reinforce a fixed mindset. It is the articulation of the thinking, and being privileged enough to hear someone else's ideas, that enable children to be able to confidently answer at random.

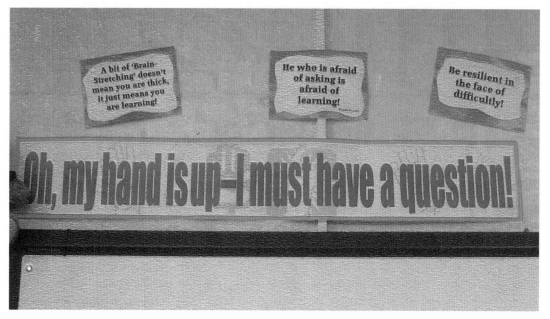

Fig. 4.1 *'No hands up' poster*

SLANT

Seamus Gibbons, a teacher referred to in the Introduction, researched strategies
for helping children focus, especially for those who for one reason or another
are in challenging circumstances. He discovered a method called *SLANT*, which
is an acronym for five common visual indicators of student engagement. The
indicators are:

- Sit up
- Lean forward
- Ask questions about the topic
- Nod your head
- Track the teacher with your eyes

Researching this myself, I see that there are many variations of *SLANT*. I like
Seamus's version, which brings in listening and answering and asks that any
speaker be tracked, not just the teacher:

Sit up

Listen

Ask and answer questions

Nod your head

Track the speaker

SLANT can be referred to as a single-word expectation and 'track the speaker' is used constantly to make sure children are focusing on whoever is speaking. In Seamus's classroom, every child is expected to turn to look at the speaker, whether they are a child or an adult. Along with the random lollysticks for who answers a question, the effect is to increase children's concentration and focus, but also to enhance their listening and therefore understanding.

Talk partner success criteria

Creating class talk partner success criteria sets the scene for discussion about what makes a *good* talk partner. Once displayed, these can then be referred to during lessons, sometimes taking the place or linking with the learning powers described in Chapter 2. The most popular method for co-constructing success criteria for talk partners is the teacher and teaching assistant, or another adult, role playing a discussion in which the teacher demonstrates how *not* to be a good talk partner. The subsequent discussion draws out the ingredients for being a good talk partner. Many teachers have self- and peer evaluation sessions before children change talk partners, either by children filling in various slips or forms or by sharing their thoughts about their skills.

VIDEOCLIP TASTER #6 Self- and peer evaluation of talk partners

Alice asks her 6 year olds to self- and peer evaluate before they change talk partners. http://bit.ly/1kbSA50

Extremely popular is some kind of 'compliment slip' on which children write a positive comment to their partner, saying why they enjoyed learning with them, kept in each child's special folder (see Fig. 4.2). The success criteria enable teachers to train children to be good talk partners, taking one at a time and looking in depth at what each means, sometimes with associated tasks (e.g. persuasion tasks or remembering what your partner said). One school videoed talk partners and found that children often told their partner something rather than explaining it, especially in mathematics. This is another training issue, which needs demonstration and role play to help children see the difference.

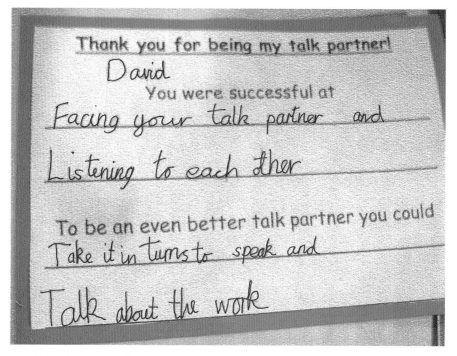

Fig. 4.2 *Talk partner compliment slip*

Examples of success criteria for different age groups can be seen in Fig. 4.3 and opposite.

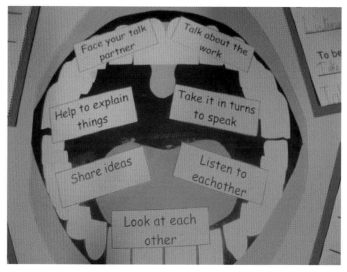

Fig. 4.3 *Talk partner success criteria*

How to Be a Great Talk Partner!
1. No moaning or sulking!
2. Sit close together and face each other
3. Speak clearly – don't cover your mouth
4. Look at your partner when they speak
5. Speak slowly

6. Let both people have a turn

7. Ask questions

8. Think about the question

9. Don't laugh at any answers

10. Remember: getting things wrong can help us learn

Our Learning Partners' Success Criteria

I am beginning to listen to my partner's advice and use it in my learning.

I am beginning to leave other learning partners alone.

I am beginning to take a shared responsibility for our learning.

I am beginning to take turns with my partner and not interrupt them.

I am beginning to help my partner by offering suggestions.

I am beginning to understand that my partner might not agree with me.

I am beginning to look at my partner when they are talking to me.

I am beginning to share my ideas with my partner.

With random talk partners changing every week, teachers have also found it easier to organise mixed-ability learning, with children often offered challenge choices, but learning from each other (see Chapter 2).

One teacher's findings after changing to random pairings and mixed-ability learning are outlined below. Her comments represent the findings of many teachers:

Impact of mixed-ability pairings

- **Exposure to 'good' examples and thinking**
  - Allows lower-achieving pupils to see how a task can be done, supporting and prompting improvement
- **Each child brings different strengths to the partnership**
  - Sharing of knowledge and skills provides support within pairings across the curriculum
- **Learning from peers**
  - Teaching another child embeds learning and clarifies thinking for the 'teacher' and provides a different (and possibly more accessible) perspective on the learning for the lower achiever
- **Provides all children with the chance to experience success**
  - Boosts self-esteem

- **Elimination of ability groups in all subjects**
  - Huge increase in motivation and engagement
  - Learners feel empowered
  - A willingness to 'have a go'
  - The learning is self-tailored to individuals' needs
  - Massive leaps in self-worth
  - No labels!
- **Provides a safe and structured situation in which to practise communication and social skills**
  - Improvement in skills of less socially able
  - Greater imagination and motivation of cultural minority groups
  - New friendships
  - Increased confidence
  - Building of teamwork and cooperative skills
  - Greater maturity in working relationships in the classroom

Quotes from children:

➤ *'When you think of an idea and they think of an idea, you can put them together and make a better idea.'*

➤ *'I like lolly-sticks and it's all about luck really. If we got to choose, I wouldn't choose a girl and I would be with the same talk-partner all of the time. I like it because you make new friends, even if it is a girl!'*

➤ *'I like working with talk partners because if you don't understand something, they can explain it to you. So, when you get "lolly-sticked" you will have something to say.'*

Finally, a Doncaster learning team teacher wrote her experiences of introducing random talk partners as a case study – useful for teachers who want to see the steps involved and for senior managers in creating a whole-school approach.

Talk Partners Case Study

1. Aims and objectives

- My initial intention was to implement a range of opportunities across the curriculum that would develop speaking and listening skills.
- Ensuring quality talk in the classroom:
  - Children need to have thinking time to answer a question, but discussing with a talk partner during that time or using mini-whiteboards makes the thinking time more productive.
  - Talk partner discussion needs to be very focused and not too long (e.g. *30 seconds to come up with one thing you can see in this writing; One minute to think of a good simile for a cat; Two minutes to decide what has gone wrong with this calculation*). This avoids pupils' losing momentum and going off task.

- My aim was that all children would become fully involved within the learning activities to enable them to make the best progress and, as a result, become more confident, independent learners.
- All research shows that when speaking and listening is well developed and encouraged, it has a positive impact on children's learning.

2. Actions/Strategies used

How could I introduce talk partners in my classroom?

- Circle-time discussion based around why it is important to talk about and share their learning with each other. It may be worth asking the children to think about what would happen if they *didn't* share their learning with anyone.
- Many teachers have found it useful to model the strategy for themselves with their teaching assistant, both good and bad talk partners. Once this modelling has taken place, it means that success criteria can be generated and displayed in the classroom.
- Introduce the idea of random talk partners.
- Share the children's experiences after week 1.

How do I select the pairings?

- The selection process can be done in a variety of different ways and it is up to the individual teacher's preference. Some suggestions:
  - Children can decorate their own lollypop sticks and then these are placed in a bag and teacher picks them out at random;
  - Photographs of the children are put into a bag and picked out at random;
  - Using match-it cards – e.g. 'high–low', 'sugar–spice'
  - Random name generator program.
- The selection process of choosing your talk partners can also be used for a number of other AfL situations. For example, choosing which child's work you are going to show under visualiser, who will answer the next question, etc. This keeps the children focused because 'it could be me.'
- Most teachers have allowed the children to choose where to sit, once the names have been drawn out. Again, this is individual preference and as the teacher you could decide whereabouts in the classroom the children sit once their names are drawn.

I like the idea but I am really worried about friends being chosen to sit together.

I have used talk partners over two academic years and I have only ever had to separate one pairing once. In one class two boys who were best friends and would always mess about if they were partners for anything ended up sitting together. I was really worried. However, these particular boys were my talk partners of the week and I asked why they had been so good together and they stated *'We are learning partners, not friends and we have to follow the success criteria.'*

3. Talk partners into practice

Initially, I introduced the concept to the class, explaining how the talk partners system would work and the rules that must be observed – e.g. sit knee to knee, listen, respond, take turns, share ideas and so on. We had a circle-time discussion based around why it is important to talk about and share their learning with each other. I asked the children to think about what would happen if they didn't share their learning with anyone.

Next, I modelled the strategy using my teaching assistant. We modelled being bad talk partners and the children shared their ideas as to how we could do it properly. Using this modelling process and the children's ideas, success criteria were generated with the children agreeing a set of rules regarding respectful speaking and listening. These are displayed in the classroom as a reminder. The idea of random talk partners was introduced and I shared the random name generator program with the children. They really liked this program and the fairness factor: they like that it is completely out of my control. There had been some issues at first with children not wanting to sit with certain children, but they really like the system now and want to sit with their friends less than before.

At the beginning of each week, I use the random name generator to identify pairings. The children choose which table and where in the classroom they want to sit. At the end of the week the children are given an evaluation which they complete to determine whether they have been a good talk partner and whether their partner was a good partner. I choose which pair I feel has worked the best and followed the success criteria and gained the most benefit from having each other as a learning partner. This pair is stood up in golden assembly and each child receives a certificate.

At the start of different lessons, either problems were set or questions asked for the talk partners to work through and the pupils were encouraged to share their thoughts and knowledge with their partner to explain how they could solve the problem. Sometimes the children are asked to whiteboards to make jottings and notes to help refine their thinking. Whilst this is happening, depending on the length of the time given, I walk around the classroom listening to children's talk and identifying any misconceptions on the spot, giving immediate feedback. I find this useful for both APP and evaluating the children's speaking and listening skills. As the pairs are random, the children have opportunities over the weeks to work with peers who had different learning styles and ways of thinking to their own.

A significant advantage in using this approach is that children never have to wait in a whole-class 'hands up' situation – they always have an opportunity to share their thoughts and ideas. I would ask the question or set the problem and then give the children their 'talk' time before using the program to decide who will answer the question. This is often open to the pair rather than the individual. I have found that as a pair they support each other in their answering and enabling me to gain higher-ordering thinking/questioning. It has also made it very difficult for children to 'switch off' during this part of the lesson, as their talk partner was depending on their interaction and the children always had the sense 'it could be me.'

I use talk partners in a variety of lessons and have found it particularly effective in literacy, numeracy, science, PSHE. and PE. Alongside talk partners, we also use the 'ask-it' baskets.

4. **What key resources would people who want to learn from my experience need access to?**
   - Teachers willing to take on new initiatives and improve their own practice.
   - Time out of class to plan implementation of new strategies.
   - Staff meeting time to feedback on progress.
   - Shirley Clarke book *Active Learning through Formative Assessment*.
   - The support of the leadership team.
   - Assessment for learning project meetings and network meetings – sharing resources and ideas with colleagues from other schools.

5. What has been the impact on learning?

The impact on learning, in a range of subjects across the whole class, has been amazing. All children have become ready and willing to talk through their thinking, and are far more able to focus on the task in hand. Social skills are improving and quieter children are being given a voice and a place in the class. The quieter children have made the most progress, and have occasionally even taken on a lead role in discussions. One boy who was usually very quiet actually led a discussion on the effects of healthy eating, and was keen to give his views.

There is a better ethos in classrooms, with greater mutual respect. No children are left out, so self-esteem is good for everyone. Beginnings of lessons are now more efficient, as children link straight away with their partner.

The amount of work produced has visibly increased, and the children are recalling more of their past learning to help them. In their independent class work, the children have increased their ability to solve problems by thinking them through and using what they know, instead of panicking! This has also meant the children are far more receptive to TASC problem-solving wheel (Thinking Actively in a Social Context: www.tascwheel.com). The amount of pupil speaking, appropriate to the lesson, has increased dramatically so that 'teacher talk' has been reduced.

Children have themselves commented that they no longer get frustrated – instead of waiting with their hands up, they can now share all their ideas with a partner, and children are more willing to tackle independent tasks more effectively, using strategies they have gained from TASC to solve problems.

Children are more confident to answer a question when they have discussed it with a partner. By asking children to say what their partners said, there has been an improvement in children's listening skills. Children are empowered to have a go. When giving explanations to lower achievers, higher achievers have to be really clear about their thinking, so each child benefits from the pairing.

I thought that the introduction of talk partners within my classroom may have been initially a problem; however, the children were not fazed and were really keen to be involved. I think my enthusiasm for the whole assessment for learning strategies rubbed off on the children and the overall atmosphere and ethos in the classroom is generally busy, respectful and purposeful. Children like the idea of being responsible for their own learning. I had won the children over: parents were my biggest worry. However, at parents evening I explained the benefits and explained that it would be a weekly change, and they liked the idea of their children mixing with other children in this way.

What the children think:

At the end of the half-term I gave the children a questionnaire to gain their thoughts and opinions on talk partners. I found that the children are extremely positive about the use of talk partners:

- *'If you have to talk, you have to think. I get to learn things from other people I didn't know.'*
- *'It's better than sitting next to the same person all the time; I get to learn things from other people.'*
- *'I like talk partners because I struggle with reading.'*
- *'We get to work with each other, rather than on our own.'*
- *'You get to discuss things and hear other people's opinions.'*
- *'I get to know people in my class better.'*
- *'We get to share ideas.'*
- *'It's better that we don't put our hands up because sometimes with hands up you can't share your ideas if you are not picked.'*

What has been the impact on teaching?

- I use talk partners daily as a natural part of my practice.
- The amount of speaking and listening has increased dramatically and has enabled me to do more ongoing assessment of the pupils' learning.
- Feedback is more immediate – as I and my teaching assistant move around the classroom we are able to listen to the children's discussions and help to clarify their thinking as appropriate.
- Less teacher talk and more focus on encouraging children to talk.
- Clearer focus for assessment.
- More time spent on assessment through observation in lessons.
- More immediate feedback given to pupils, clearing up misunderstandings.
- Reviewing marking of work practices as a result of the talk partner work, to give clearer feedback to children after their independent work.

6. **Plans for the future**

- The initial training and implementation of AfL has just been introduced to the whole school and is led by the Assessment Coordinator and Year 5 teacher as a result of taking part in Shirley Clarke's learning teams for Doncaster.
- Teachers involved in the research project have worked alongside their year group partner on a one-to-one basis to help them introduce it in their classes.
- A class of children involved on the project could help introduce the strategy to other children in school. Workshops could be led and organised by the year 5 children, where they produce some displays, and each child be partnered with a child from another class to 'talk' them through the talk partner process.
- Parent workshops to explain the approach.
- All children in year 2 and year 5 within school are fully involved with AfL, especially peer and self-assessment and sharing ideas with 'talking partners'. This will be rolled out to the rest of the school, initially with a focus on mindset and talk partners, followed by the use of learning intentions and success criteria.
- To ensure that AfL is completely embedded in all aspects of teaching and learning.

Lorraine Sutton, Kingfisher Primary School (10 year olds)

Summary

Talk partners create a culture in which pupils do more talking than teachers, cooperatively discussing, answering questions, learning from each other and improving. To maximise their success the following elements need to be in place:

- Random pairings which change weekly
- Co-constructed talk partner success criteria which enable talk training and self- and peer evaluation
- Random choosing of who answers questions, which eliminates the damaging 'hands up' culture

Effective starts to lessons: learning objectives, success criteria, developing excellence, beyond the success criteria in writing

How lessons begin sets the tone for the rest of the lesson – will it be teacher-led or pupil-led, performance-led or learning-led? Will it start with teacher input and quick-fired questions, or an immediate task to establish prior knowledge? Will it engage pupils immediately or pave a path of boredom?

Learning objective first?

The most damaging learning objective myth of the last decade has been that learning objectives must be written on the whiteboard before the lesson begins, and that the words of the learning objective should be the first words uttered in a lesson. For many subjects, beginning with the learning objective would fill the children with dread or boredom. In science, revealing the learning objective too early would 'give the game away'. For mathematics, however, it does usually make sense to start with the learning objective.

The guiding principle is that children should know the learning objective at the point at which they will be judged against that learning objective.

Starting a lesson by capturing their interest or giving them a calculation gets all the children instantly engaged and thinking about the subject matter of the lesson. That is not to say that learning objectives should be left till the end of the lesson, then left as a 'guess what you were learning?' game, where knowing what they were learning would, in retrospect, have altered their approach to the task. If children do not know the key objective at the point at which they are engaging with any task which will be judged in some way, they will have little chance of fulfilling the expectations of that objective.

Teachers need to decide for themselves whether it would be better to start with the learning objective or delay it. For mathematics lessons, teachers often choose to start with the learning objective, asking children to traffic light their understanding at this moment. By holding up whiteboards, the teacher can see instantly what the children think. The following lesson start description shows the appropriateness of starting with the learning objective for this particular lesson, where it might not be for others.

A Year 5 teacher in my first DVD, Natasha Boult, is seen beginning a lesson on equivalent fractions by asking children to traffic light, on their whiteboards, their understanding at this moment. She looks at their held-aloft whiteboards and confirms that two boys have green. She then asks those boys to prove it by writing some equivalent fractions, while the rest of the class (all amber or red) discuss in pairs an 'odd one out' starter she writes on the whiteboard:

Which is the odd one out? 25/50 1/2 10/20 1/3

After 30 seconds she draws a random lollystick out of a tin and asks one of the 'green' boys for the answer. He says 1/3, which, incidentally, now confirms for the other pupils that the answer is almost definitely 1/3, as he is clearly one of the two highest achievers for maths in this class. She then asks if anyone put anything other than 1/3 and ascertains that two children indicate that they have put a different answer. The moment when the two children put their hands up to say they have the wrong answer is, for me, the absolute proof that the culture of this classroom is a growth mindset, in which children are not afraid of failure, but instead see revealing their mistakes as a necessary act to ensure that something is done to enable them to achieve. That is exactly what happens next, as the teacher then pairs those with the wrong answer with children with right answers and asks everyone to discuss why they got their answer. Talk partner power means that those two children will soon have explained to them, in child language rather than school language, what an equivalent fraction is. Those who got it right are articulating their thinking and explaining in depth what an equivalent fraction is.

VIDEOCLIP TASTER #7 Effective lesson start

Natasha asks her 10 year olds to traffic light their understanding of equivalent fractions and gives them an odd-one-out starter. http://bit.ly/1kkzEm7

The big picture

Knowing the 'big picture' is important for all learners, so that the subsequent pieces can be mentally placed as they evolve. The first minutes of every day can usefully outline in brief the order of play for that day. The first minute of a lesson can briefly show where the topic/subject/theme has been and where it's going. So a week of fractions, for instance, will have a number of elements, all of which can be shared at the beginning of the week and then at the very beginning of every lesson.

Gauging understanding

'The most important single factor influencing learning is what the learner already knows. Ascertain this and teach him accordingly.'

Ausubel et al (1978)

Finding out what children already know or understand, on a lesson-by-lesson, minute-by-minute basis, is a priority, to avoid assuming that what we have planned is appropriate for each learner – so a prior knowledge task is an important starting point to get some idea of the learning needs for that lesson. In mathematics, this could be a question, a calculation or problem to solve; in literacy, this might be a question or instant engagement with a text or 'good' and 'not so good' examples, looking for features or 'best bits'. In science, it could be a question or exploration of some resources to see what they do, or to make something work. In art, it could be talk partner discussion over an artist's techniques, looking at examples of their work, or possibly experimenting with certain materials to find out what works and what doesn't. While these starter tasks are underway, the most effective role of the teacher seems to be observation, listening and questioning children as they engage in the task, quickly moving around the classroom to find out as much as possible about the ways in which children are thinking. Questions such as *'What have you found out so far?', 'Tell me how you are going to work that out...', 'What do you mean by...?'* (even if you know what they mean) encourage children to explain their thinking in an explicit way, giving vital clues to teachers about both misconceptions and clarity. By engaging children in starter tasks, problem solving or exploration, we are not only engaging them and finding out what they know, we are also standing lessons on their head: instead of teaching followed by task, task is followed by teaching, but with the advantage of wisdom rather than guesswork.

In this section on effective starts to lessons, four elements are described:

- **starter questions and activities** (Chapter 5)
- **sharing learning objectives and co-constructing success criteria** (Chapter 6)
- **developing excellence** (Chapter 7)
- **beyond the success criteria – developing excellent writing** (Chapter 7)

All or some of these typify the beginning of a successful lesson. It might be more useful to think of these elements as what might or could take place before children are engaged in the production stage of the lesson. The 'beginning', therefore, could take up to half the lesson time, all of it, or several lessons if we were building a number of lessons around a particular theme – especially if the success criteria are being generated for the first time and there are 'analysis of excellence' examples.

5 Questions and activities

Building on the preceding pages, this chapter gives practical examples of questions and activities which can help teachers to gauge prior knowledge, promote discussion and capture interest.

Questions

Some years of experimentation of effective question starters have led to a number of useful templates being invented by teachers, as seen below. These can be used in any subject for any age group. If starter questions are to be worthwhile in engaging children, furthering their thinking and revealing current understanding, they need to be planned rather than asked 'on the hoof'.

Question templates

- Starting from the end
- Where did I go wrong?
- Statement
- Range of answers
- Odd one out
- Order these
- Right and wrong
- True or false?
- Opposing standpoint
- Always/sometimes/never true?

Examples of effective starts, using the question templates

Mathematics

- **Starting from the end**

For a lesson on number bonds: *'5 is the answer. What might the question be?'*

- **Statement**

For a lesson on percentages: *'45% of 365 is greater than 54% of 285. Agree or disagree?'*

For a lesson on angles: *'All angles of a triangle add up to 200 degrees. Agree or disagree? Prove your answer.'*

■ *Odd one out*

For a lesson on properties of 2D shapes: *'Which of these shapes is the odd one out? How many different answers can you find?'*

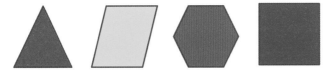

■ *Range of answers*

For a lesson on range and mode:

9, 2, 7, 5, 2, 3, 9, 1, 4, 8 – What is the mode?
The mode is 8 because that's the difference between the smallest and largest numbers.
The mode is 9 because that number appears most often.
It's 5, because when you put the numbers in order, that is the middle number.
It's 5, because 50 divided by 10 is 5.
Which is right?

For a lesson on unit based length: *'What can we use to measure the gruffalo?'*
(Cubes, bananas, dice, oranges, marbles)

■ *Where did I go wrong?*

For a lesson on multiplication grids:

'How many sweets altogether?' 26, 26, 26, 26, 26, 26, 26

×	20	7
6	120	42

26 × 7 = 162

VIDEOCLIP TASTER #8 'Where did they go wrong?' starter

To see how much they know and help them break down the steps involved, Seamus presents his 11 year olds with success criteria and an incorrect calculation. http://bit.ly/1hHoJyw

Science

■ *True or false?*

For a lesson on electricity:

> You can see electricity.
>
> Electricity flows through wires.
>
> Electricity buzzes around us.

■ *Range of answers*

For a lesson on insulation: *'What makes a good insulator? Plastic/cotton/wool/ tinfoil/paper.'*

■ *Statement*

For a lesson about health: *'Exercise leads to a healthy lifestyle. Agree or disagree?'*

■ *Right and wrong*

For a lesson on predictions and generalisation: *'Why will this car move easily down this ramp and not easily down this one?'*

PSHE

■ *Opposing standpoint*

For a lesson on bullying: *'Is it OK to hit someone if they have hit you? Should bullies be treated differently to those who don't bully others?'*

History

■ *Statement*

For a lesson about the key events of the Gunpowder Plot and a balanced argument: *'Guy Fawkes was a good guy. Agree or disagree?'*

For a lesson on World War 2: *'It was a good idea to bomb Berlin in the war. Agree or disagree?'*

For a lesson on understanding the past: A picture of Mary Seacole was displayed with the statement *'This is a person from the past. Agree or disagree? How do you know?'*

Literacy

■ *Starting from the end*

For a lesson about prediction: given the final verse of 'Romeo and Juliet' children had to predict what might have happened before this.

■ *Statement*

For a lesson on different points of view: *'Wolves should be banned from fairy tales. Agree or disagree?'*

For a lesson on poetry analysis in secondary: One teacher read the students *Nettles*, by Vernon Scannell, a poem about a father's love for his child and said '*This is a poem about nettles. Agree or disagree?*'

Activities

Effective starts are sometimes engaging activities, which might or might not be linked with one of the question types outlined so far: their main purpose is to capture interest and reveal prior understanding. The following list is a collection of tried and tested activity starts from teachers across my learning teams. There are many more possibilities....

- **Changing the setting** (e.g. classroom becomes a castle)
- **Exploring resources** (e.g. magnets and metals)
- **Deep-end task** (e.g. make a plant grow sideways)
- **Box of objects/artifacts** (e.g. clues for a character or event in history or a story)
- **Surprise letter/invitation/message in a bottle** (e.g. incomplete invitation)
- **Class visit or trip** (e.g. to look at the houses in our street)
- **Role play** (e.g. teacher arrives as a character from history or nursery rhyme)
- **Story** (e.g. beginning of a story read aloud)
- **Play a game** (e.g. short playground game before discussion about defence skills)
- **Crime scene** (with clues added one by one)
- **Jigsaw the pieces** (e.g. cut out paragraphs of a newspaper report)
- **Sorting cards** (e.g. science vocabulary for liquids and solids)
- **Web page/Twitter** (e.g. response from famous poet about our class poems)
- **Sorting success criteria** (e.g. muddled steps for chunking in division)
- **Success criteria bingo** (e.g. all the elements of a balanced argument are gradually revealed and discussed after children first write them from memory)
- **Gradually reveal a map or picture** while children guess what/where it is
- **Given headlines, guess the story,** gradually adding more sub-headings

Mathematics

- *Picture for discussion*

For a lesson on probability: A picture of a robbery in a museum was discussed to see what had happened, clues gradually added, leading to probability statements.

Science

- *Explore equipment*

For a lesson on electrical circuits: Children were given a list of equipment they would use to make a circuit, but included on the list were some things they would not need.

■ *Demonstration*

For a lesson on recognising the variables to change in a scientific experiment: Children watched two Mentos being dropped into a litre of cola, which exploded. They were then asked, *'If you were to have a go, but you have to do something different, what would you do?'* Children wrote suggestions on sticky notes (e.g. different sized bottle, different temperature of cola, etc.).

Literacy

■ *Play detective*

For a lesson on newspaper articles: Given chopped-up headlines from a newspaper article, children had to guess what the story could be about.

PSHE

■ *Order these*

For a lesson on human rights: Children used a 'diamond nine' to order some statements about children's rights. Top of the shape is the most important, and so on.

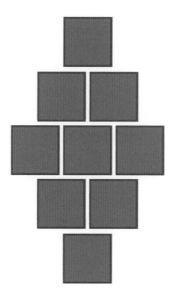

History

■ *Sort these*

For a lesson on the history of Brighton: Sort these pictures (of Brighton at various points through history) in different ways.

■ *Play detective*

For a lesson on historical evidence: Given a box of artifacts, try to decide what the lesson/character/place, etc., will be about.

Examples of practice

The following examples of effective starts to lessons include quotes from children recorded during the discussion, giving a fuller idea of the impact they have had on children's thinking, reasoning and communication skills.

Example 1

At the start of a topic on light, the children were asked 'Which is the odd one out, and why? The sun, stars, electric eel, fire, lightbulb, torch.'

'The electric eel, because it's an animal.'

'Fire, because you have to make it.'

'The torch, because it needs batteries.'

'The sun, because we would die without it.'

'Stars, because they make patterns in the sky.'

'A light bulb, because they have to be plugged in.'

Example 2

'The children at Chater Infant School have healthy packed lunches. True or false?'

Persia: 'No, because some children have too much chocolate.'

Cara: 'I think that children only need a little bit of chocolate. I have seen someone with two Haribos and one chocolate and I think that's too much.'

Nidah: 'I think yes because my brother has an apple, a pear and a banana.'

Saffa: 'No, because people have crisps and chocolate biscuits.'

Max: 'I think they should have something from the 5 different food groups because they will get healthier.'

Adama: 'No, because some children have chocolate every day.'

Maitreyan: 'Yes and no because some are healthy and some are not.'

Example 3

'During a science lesson on variation with 7 year olds, the children were grouping animals with their talk partners. One child said *'A fox is more like a cat than a dog'*. I put this on the whiteboard and asked for feedback. After talk partner discussion, I recorded their responses on the board, quickly adding a picture of a dog and a fox. They began developing their statements, concluding that a fox was more like a dog than a cat.

Some examples:

- *'It's more like a cat, because it has long whiskers.'*
- *'It's more like a cat, because cats can jump into trees but dogs don't bother. And foxes live underground.'*
- *'Foxes normally go up near branches and so do cats.'*
- *'A fox is more like a dog, because cats bury their business but dogs don't.'*
- *'I think the dog looks more like a fox, because they both have long snouts.'*
- *'The dog and fox both have black noses.'*
- *'The dog and fox have long tails the same.'*

Impact:

Pupils developed their own learning. I could easily assess the learning as it happened. I did less work, they did more.'

Kirstin Greygoose, Bidford-on-Avon Primary School

Summary

- How lessons begin establishes whether the lesson will be learning- or performance-focused.
- Effective lessons often begin with a question or activity, either to establish current understanding or to capture interest and to engage the pupils in thinking and discussion.
- There are a number of powerful question and activity templates which can be applied to any age group or subject.

6 Learning objectives and success criteria

Rationale for learning objectives

For teachers

The introduction of national curricula – such as the National Curriculum in England in 1989 or the Common Core Standards in 2013 in the USA – necessarily focuses teachers on learning objectives. Much excellent teaching used to be instinctive, with learning objectives not stated explicitly and children mostly involved in *activity-based learning*. Learning objectives were rarely articulated and may or may not have been known by teachers. Specifying learning objectives – as targets, standards, or statements of attainment – has been a route to a more rigorous approach to coverage and – one of the key purposes – more chance of equal opportunities for pupils. Compulsory learning objectives have often led to overloaded coverage and more time spent on surface than deep learning, in order to get through it all.

For pupils

The importance of children *knowing* what they are learning, as well as what they are doing, is backed up by many studies (for instance, Crooks, 1988; Hillocks, 1986; Ames and Ames, 1984; Butler, 1988). In order to judge the quality of a pupil's achievement, the teacher must have a clear understanding of what the learning objective *means*, what *quality* for that learning objective would look like and be able to *compare* what they witness to that concept. However, it is not enough for the teacher to hold this idea of 'what makes good', as the feedback would be one way only, limiting the pupil's ability to develop independently. The *pupil* must also understand the learning objective and the definition of quality held by the teacher, so that he or she can monitor his or her own progress during its production. A defining description of what amounts to the raison d'être of formative assessment was articulated by Royce Sadler (1989). Stated explicitly, the learner has to:

❝● Possess a concept of the standard (or goal, or reference level) being aimed for
● Compare the **actual** (or current) **level of performance** with the standard, and
● Engage in appropriate **action** which leads to some closure of the gap.❞

Many years of my work with teachers have been about unpicking and fulfilling these words and ideas. In practical terms:

- the **learning objective** is the starting point for the teacher's or teacher and pupils' *planning*, although the starting point of a *lesson* is often to capture interest first before the learning objective is made clear, which establishes prior knowledge and understanding;

- the learning objective is broken down into mini-goals or ingredients, commonly known as **success criteria**;

- using published or old, anonymous examples of excellent and 'not so good' pupil work allows the concept of quality to be known;

- talk partners, good questioning, on-the-spot self, peer and teacher feedback, often via 'mid-lesson learning stops', enable improvements to be made during the learning.

The learning objective, therefore, focuses the teacher thus:

- What do I want them to learn?
- How do I articulate that?
- What would be a good way of learning it?
- What do I think a range of excellent finished products would look like?

The learning objective, and or/starter question, focuses the pupil to be able to recognise how much they already know about it, anchor them throughout its learning, and encourage self-assessment.

Rationale for success criteria

Success criteria are well established as a useful breakdown of the learning objective. Once the learner has success criteria, they have a framework for a formative dialogue – with peers or adults – which enable them to:

- Know what the learning objective means;
- Know the steps involved with a closed learning objective (e.g. to find percentages of whole numbers) or the elements of a particular writing form (e.g. a newspaper report);
- Know the possible ingredients for an open learning objective (e.g. a ghost story opening);
- Identify where success has been achieved and where help might be needed;
- Be clearer about where improvements can be made;
- Discuss strategies for improvement;
- Reflect on progress.

For *closed* learning objectives (see page 84), success criteria are particularly useful, as they are usually compulsory elements and can therefore be tracked throughout a task. For *open* learning objectives, where inclusion of the success criteria does not in itself ensure quality, the concept of excellence needs to be modelled. Moving beyond the success criteria in writing is discussed at length in the next chapter.

Acronyms and characters

The introduction of learning objectives and success criteria – a new and complex idea after the introduction of the National Curriculum in England – saw many cartoon characters such as WALT *(We are learning to...)*, WILF *(What I'm looking for...)* and TIB *(This is because...)* springing up, which made the whole thing more accessible for teachers, even though at the time it was thought by teachers to be the best way of introducing the new concepts to children. Looking back, I believe these acronyms and characters were a support for teachers more than children, and the teachers I remember inventing them were tired of them within about six months, realising that they were unnecessary and distracting.

By 2001, my huge Gillingham Evaluation Project (2000) established that these gimmicks were getting in the way of children realising that they were learning for *themselves*, not a character or a teacher. *'This is because...'* became a repetitious encumbrance and clogged up beginnings of lessons. I worked with teachers on new, simpler ways forward and, for some years now, the preferred way in for many teachers has been: *'We are learning to...'* or *'L.O. (learning objective)...'* or *'L.I. (learning intention)...'* for **the learning objective/s of the lesson** and *'Remember to...'* (closed learning steps) or *'Choose from...'* (open choice ingredients), *'Top tips'* for very young children, or simply *'Success criteria'* for the accompanying **success criteria**.

As with everything, what matters is the meaning implied by the words, rather than the words themselves. As long as the principles are fulfilled, the method used is irrelevant, although whole-school or key stage consistency is clearly preferable.

Unpicking learning objectives 1: skill, not context

When making learning objectives clear, it seems necessary to make sure it spells out a skill or knowledge, without including the context within which the skills will be taught. So, *'learning to write a set of instructions about making a sandwich'* should be *'learning to write instructions'*. There are two reasons for decontextualising learning objectives in this way:

1 Once the skill is revealed in its 'clean' form, the success criteria, or breakdown of mini-skills, become *process*- not *content*-based. These are processes we want pupils to have embedded so that they can apply them to any future learning, regardless of the context.

2 If the context (the sandwich) is included, children often see the skill as untransferrable, relating only to the context in hand, so that the next time that skill is revisited, in a different context, children don't make links and in effect have to start again.

***Contextualised* learning objective and success criteria: unlikely to be seen as a transferrable skill**

We are learning to write instructions for making a jam sandwich *Remember to:* • List the ingredients needed for the sandwich • Write in order how to make it (e.g. butter two slices of bread, etc.) • Provide a picture of a jam sandwich	*I know how to make a jam sandwich now, but if you ask me to tell you instruction criteria I won't know them....*

***Decontextualised* learning objective and success criteria: a transferrable skill to any context or subject**

We are learning to write instructions *Remember to:* • List what you need • Use 'bossy' verbs • Use numbers, bullet points or similar • Use time connectives • Write instructions in order • Include diagrams/pictures, if appropriate	*I can create instructions for making a jam sandwich, putting up a tent, making a paper hat or anything else I know how to do. I can also tell you the instruction criteria....*

Unpicking learning objectives 2: does this really say what I want them to learn?

One of the problems with learning objectives is the language used in official documents. As long as the meaning is clear, we should be using whichever words feel most accurate in describing what we want them to learn. A greater issue, however, is being clear in the first place about exactly what that is. I often hear teachers say that their mathematics learning objectives tend to have too many elements, covering both a skill and its application, or observing, recording and interpreting data, for instance. The lesson is unsuccessful because the children were confused and the success criteria were unfocused. Without clear success criteria, children cannot take ownership of the skill and monitor their performance against them. The learning objective with multiple elements can still be introduced, but then broken down into smaller learning objectives as each is tackled for each lesson, keeping the connections clear between the parts. In this way there might be a blanket learning objective for the week, with breakdown learning objectives each day. The same is true for literacy learning objectives, where an overarching objective can be built up during the week.

A more difficult issue is where the learning objective is given, in good faith, but the children's focus is not on your intended focus. One teacher, for instance, told the children they were learning to sort shapes. She gave them Venn diagrams and shapes to sort and talked about the Venn. Their entire focus was on the shapes and their properties, whereas the teacher wanted them to understand about the way a Venn diagram works. She realised that by simply changing the learning objective to *'We are learning about Venn diagrams'*, the entire focus would be shifted. She can now consider whether all children have to sort shapes or whether some other resource would be better. Perhaps by having different groups with different sorting resources, their focus would be more tuned to the intersections than the materials.

Another teacher told children they were *'finding out the temperature between their toes'*, resulting in a focus on their feet, rather than *'To be able to use a thermometer'*, which would have led to success criteria focused on the way to use a thermometer, regardless of how or where it was used.

Bringing short-term plans to a staff meeting and deciding in pairs whether or not learning objectives of previous lessons, or lessons to come, really describe the learning objective is a very useful process.

The learning objective's link with success criteria is critical in making sure it really says what you want to be learnt. If the objective is about **sorting shapes**, then the success criteria will be a breakdown of that (e.g. listing the different ways you could sort the shapes). If the objective is about **Venn diagrams**, the success criteria will be a breakdown of the functions of a Venn diagram (e.g. where to place the objects, what the intersection means, things that belong outside the Venn, etc.).

Knowledge and skills

Although there is usually one learning objective for a lesson (the main focus for the learning), there are times, especially for subjects other than literacy or mathematics, where there are *two* learning objectives at play: the **knowledge** you want them to acquire, and the **skill** they will use either in acquiring that knowledge or in applying it. The important thing to remember here is that both learning objectives need to be known, at the appropriate time, but the skill-based learning objective will be the one which has accompanying process success criteria. Knowledge is important, even though we later forget much of it, because it engages us and provides a meaningful and often exciting context for our all-important skill learning. The skills set us up to be able to apply them in life situations in any context and to be able to learn anything we want to, again in any context. So knowledge learning objectives might look like this:

> To know the key events of World War 2
>
> To know the names of the key parts of a plant
>
> To know properties of 3D shapes
>
> To know what a volcano is

These objectives contain short pieces of information, but we want children not only to know these facts, but also to be able to use that knowledge when they are practising or exploring skills. Rarely is information just given to children. We usually ask them to do something with that knowledge, present it in some way or use it in tandem with another skill, often from another subject domain (e.g. literacy). Possible skills which would be linked with these knowledge learning objectives might be:

> To know the key events of World War 2 + **To be able to write a diary (context: an evacuee)**
>
> To know the names of the key parts of a plant + **To be able to label diagrams (context: a flower)**
>
> To know properties of 3D shapes + **To be able to use a Venn diagram**
>
> To know what a volcano is + **To be able to write an explanation text**

Thus, both learning objectives would be displayed, but only the skill would usefully have associated success criteria which, as a breakdown of the learning objective, break the skill down into its component parts or possible ingredients.

Closed and open learning objectives and related success criteria

Closed learning objectives and mathematics

Learning objectives tend to be either **open or closed**. It is only important to know this because of the impact on success criteria, feedback and quality.

Closed learning objectives, such as specific maths skills, always have compulsory elements for the learning objective to be fulfilled (e.g. every step of a calculation must be followed to attain the objective). If the success criteria have been achieved, with accuracy, the learning objective will be achieved. However, although the answer is either right or wrong, success criteria might need to be supplemented on the hoof for some children.

Imagine, for example, the success criteria for *adding two-digit numbers on a number line:* we might have:

- Start from the biggest number
- Jump in tens first (e.g. 36, 46, 56, etc.)
- Jump the ones next (53, 54, 55, etc.)
- Record where you land

Some children, however, might individually be asked – if the teacher sees some difficulty – to make extra recordings to keep track of their jumps or to use arrow marks on their jumps. It is better to have fewer main steps for mathematics success criteria, and then supplement them according to need, than to have an endless lists of steps or ingredients which children can lose track of, find hard to read or be intimidated by. One of the issues peculiar to mathematics seems to be the notion that every single step should be included, even when that mathematical skill has been known to the children for years. So, when measuring length, for instance, the key elements might be:

Remember to:

- start from 0
- record the exact measurement
- use the correct unit.

It would be unnecessary to include getting the ruler, laying out the thing to be measured, counting along the ruler, etc., if those steps can be assumed for most children.

Feedback for closed skills focuses around mastery and checking for errors, re-teaching or more input, either from a peer or a teacher. Improvement is simply 'getting it right', as there is no continuum of achievement with closed skills – only right or wrong elements. New thinking about effective feedback for maths skills and secretarial skills, fully exemplified in Chapter 9, puts the main feedback at the point at which children appear to have mastered the skill and are then asked to create *their own individual success criteria* for the objective. This is an effective technique once children can write independently and enables misconceptions to be illuminated by asking children to explain, in their own words, how the procedure works or what something means.

Open learning objectives for mathematics still have right or wrong answers, of course, but the openness is in the choice of method used. So, when a **specific skill** is being taught, the criteria would necessarily be compulsory. Once pupils have **a range of techniques** for calculating a specific area of mathematics (e.g. addition), however, the learning objective and the success criteria become more choice-oriented:

To add two-digit numbers

Choose from:

- A mental method
- Using a number line
- The column method
- Adding tens first, then units, then both together.

What was once a specific learning objective (using a number line), once learnt, becomes one of the success criteria for a more open learning objective. Success criteria often nest in this way.

If the mathematics was focused on a problem or word sum – even more open ended – again, although the answer must be right, the focus is now more likely to be on the problem-solving strategies used, which will be reflected in the success criteria. Success criteria for solving a big problem, such as *'How many minutes have you been alive?'*, might look like this:

To solve a mathematical problem

Remember to:

- Estimate the answer
- Underline the key words
- Choose a method
- Choose resources
- Change your strategy if it doesn't work
- Check your answer a different way
- Compare your answer with your estimate

Table 6.1 exemplifies all three types of success criteria outlined above.

Closed success criteria for a specific skill	Open success criteria when pupils have learnt a range of techniques	Open success criteria which focus on problem-solving processes and decision making
To add two-digit numbers on a number line	*To add two-digit numbers*	*To solve a word problem: how many hours have you been alive?*
Remember to: ➤ Start from the biggest number ➤ Jump in tens first (e.g. 36, 46, 56, etc.) ➤ Jump the ones next (53, 54, 55, etc.) ➤ Record where you land	**Choose from:** ➤ A mental method ➤ Using a number line ➤ The column method ➤ Adding tens first, then units, then both together	**Remember to:** ➤ Estimate the answer ➤ Underline the key words ➤ Choose a method ➤ Choose resources ➤ Change your strategy if it doesn't work ➤ Check your answer a different way ➤ Compare your answer with your estimate

Table 6.1 *Mathematics success criteria*

The issues surrounding success criteria and Writing are fully explored in Chapter 7.

Co-constructed success criteria

Success criteria are internalised and used by pupils if they have had a stake in their generation. I now have an ever-growing number of excellent strategies for co-constructing success criteria with pupils, detailed below.

The impact of co-constructed success criteria is that:

- Pupils become more independent;
- Pupils have more ownership over their learning and ongoing assessment;
- Pupils can decide criteria for which help is needed;
- There is higher achievement when pupils have seen good examples and can follow or choose from the success criteria they have generated;
- Older children can teach younger children more effectively;
- Higher achievers can teach lower achievers more effectively.

Strategies used by teachers to co-construct criteria include:

■ Showing excellent, different examples of the same skill

One teacher showed her class three examples of word sums and their solutions. Each one had key words highlighted, a diagram and some calculations. Children identified these criteria and could apply them immediately.

■ Demonstrating a technique or skill

Demonstrating at the visualiser – a particular art technique, for instance, or specific skill such as looking up words in a dictionary, with the teacher thinking out loud throughout – helps children identify the steps or ingredients of the skill. They can be asked repeatedly *'What did I just do?'* as a way of gathering the criteria. Older children can compile their own success criteria during the demonstration. This technique can also be used to develop quality in writing, for instance, where the teacher thinks aloud her choice of words, encouraging children to call out better words or phrases.

■ Demonstrating good and bad

PE, music, art were examples of subjects for which a practical demonstration of how to do the skill well and how to do it badly both entertained children as well as helped them identify key features.

■ Doing it wrong

The teacher, often at a visualiser or document camera, demonstrates how *not* to do the task in hand, inviting children to correct her and draw up the criteria as they go along (especially good for mathematics with closed elements).

■ Showing a wrong example

One teacher showed her class a really bad example of how to film someone. Children offered advice to the film-maker, thus generating the success criteria.

Another teacher showed a recording the class puppet had done of his experiment to see which liquids rot teeth the fastest. None of the variables were constant and children could see what should stay the same and what should change, so were able to generate the criteria for a fair test.

N.B. Showing children just a bad example of writing can be unsuccessful and time-consuming as a way of getting them to (a) create success criteria and/or (b) improve the writing. Showing them an excellent and a bad example, by contrast, is extremely successful in modelling good writing and seeing how improvements can be made.

■ Working through it

Analysing a bar graph, for instance, and discussing what helped children to interpret it, is a good way of pulling out its elements.

■ Recounting practical experience

Children were asked to play a playground game then had to explain how the game was played to their partner. Their discussions were then analysed as a class (they had used time connectives, ordering steps and so on) and instruction success criteria were generated, with examples.

■ Incomplete surprise letter or invitation

By providing a surprise which is incomplete, children instinctively want to include the missing elements, which amount to the success criteria.

VIDEOCLIP TASTER #9 An incomplete surprise starter

Jen 'finds' an incomplete invitation in the room.
Children's questions will amount to the success criteria
for an invitation. http://bit.ly/1pG00V9

■ Jigsaw the pieces

By cutting up the pieces of, say, an excellent newspaper report, an invitation, a letter or a persuasive letter, and inviting children to reassemble them, they are involved in analysis of the content matter. This leads to the generation of the ingredients, but also gives an example of what a good one looks like.

■ Success criteria bingo

To revisit previously generated success criteria, ask children to quickly write the criteria from memory on a blank bingo card grid. Have the criteria hidden behind coloured shapes on the smart board.

Choose children randomly, one at a time, to choose a shape, read out the now revealed criterion and give an example of its meaning. Every child who has written that criterion crosses it out. Play continues in this way until someone wins. The explanation of the criterion each time is the crux of the learning, cementing the understanding of the criteria.

■ Reordering given success criteria after practical experience

One teacher of 5 year olds presented the children with three success criteria cards for a science experiment, which she needed to be put in order. They had previously conducted a simple experiment, made predictions and so on, so the task had that previous experience for them to hook the criteria on.

■ Eavesdropping talk partners

Asking children to decide the success criteria for a learning objective, and simply walking around jotting down their ideas, is an efficient way of gathering success criteria.

■ Sloppy success criteria

Especially good for mathematics, a calculation with errors is presented alongside its success criteria. The success criteria have been followed correctly, so what has gone wrong? Children have to analyse the steps, the errors and put right the success criteria.

Examples of success criteria co-constructed with pupils across the age range and subjects

Top tips: Treasure Island (nursery: 3–4 year olds)

- 4 people can play here
- Don't tread on the toys with your feet
- We should share
- We talk to people nicely
- Don't touch the trees
- Tidy up when the music is playing

Top tips: Let's get ready to write (nursery)

- Use which hand feels the comfiest
- You need to sit on the chair properly
- Put your thumb underneath the pencil and the first finger on the top
- Hold the paper with your other hand or it might move

To construct a bar graph (7 year olds discuss first an accurate, then later an inaccurate bar graph)

> 'In the first lesson on bar charts, we looked at an example of a graph and identified the features. These became our success criteria (e.g. **scale, title, labelling the axes,** etc.). After marking the graphs, all children had included these features but with some inaccuracies (e.g. scales drawn inaccurately, different width bars).'
>
> 'In the second lesson we looked at an example of a graph similar to the one children had drawn. We discussed how this met the success criteria but not accurately. After this recap about accuracy, ALL children produced an accurate graph.'
>
> Emma Hancock, Tunbridge Wells Team

To write a story opening for a scary story (8 and 9 year olds having discussed a good and a not so good example)

Choose to include:

- A flashback
- Dialogue
- Description
- A significant event
- Your own idea

To solve word problems (8 and 9 year olds analysing three excellent examples of solved problems and what they had in common)

Choose to:

- Highlight key words
- Draw a diagram
- Use symbols
- Make a chart

To write an invitation (8 and 9 year olds having compared successful and unsuccessful invitations)

VIDEOCLIP TASTER #10 Co-constructing success criteria

The class of 8 and 9 year olds finally write up the success criteria for an invitation after a number of class activities.
http://bit.ly/1hG9B95

To create a collage (11 year olds analysing a number of excellent collages)

Remember to:

- Stick materials on the paper
- Cover most of the paper
- Choose colours, materials and design
- Make it eye-catching

To solve a quadratic equation with real roots using the quadratic formula (17 year olds)

Remember to:

- Put equation in $ax^2 + bx + c = 0$ form
- Identify the values of a, b, c
- Substitute values into quadratic formula
- Simplify
- Express roots appropriately
- Consider a method to check your solutions

Finally, a Doncaster learning team teacher wrote his experiences of introducing success criteria as a case study:

Year 6 Success Criteria Case Study

Focus of the case study

The focus for this case study is the pupil generation and use of success criteria.

Aims and objectives

- To explore the various ways in which success criteria can be generated by pupils.
- To evaluate the impact on learning of pupils' input into the generation and subsequent application of success criteria.
- To focus initially on writing – as this was a focus in the School Improvement Plan.
- To then extend into other areas of the curriculum.
- To disseminate and share good practice with colleagues.

Timescale

This research took place during the Spring and Summer terms.

Actions/Strategies used

We were asked to investigate the various ways of generating success criteria as outlined by Shirley Clarke.

There are several very high-quality techniques for getting pupils to generate success criteria, namely:

- Prove it/Do it wrong
- Finished piece of work
- Two pieces of finished work
- Poor quality success criteria
- Demonstration/Retrospective creation
- Revisiting existing success criteria

I focused on generating success criteria from a finished piece of work initially and then developed this to using two (or more) finished pieces of work, side-by-side, to consider quality. I started with English/Literacy as the subject area, with a focus on writing across the different genres.

Writing skills are an area for development within our school and was a focus in our School Improvement Plan. Mathematics and IT are my subject specialisms so I decided to work out of my 'comfort zone'.

Children generating success criteria through a finished product has implications for resourcing. Where do you get a 'finished product' from? In schools with more than a one-form entry, then work can be taken from a parallel class, provided the work has been completed. In single-form schools, then it becomes more difficult. The teacher could 'create' such examples of work, but there is more impact if it is clearly from another pupil. This means *saving* examples of work to be used the following year – ideally stored digitally, scanning the work so that that it can be saved and then subsequently projected, or keeping a hard copy and using a visualiser, or photocopied to show to the whole class.

As my school is a single-form entry I used a mixture of both – creating examples of work and using children's work from the previous year. I was fortunate because it is school policy to keep all the work done by three children from every class – high, average and low achievers – so I had a 'stock' of examples.

As the focus was initially on literacy and writing, I could also draw upon the mark schemes from the English Key Stage 2 SATs papers, as these provide examples of pupils' scripts at different levels and over the years have covered different genres. They are also annotated, too, picking out features of the writing.

The following is the way I structured my lessons (or series of lessons) to enable the pupils to generate success criteria:

Prior to the lesson

- Learning objectives decided upon
- Success criteria 'roughed out'
- Examples of finished products sourced

During lesson

- I refer to the 'bigger picture' – bringing in previous learning and where the learning is going.
- Learning objective is shared with the children and discussed with their learning partner.
- The finished product/s is/are then shown and discussed and analysed.
- Pupils, in their pairs, start formulating the success criteria.
- These are then shared with the class – I act as 'scribe', writing them on pieces of paper which I hang on a 'washing line' – this allows us to discuss the importance of each success criterion and maybe, if appropriate, order them as to importance.
- Pupils then work on their own piece, referring to the success criteria as they are working.
- During this independent working time, I may select pupils' work and show it to the class, using the visualiser to compare against success criteria.
- Plenary – revisit learning objective/adaptations to success criteria, if needed.
- Discuss improvements made. Reflect on their learning.

The success criteria I then transfer to our 'learning ladders' (see example below). I then give copies of this to the children to use as a way of self-evaluation and peer evaluation in discussion with their learning partner. There is also a section for a written comment detailing their next learning focus.

Resources used

- Examples of 'finished work' from either:
  - a parallel class,
  - previous year's work, or
  - teacher created
- Visualiser
- Washing line to display success criteria and order, if necessary
- Learning ladder – see *following example*:

Name _____   Date _____

Self-evaluation Ladder

Success Criteria – Writing a **play script**

Character's name written in the margin to show who is speaking.
Stage directions written inside brackets.
Each speech written on a new line.
No speech marks.
No use of the word 'said'.
Stage directions describe the setting.
Stage directions tell the actor how to say their speech and what to do.
Use adverbs/adjectives in stage directions.

Outcomes – impact on learning

- To have maximum impact, success criteria must be generated by the pupils.
- Pupils have more ownership of their work – they are generating their own success criteria, so it is more relevant to them – rather than being teacher-directed.
- Raises self-esteem – they set the targets (i.e. success criteria) and get positive feedback when they self-assess and see that their work satisfies the criteria.
- Children are more confident and the quality of work has improved – more revisions and self-corrections.
- Use of learning (talk) partners has improved the quality of discussion.
- They remember their input and refer to the success criteria when working.
- Seeing a child's previous work inspires them – but also they want to do 'better'.
- Success criteria provide a platform for both self- and peer assessments.
- Success criteria are a way of generating 'personal' targets.
- Pupils are becoming more reflective thinkers and becoming more critical thinkers – analytical skills are being developed.
- Children become more independent and self-reliant.
- Differentiation is addressed – once success criteria have been formulated, lower achievers might focus on maybe two or three key criteria – not all of them.
- Learning becomes more personalised, but yet manageable.

Plans for the future

To share with colleagues within school the 'Shirley Clarke experience'. Development of active learning has been written into the School Improvement Plan and will be delivered to the remainder of the staff by myself and my colleague who undertook the research project with me.

This training is to follow the model adopted by Shirley Clarke – namely, a series of training sessions with gap tasks for staff to experiment with/try out and then feed back at the next session. The strategies and techniques that Shirley shared with us do work in the classroom – they have been trialled and developed by teachers. They are practical, relevant and manageable.

They promote pupil engagement, effective discussion and dialogue and reflective thinking.

Monitoring and Evaluation will be done through lesson observations, pupil works scrutiny and pupil interview.

Graham Rhodes, Deputy Headteacher, Mexborough Highwoods Primary School

Summary

- In order to judge the quality of a pupil's achievement, the teacher must have a clear understanding of the learning objective.
- Pupils must also understand the learning objectives and the definition of quality held by the teacher in order to have any chance of fulfilling them.
- Success criteria are a breakdown of the learning objective and enable monitoring of progress and self-assessment.
- Although knowledge objectives are important, only skill-based objectives are usefully linked with success criteria, helping pupils internalise the elements of the skill so that they can be transferred to any subject or context.
- Success criteria are more effective if they are decontextualised and a true reflection of what the teacher wants pupils to learn.
- Success criteria for closed learning objectives are compulsory elements, often in chronological order.
- The more open the learning objective, the broader the success criteria.
- 'Remember to…' and 'Choose from…' seem to be the preferred language for introducing success criteria, so that pupils are not distracted by acronyms or characters.
- Co-constructed success criteria, between pupils and teacher, are more effective than those simply given.
- Using success criteria enables pupils to be more independent, to identify successes and improvement needs, to facilitate self- and peer assessment and to track their inclusion, if closed.

7 Developing excellence... for all subjects, and beyond the success criteria for Writing

Developing excellence in all subjects

Only by modelling excellent examples can children develop a sense of what the end product might look like and the different ways in which excellence might be achieved. Some lessons might begin by showing children one or more excellent examples (e.g. three excellent watercolour paintings from last year's class), analysing them and discussing what makes them good. They could also start by comparing an excellent example with one which is average. These strategies are possible across every subject and every age range. Particularly popular is the process of discussing the difference between a good and a not so good example – and the younger the children, the wider the gap between the two examples. Teachers have used a huge range of contrasting products, sometimes comparing three, from videoclips comparing good and bad dance or sporting moves to varying science experiments, one excellent, one not – to a dreadful reading of a poem compared to an excellent reading. It is the explicitness of the comparison that helps children see clearly *why* one is better than another. At all levels our learning is enhanced if we can be shown an example of one that is deemed excellent with one that is not. Imagine beginning photography classes and being shown two contrasting photos of a person, one appalling and one pleasing, then analysing and discussing the differences between them. No amount of lecturing *without* the examples will be as good as this comparison of products. How much easier would our college courses have been if we had been presented with good and poor examples of academic assignments?

VIDEOCLIP TASTER #11 Comparing 'not so good' with excellent

Seamus's class compare and analyse his collage and the teaching assistant's collage. http://bit.ly/1kbSII3

Although comparing one excellent example with one not so good is powerful in creating an in-depth analysis, we have learnt that all learners need to see more than one example of excellence, to avoid their being constrained by the style of only one version of excellence. Whereas children do not copy the piece analysed, they might be influenced by its general style if they are not exposed to other, different excellent versions of the same context. My advice is to save three excellent and one not so good for future classes every time a product is produced that can be scanned or photographed. The aim would be for every teacher and school to have access to a wide range of pupil examples.

Chapter 9 of my book *Active Learning through Formative Assessment* has extensive examples of teachers' comparisons of products across the age range and subjects, which fully illustrate the potential of this strategy and its immediate impact on the quality of children's achievement and their relief at seeing what end products should look like.

I include here just a few new examples from recent action research teams:

- A teacher of 5 year olds showed the children writing from last year with finger spaces and one without finger spaces.

- Another teacher of 5 year olds invented a fictitious child, Henry, who started off with poor handwriting, but after three attempts had improved, thus comparing three examples.

- A full skeleton picture was shown to a class of 6 year olds and compared to a simple stick man. Children's resulting skeleton pictures were highly detailed.

- DT kite models, adverts for smoothies and self-portraits from other classes had been used to compare good with not so good.

- Recordings of last year's news broadcasts made by children were compared, also science conclusions and accurate and inaccurate geometry diagrams.

- PE (gym) videoclips were used to compare and discuss using *Aspire*.

- One teacher as a DT project made a lunar buggy which had many flaws. This helped children develop success criteria through their analysis of it and seeing what was expected.

- Good and not so good photo frames in DT and designs of sandwich boxes were also compared.

- Special school teachers used puppets that had created art works or aspects of food technology to compare.

- One teacher described a drama lesson in which good and bad talking was demonstrated, which led to children thinking more carefully about their own performance.

Beyond the success criteria – developing excellent writing

With thanks to Pie Corbett for his commentary (in blue)

When I first started teaching – before the National Curriculum and specific content requirements – children's writing tended to be judged by personal criteria: was it good to read, did it make sense, was it properly spelt and punctuated? With the advent of level descriptions and national tests, teachers had to more formally introduce children to the technical features of writing, such as adjectives, adverbs, complex sentences, similes and so on. This gave teachers and children a vocabulary about writing, but not about *quality*.

Success criteria emerged, as a breakdown of the learning objective, and were helpful in listing key elements to include – either compulsory or optional, depending on the nature of the learning objective (closed or open). In all subjects there are success criteria which detail the features of the particular skill in hand, which are necessary for children to know what the learning objective consists of. The elements of a newspaper report, for instance, are what makes a newspaper report, the elements of characterisation are what makes a characterisation, the elements of a collage are what makes a collage, the elements of a science investigation are what makes a science investigation. A completely different aspect, however, is what makes those things *excellent.*

Because Writing is the most controversial in the inclusion of success criteria – sometimes accused of stifling creativity – I am going to look closely at the issues here. I believe there are three success criteria-related components of good writing:

1 the included success criteria for that particular writing form (e.g. a newspaper article has headline, sub-title and so on);

2 the everyday secretarial features of spelling, handwriting, grammar and punctuation; and

3 the almost intangible elements of excellent writing that make you enjoy reading it and make you want to read on – incorporating technical features such as short sentences, adjectives and so on, and being clear about the impact on the reader and the suitability for the genre or writing type.

The first, the success criteria for the genre or writing form, is a given and helps children and teachers know what should be included in the structure of a particular piece. Looking at good examples helps children not only to generate the success criteria, but also gives them an idea of what a good piece might look like. Teachers' feedback about analysing products is consistent: the impact on quality will be evident in children's immediate attempts, within that lesson. This is not surprising, because children now have some exposure to what a good example looks like.

The second, the everyday features, are often seen on classroom posters entitled *'Every time we write'.* These are useful, because they point out the secretarial features children should always be checking and moving forwards in. The poster would typically consist of: correct **punctuation, spelling, handwriting** and **grammar**. These are also usefully displayed because they stop children talking about the wrong things when you want them to spot the features of a particular genre or writing construct when co-constructing success criteria. Ask children what features they can see in a characterisation, for instance, without the reminder that we are not looking for the things on the poster, and they will typically point out spelling and handwriting rather than features of a characterisation, such as personality and likes and dislikes.

The third, what makes *good* writing, needs some unpicking as there are some historical issues. Wherever there are high-stakes tests, teachers inevitably teach to that test – this, in England, was the case for the previously compulsory Writing paper for 11 year olds, which, for some years, awarded credit to vocabulary, connectives, openers and correct punctuation, even if those were used inappropriately, so that became the key focus in teaching children's writing. The rules suddenly changed and children were penalised for using these things inappropriately. The upshot has been that writing is now teacher-assessed only, so, at last, teachers in England can focus on what good writing should really look like.

After such pressure from a testing regime, teachers and children now find it difficult *not* to identify adjectives, short sentences, similes and so on as a measure of excellence when deciding on the quality of a piece of writing. It is the tests rather than success criteria that have stifled creativity. Rather than simply listing these technical elements, any class success criteria for 'good writing' might be more appropriate if it asked, for instance:

What makes good writing (for any genre)?

- What effect do you want your opening to have on the reader?
- What will do this best? (e.g. dialogue/flashback/descriptive setting/significant event, etc.)
- Have you avoided obvious or clichéd descriptions in your writing?
- Have you made sure your adjectives tell the reader something they would not have known?
- Have you chosen interesting, informative nouns and verbs (e.g. 'the policeman stared at the golden eagle' rather than 'the man looked at the bird')?
- Have you shown the reader how characters feel or look, rather than telling them?
- Does your writing make the reader want to read on?
- How do you want the reader to feel when they read your ending? Choose the best way of doing this.

Teachers from St Thomas of Canterbury R.C. Primary School in Salford have been using Pie Corbett's *Talk for Writing* and the idea of different types of success criteria for writing, resulting in outstanding outcomes. Fig. 7.1 shows an example of typical success criteria (toolkits) for writing, with the results shown in Figs 7.2–4. The columns in the biography success criteria are simply ticked to show the different people who have given feedback about the piece.

The writing toolkits are an attempt to draw attention to how a writer structures text and uses certain features but also involves what I would call 'writer's knowledge'. By this I mean things such as knowing that it is often more effective to 'show' how a character feels by describing their reaction to something rather than 'tell', e.g. Joanna gasped. I would have the toolkits for things such as suspense as a list of writerly options (tools not rules) that can be drawn on when writing.... but leave the possibility open that the child may find other ways to create suspense. P.C.

To write a biography you can:	Me	My peer	Mrs Abbott
The structure			
— introduce the person and why they are famous			
— share significant facts about their life in chronological order			
— include a closing statement that links back to the opening; (L5) may give writer's opinion			
Genre features			
— use 3rd person, past tense			
— include quotations			
— use connectives to link ideas			
— include a range of sentence types			
Consider the effect on the reader			
— (L5) engage the reader rather than just listing facts			
— show some of your opinions without being personal			
My personal writing targets are:			

Fig. 7.1 *A writing toolkit*

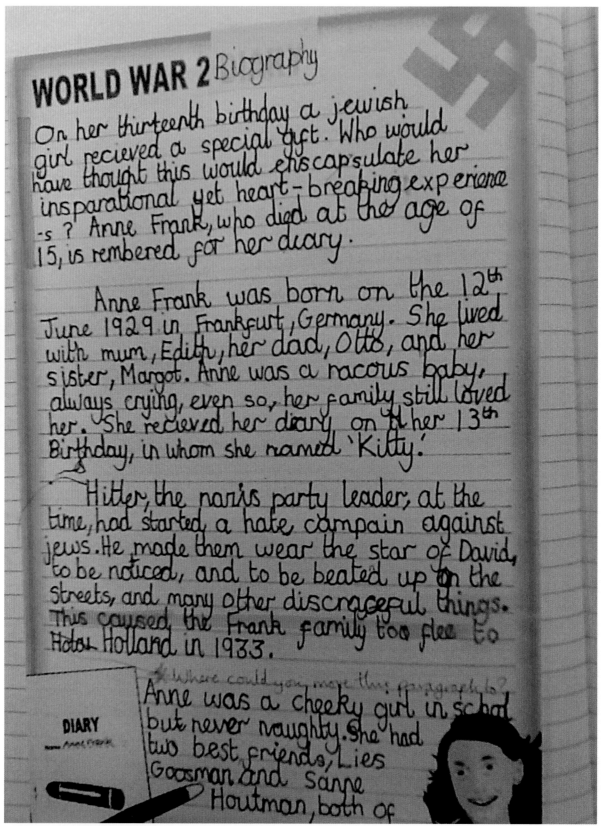

WORLD WAR 2 Biography

On her thirteenth birthday a jewish girl recieved a special gift. Who would have thought this would enscapsulate her insparational yet heart-breaking experience-s? Anne Frank, who died at the age of 15, is rembered for her diary.

Anne Frank was born on the 12th June 1929 in Frankfurt, Germany. She lived with mum, Edith, her dad, Otto, and her sister, Margot. Anne was a racous baby, always crying, even so, her family still loved her. She recieved her diary on her 13th Birthday, in whom she named 'Kitty.'

Hitler, the nazis party leader, at the time, had started a hate campain against jews. He made them wear the star of David, to be noticed, and to be beated up on the streets, and many other disgraceful things. This caused the Frank family too flee to Holland in 1933.

Where could you move this paragraph to?

Anne was a cheeky girl in school but never naughty. She had two best friends, Lies Goosman and Sanne Houtman, both of

DIARY
ANNE FRANK

Fig. 7.2 *Biography writing: opening*

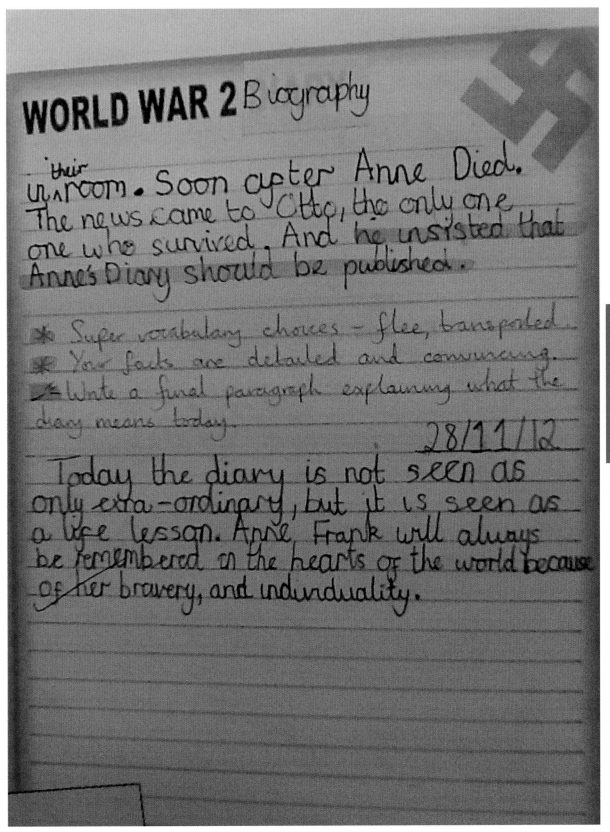

WORLD WAR 2 Biography

their
u room. Soon after Anne Died.
The news came to Otto, the only one
one who survived. And he insisted that
Anne's Diary should be published.

* Super vocabulary choices - flee, transported.
* Your facts are detailed and convincing.
* Write a final paragraph explaining what the
diary means today.
28/11/12

Today the diary is not seen as
only extra-ordinary, but it is seen as
a life lesson. Anne Frank will always
be remembered in the hearts of the world because
of her bravery, and individuality.

Fig. 7.3 *Biography writing: conclusion*

A newspaper report could:

- Include a short, catchy headline
- Report factually about the news
- Be written in the past sense
- Have an introduction with the five 'W's
- Explain in the main text each 'W'
- Include a quote
- Include a final paragraph looking to the future
- Remain impersonal
- Include 'If...' and 'When...' openers

Consider the effect on the reader:

Does it *sound* like a newspaper report? Is the reader now informed about the event?

Overwritten and clichéd prose

Pie Corbett, the master of children's writing, tackled the issue of clichéd and overwriting in *Teach First* (2013):

'*Consider this:*

The slender, elegant, graceful flamingo stood on one leg.

Many children might well say that this is a good sentence because it has lots of 'good' words in it. However, it is overwritten. Which adjective might we choose? Do we need an adjective? It might be worth saying 'the dishevelled flamingo' because that adds something that the reader could not possibly have known. Adjectives must earn their place, bringing something to a sentence that is new, and needed. Just chucking them in for the sake of it may well lead to poor writing.'

This certainly resonates, but, for young writers, including obvious adjectives is a rite of passage to get them beyond simple three- or four-word sentences and into learning to use them at all. Similarly, young children learn the colours red, blue, yellow, green, which are easily recognizable, before they can discern more subtle shades. Teachers of young children know only too well how often children begin by writing or articulating simple sentences like '*It was big*', '*I felt happy*', '*The dog is nice.*' By encouraging them to 'magpie' ('borrow') good adjectives from excellent examples, for instance, and brainstorm all the words we *could* use to describe the dog, using all our senses, we move them to a higher plain. Now the writing has obvious, clichéd adjectives, perhaps, but is greatly improved: '*The brown, fluffy dog with a waggly tail was nice and friendly*' would be a cause for celebration compared to '*The dog was nice.*' All features introduced need to go through this rite of passage, I believe – where their use is first overloaded and clichéd – in order to learn how to write more maturely.

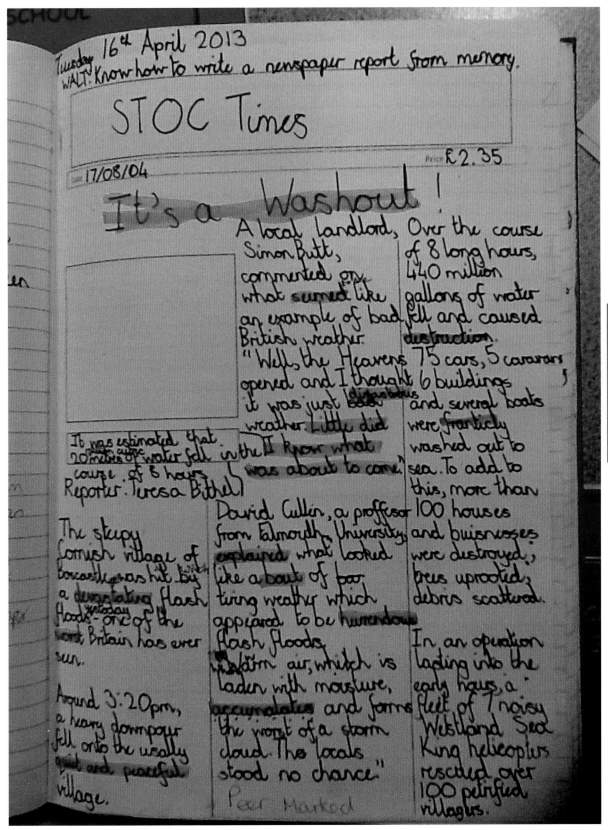

Fig. 7.4 *Newspaper report writing (provided by Danielle Abbott)*

'Overwriting', especially overuse of adjectives, is a welcome aspect of a young writer's development. It means that the child is enjoying the words and is able to generate synonyms. The next step on is to activate the inner reader that every writer needs, to help select which word is the best choice. I see writing as both generative and judgmental. It is the inner critic that needs as much development as the generator of ideas and words and images. In a way, how can you choose unless you can generate a range of possibilities? P.C.

I remember a secondary teacher who had never taught primary children complaining that children would come from primary school writing ridiculously 'purple' sentences and that what she was looking for was the ability to pull back, use fewer, more powerful words and sometimes even subvert the genre. What she failed to realise was how much work had been put into children's writing in primary to include all these words at all! Also, how relatively easy it is – once the teacher has decided that children are ready for more sophisticated dialogue about their writing – to get them to choose their words more carefully. As their reading improves and they have access to more examples of wonderful writing, children can consider using less obvious, more interesting and more appropriate description. What is certain is that to aim for excellent writing far beyond any technical ticklist must be every teacher's goal.

To write well, children have to read widely, deeply and regularly, so that the rhythms and patterns of effective prose become part of their linguistic bank – and so that their imaginative world is deepened and broadened. This helps when editing because we can 'hear' whether it 'sounds right'. Reading is the writer's yardstick. P.C.

When comparing good and not so good sentences with young children, Pie suggests that instead of one sentence without adjectives being compared to one with lots of them, the focus could be on using *more precise* nouns and verbs, a refreshing alternative to lists of adjectives.

Pie's example of refining nouns and verbs:

The man saw the bird.	The policeman stared at the golden eagle.

Corbett (2013)

I tried this with my young daughter, Katy, given the sentence *'The woman ate the food'*. Taking the nouns and verb one at a time, and asking for a better one, she came up with *'The hairdresser gobbled up the 25 sausage rolls!'*

Examples of modelling and analysing excellent writing

Comparing good with not so good

When comparing excellent and not so good examples of writing, we have a perfect opportunity to get children to talk about why one sentence is better than another *because of other things* – how it makes the reader feel, the rhythm of the words, the choice of certain words, the implied meaning, and so on, always bearing in mind how the sentence fits the whole paragraph.

We can only know if a sentence works when it is in a paragraph – so the idea of working on a sentence to make it into a stronger picture for the reader is fine – but in most cases, sentences sit inside paragraphs, so we only really know if a sentence works when it is seen in context. Having said that, good sentences do something to the imagination – writing is an experience. P.C.

Good and not so good examples of writing can be highlighted across similar elements so that specific comparisons can be made, as in Fig. 7.5a, with questions which aim to help children talk about good writing beyond the technical features. I have included possible questions a teacher might ask talk partners to discuss. Notice that technical elements are not mentioned, only the impact of the writer's intent.

Torah woke with a start. He hadn't meant to fall asleep. The fire had almost gone out and didn't give much light any more. He crouched down and peered into the dark forest. He couldn't see anything or hear anything. Had it come back? Was it out there now watching him with hot, murderous eyes?	Torah woke with a jolt from a sleep he never meant to have. The fire had burned low. He crouched in the fragile shell of light and peered into the looming blackness of the forest. He couldn't see anything, couldn't hear anything. Had it come back? Was it out there now, watching him?

Fig. 7.5a *Specific comparisons of quality*

First example	Second example	Things we might point out beyond technical features
Torah woke with a start. He hadn't meant to fall asleep.	Torah woke with a jolt from a sleep he never meant to have.	*Why is jolt better than start? What image does it give you? What is the difference in meaning between 'hadn't meant to fall asleep' and 'sleep he never meant to have'? What does the word 'never' seem to imply? How does the second sentence make you feel about his situation? What makes us feel uneasy in the words he has chosen?*
The fire had almost gone out and didn't give much light any more. He crouched down and peered into the dark forest.	The fire had burned low. He crouched in the fragile shell of light and peered into the looming blackness of the forest.	*What information is unnecessary? Why is 'looming blackness' better than 'dark'? Is it more effective to **tell** us it's dark or **show** us? How does each word affect you? Which words give us a sense of his anxiety? How does the word 'looming' sound? Would the word 'approaching' or 'gleaming' have the same effect? Why not?*
He couldn't see anything or hear anything. Had it come back? Was it out there now watching him with hot, murderous eyes?	He couldn't see anything, couldn't hear anything. Had it come back? Was it out there now, watching him?	*What sense does the repeat and rhythm of 'couldn't see anything, couldn't hear anything' give us? How would you say those words? What emotion do they convey compared to 'he couldn't see anything or hear anything?' Which of the two last lines has most impact? Which makes you feel more uneasy? Should the writer always describe the terrible thing or should it be implied and left to the reader's imagination?*

Fig. 7.5b *Discussion possibilities*

After this discussion, presenting the class with further examples of excellence will yield a more powerful discussion because of what they have learnt during this analysis.

Excellence in action

Seamus Gibbons, a teacher from St Luke's School in Westminster, London, helped children to identify quality writing in the context of a balanced argument by providing them with, first, a copy of his very own balanced argument, written when he was 11! The children were intrigued, of course, and Seamus pretended that he thought his work was spectacular. They were asked to whiteboard his level for the piece and he then revealed that it had been awarded Level 3 – below expectation for an 11 year old. He pointed out that his balanced argument had all the features listed in the success criteria – a question as a title, for and against, connectives, percentages and so on. He then showed them a piece written by a child from the previous year, which had been deemed Level 5 – above expectations for an 11 year old. The lesson continued with the children discussing and summarizing, in pairs, why one was better than the other in specific terms and how Seamus's example could have been improved. The lesson can be seen in full on my DVD *Outstanding Formative Assessment*. It is a wonderful example of the different elements of formative assessment being brought together, and the children's understanding of quality is tangible. The two balanced arguments he used can be seen in Figs 7.6 and 7.7.

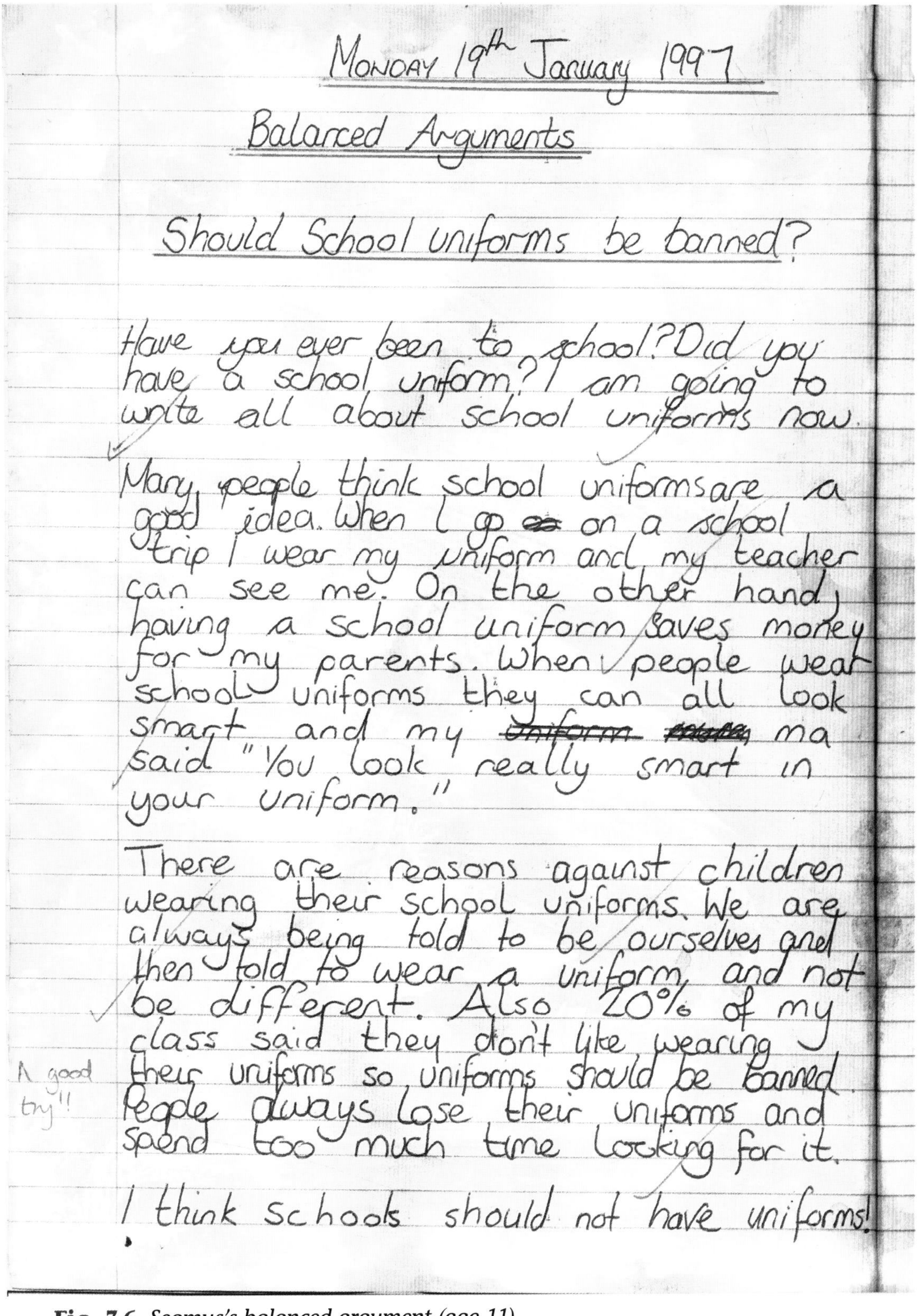

Monday 19th January 1997

Balanced Arguments

Should School uniforms be banned?

Have you ever been to school? Did you have a school uniform? I am going to write all about school uniforms now.

Many people think school uniforms are a good idea. When I go on a school trip I wear my uniform and my teacher can see me. On the other hand, having a school uniform saves money for my parents. When people wear school uniforms they can all look smart and my ~~uniform~~ ~~~~ ma said "You look really smart in your uniform."

There are reasons against children wearing their school uniforms. We are always being told to be ourselves and then told to wear a uniform, and not be different. Also 20% of my class said they don't like wearing their uniforms so uniforms should be banned. People always lose their uniforms and spend too much time looking for it.

I think schools should not have uniforms!

A good try!!

Fig. 7.6 *Seamus's balanced argument (age 11)*

Should school uniforms be banned in schools?

For as long as we can remember, children have been wearing school uniforms. However, in the last few years there has been an explosion of fashion styles – making school children more passionate about having an individual style. As a result, considerable debate has taken place recently, as to whether pupils should have to wear school uniforms or not.

No one can deny the importance of having an identity and this includes a school identify. Wearing school uniforms provides children with a strong connection to their school, giving students a sense of belonging. Equally it is cheaper for parents to buy school uniforms for their children, meaning parents don't have to worry about money. For instance, in supermarkets such as ASDA – you can buy school uniforms for as cheap as £2, this helps parents who have financial issues. Another reason for the importance of children wearing uniforms is that it provides teachers with reassurance on school trips. When a school is on a trip, the children's safety is the most important thing for teachers. If they can easily recognize their children because they can see the school uniform, it reassures them. David Cameron, the Prime Minister, stated that "When children are wearing school uniforms on trips, the likelihood of one getting lost is much less. Of those children who have gotten lost on a school trip, 92% of them were not wearing a school uniform."

On the other hand, there is much evidence to support reasons for children not wearing a school uniform. The government and parents are always encouraging children to be more individual and independent, by children being allowed to choose their own clothes they are encouraged to do this. Similarly, uniforms are made from very itchy material which can be uncomfortable to wear and distract children from their learning. For example, in a survey carried out online, 96% of children stated that they found their uniform to be uncomfortable. In addition to this, teachers report that much time is wasted searching for lost uniform. Items such as ties and jumpers are constantly being lost and children spend their learning time looking for these objects.

Without a doubt, there is strong evidence to support both reasons for and against children wearing school uniforms. However, it is my opinion that children need a sense of belonging in their school and by wearing a school uniform children are provided with this. Therefore I believe school uniforms should not be banned in schools. What do you think?

Fig. 7.7 *An 11 year old's contrasting balanced argument*

Seamus's thoughts:

'For every writing genre I will ensure all the examples I show identify high-quality features. I will then do a lesson on comparing and contrasting two different types of writing, with one displaying excellence. I have now purposely started to put "wow" words and random sentence-openers in the bad example to draw discussion out. I will then show them more examples of good-quality pieces (so by this stage they have seen about seven) and on top of that I will ensure my guided reading links with the writing, so they see even more examples of excellence. This is why, if they have their writing journals alongside them all the time and are constantly writing and magpieing those ideas, they have an incredible bank of excellence at their fingertips to support their writing.'

Comparing equally 'levelled' writing

Another strategy many teachers use is to present children with two equally levelled pieces of writing – in terms of test criteria and success criteria – and ask them to analyse which is the one most likely to make you want to read on. Doing this gives a powerful message that the success criteria and use of secretarial features only go so far and certainly do not guarantee that the reader will want to continue reading. As part of a focus on the popular horror genre, Seamus used the Level 5 pieces from the previous year's class (Fig. 7.8).

A sheet of darkness took over the sky. Quivering, Paul lay awake in bed. If he dared to sleep, would it come back again? He sat up in his bed to try and calm the rapid beating of his heart. 'It's just my imagination,' he whispered to himself. Just as he finally began to relax, he felt a chilling drop in the temperature of the room. The hair on the back of his neck rose. It was back.	Night time had finally come. Paul knew now he had to do his dare! It was time to walk through the crumbling graveyard. 'Why did I agree to do this stupid dare?' wondered Paul. He was petrified! He opened the rusty gates and slowly stepped in. Paul was desperate to turn around, but knew Christian and his gang would never let him forget. He had to brave the graveyard.

Fig. 7.8 *Two equally 'levelled' openings used for quality comparison*

VIDEOCLIP TASTER #12 Comparing two excellent examples

Seamus shows the class of 11 year olds two excellent ghost story openings and asks which one is the most engaging and why.
http://bit.ly/1j6Qc1a

The difference between the two is not immediately obvious, and both have recognisably 'excellent' features. Even though we could decide that the first is better written, the context might resonate with one reader and not another. I might be interested in the gang, for instance, even though the writing in that piece is more 'obvious'. Choosing a book to read is not governed just by the quality of the writing, but also the context, setting and genre – all personal preferences. The main difference Seamus's class identified was that in the first piece the reader was *shown* how the author felt (sheet of darkness, rapid beating of his heart, hair on the back of his neck), whereas the second *told* the reader (night had come, he was petrified, Paul was desperate). This kind of analytical session can be carried out with children of any age. Old pupil work is particularly effective because it lends credibility to teachers' and children's aspirations. The impact of comparing products in this way is that children's writing is considerably improved and they become more confident and independent writers.

By widening the teaching repertoire of reading, identifying and writing excellence in the ways outlined so far, we will be able to create writers who know how to write far beyond the success criteria.

Finally, to bring together all the elements that makes good writing – not just the link to success criteria and beyond – a teacher from a school which had been involved in Pie Corbett's 'Talk for Writing' project described to me the amazing progress that her children had made in one year. She focused in on one child who had made a leap from 3a to 5c (five sub-levels), which is way beyond the expected progress for a child for a year in England. Her questions to the child:

> T: Alex, are you a good writer?
>
> A: Yes, I'd like to think so.
>
> T: What has made you a good writer?
>
> A: I'd have to say **toolkits** (see Fig. 7.9) have really helped. They help me to know what to write now, not just reminding me about punctuation. Also **shared writing** with Miss and also **working in pairs**. I love 'magpieing' from other people. I'd also have to say **AFL marking in pairs** and with Miss has really helped. It shows me what is good about my writing and what I need to do to improve.

What the child calls 'AFL marking in pairs' is fully outlined in Chapter 9.

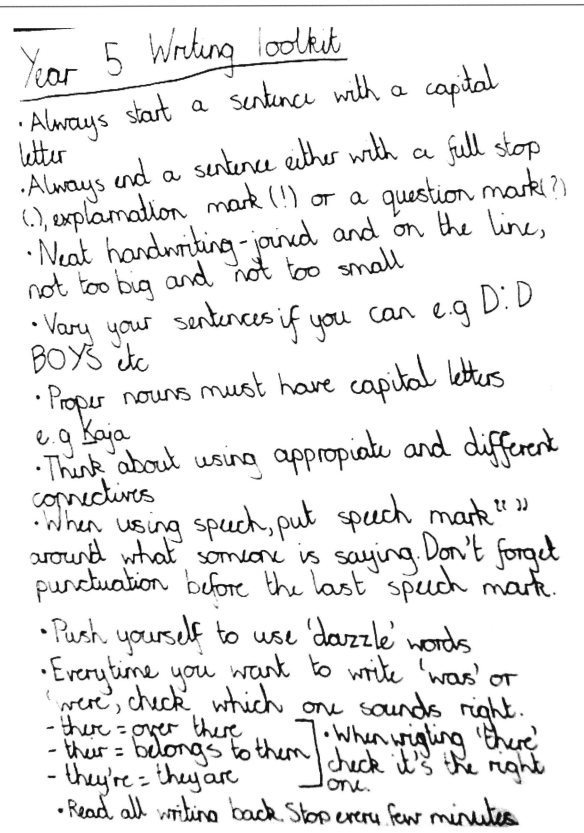

Year 5 Writing Toolkit

- Always start a sentence with a capital letter
- Always end a sentence either with a full stop (.), explamation mark (!) or a question mark(?)
- Neat handwriting-joined and on the line, not too big and not too small
- Vary your sentences if you can e.g D:D BOYS etc
- Proper nouns must have capital letters e.g Kaja
- Think about using appropiate and different connectives
- When using speech, put speech mark " " around what someone is saying. Don't forget punctuation before the last speech mark.

- Push yourself to use 'dazzle' words
- Everytime you want to write 'was' or 'were', check which one sounds right.
  - there = over there
  - their = belongs to them] · When wriging 'there'
  - they're = they are   ] check it's the right one.
- Read all writing back. Stop every few minutes

Fig. 7.9 *Writing toolkit*

Toolkits can make writing hard if there are too many things to worry about and they are not seen as options (though punctuation is not optional). Ideally, the tools need to be noticed and discussed in reading (and read aloud and dramatised), practised on mini-whiteboards many times, so that they begin to become internalised as part of the child's repertoire – becoming increasingly automatic. P.C.

Building on the exposure and analysis of writing, the next two chapters – *Ongoing questioning* and *Feedback* – look at ways in which we can bring the feedback from the pupil to the teacher and how children can become constant reviewers and improvers of their writing and all other learning, through appropriate and effective self-, peer and teacher feedback.

Summary

Sharing, analysing and discussing models of excellence, across all subjects, is a powerful way of helping children see what a good example might look like, and giving them a tangible understanding of quality.

Teachers use two main strategies:

- whole-class sharing and analysis of many excellent examples from the same context and skill;
- sharing and analysis by comparing products: excellent and not so good, good and excellent or equally assessed pieces.

There appear to be three success criteria-related components to good writing:

1. the included success criteria for that particular writing frame (e.g. a newspaper article has headline, subtitle and so on);

2. the everyday secretarial features of spelling, handwriting, grammar and punctuation; and

3. the almost intangible elements of excellent writing that make you enjoy reading it and make you want to read on, incorporating technical features such as short sentences, adjectives and so on.

Once success criteria for the features of the writing form are established, excellence can be achieved by exposure to excellent examples of writing. Comparing good with not so good is particularly powerful, because what makes good writing can be analysed beyond any technical or secretarial features.

PART TWO
Lesson Culture and Structure

Developing the learning

8 Ongoing questioning

A constant theme in formative assessment is the continuing quest to try to understand children's understanding. This is usually interpreted as a need for constant summative assessment, such as giving further examples after the teaching: effectively classroom tests, to ascertain levels of achievement. While this can be helpful, it is usually true that a child's performance during regular class activities is unlikely to be different in a test scenario. Although analysis of children's efforts can isolate particular weaknesses, the information is often hollow, leaving more unanswered questions than answers. Why did the child get this one wrong? How were they visualising it at the time? Why did they not see the pattern? How can they have made that mistake? Why can't they remember where to put apostrophes? Why did they start this section again? Why did they change this word for one that wasn't as good?

As Hattie (2009) reminds us, the most important feedback is what teachers learn from students, so that we can rethink our strategies.

Talk partner opportunities

Eavesdropping

Talk partners have made children's thinking more transparent, as they are given many opportunities to articulate their thinking, so partner discussion moments present frequent golden opportunities for the teacher to walk around the classroom *eavesdropping* on those often illuminating conversations. Interesting ideas can be shared with the whole class, misconceptions can be noted and 'on the hoof' changes in the direction of the lesson made. Without this opportunity to hear what children are thinking, we might carry on the lesson with misconceptions being built upon misconceptions.

One-to-one dialogue

With more extended talk partner activities (e.g. *'Take turns explaining your method of multiplying'*, or *'Cooperatively improve your sentences one at a time'*), the teacher has a powerful opportunity to *engage individual children* in discussion. What should the teacher ask to make the most of those few minutes? Seamus Gibbons, the subject of many of the videoclips throughout this book, uses a number of effective questions to individuals throughout lessons, which reveal children's thinking and understanding:

➤ *'Tell me what you have done?'*

➤ *'Tell me what you're going to do first?'*

➤ *'What do you mean by…?'* *(key question, even if the teacher thinks s/he knows what they mean by it)*

➤ *'Why do you think…?'*

➤ *'Give me an example of what you mean'* *(key question, as often reveals misconceptions)*

➤ *'Can you develop on that?'*

➤ *'So why is this one better than that?'* *(key question, as a concrete example is available)*

➤ *'How could you change this to make it clearer?'*

VIDEOCLIP TASTER #13 Ongoing effective questioning

Seamus continually asks individuals about their learning, helping them by his questioning to clarify their thinking.
http://bit.ly/1lZugVh

The more you probe, the more is revealed, so *'What do you mean by…?'* is a simple way of getting to the heart of children's understanding. Many answers given by children are correct but don't reveal the level of their understanding. For example, the answer *'connectives'* or *'numerator'* might be right, often picked up by knowing it's the right word to say, but *'What do you mean by a connective/numerator?'* or *'Give me an example'* as a follow-up to either answer will reveal the child's real understanding. If this is a constant feature of a lesson, all children, over time, will get a good deal of face-to-face informative questioning by the teacher and lessons will be more effectively redirected as children's understanding is continually revealed. *'So why is this one better than that?'*, used when children have examples of good and not so good in front of them, helps focus them by referring to concrete examples. A child struggling to explain how one of the balanced arguments could be improved, for instance, can be directed to a specific comparison of, say, the use of percentages in each, where the improvement need is now obvious.

Table/desk configuration

The ability to question children in this way is greatly affected by the configuration of the tables in the classroom. As stated in Chapter 2, our tradition has been, in primary schools, to group children around tables of four or usually six. Although talk partners can easily learn together at these tables, there are disadvantages to the model. Half of the children around the table have their back to the teacher, or are sideways on, having to constantly turn their neck or lean to avoid staring at the back of the head of the child in front of them. While they are concentrating on individual learning, facing another child at the table is an unnecessary distraction. Even facial expressions can be enough to put someone off their thinking. If we look at the role of the teacher in questioning individual children, moreover, the six-round-a-table configuration is not conducive to effective teacher to pupil discussion. The teacher has to either *(a)* crouch in-between two children, thus distracting the next-to child and probably all the other children around the table who can now clearly hear everything the teacher is saying to the child, or *(b)* talk over the top of the child's head while standing behind them looking at their work, the child in question looking up and round to hold any eye contact with the teacher – usually not attempted because of that difficulty.

By organising the tables in the room to facilitate the learning, these problems can be easily fixed. The configurations illustrated in Chapter 2 and again here (Fig. 8.1) enable children to see the whiteboard, the teacher at the front and still be able to talk and learn with their partner but not be distracted by other children facing them. The teacher, in each configuration, can walk to individual children at any time, get directly in front of them, hold eye contact and ask them to talk about their learning in as private a setting as is possible in a busy classroom. Remembering the importance of the student/teacher relationship (Hattie, 2009), the face-to-face communication is critical in establishing a sense of the teacher really listening and therefore caring about the learning for each child.

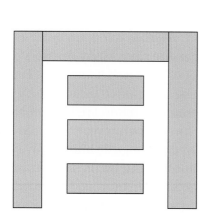

Fig. 8.1a *U-shape with rows*

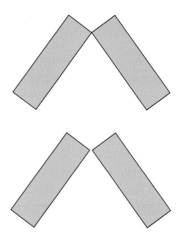

Fig. 8.1b *Arrow shapes*

Using Bloom's Taxonomy and Thinking Hats to ask higher-order questions during lessons

Bloom's Taxonomy

Bloom's Taxonomy is a well-known vehicle for planning questions through six levels:

- Knowledge
- Understanding
- Application
- Analysis
- Synthesis and speculation
- Evaluation

Analysis of questioning: *Each Peach Pear Plum*, by Allan and Janet Ahlberg

Type of question:	Question asked:	Examples of children's answers	Comments
Knowledge	Where is Tom Thumb hiding? What is a cellar?	"In the tree" A.A/I.C/A.P (and pointed to the tree) "Might be like celery" — M.T "It's where you keep your butter" — L.C "It's up the stairs and in the roof" J.A	This question focussed and engaged the children — opened up a dialogue Important to ask these questions as can identify misconceptions
Understanding	Why were the bears out hunting? What is happening in this picture?	"They need to find their dinner" — L.P-H "They might be looking for bunnies" — M.T "When they are hungry they look for food" — K.W "They were looking for the baby...hidden in water... saved the baby" J.A "The baby is floating away" — L.B	These children showed a good understanding This child was familiar with the story and was retelling This was one of only two EAL children who offered a comment — would TPs help in this situation?
Application	Where do you think the wicked witch would live? What do you think Cinderella will dust?	"A tree house" A.A "A scary house" A.F "A castle" C.C "Upstairs" — D.H "The wall" I.C "The windows" A.P/H.T "The roof" D.B "The taps" A.F	Adult encouragement needed for children to think beyond the story
Analysis	How are the bears feeling?	"Happy" — then "sad" I.C "Happy" A.H "They want to take Baby Bunting away — they are saving him" — L.P-H "They are going to carry him home" — K.W	These children were older and had some experience of working with this language Not clear use of emotion vocabulary but had a good sense of what was happening in the story — further learning opportunity
Synthesis and speculation	What do you think Bo Peep is doing in the field?	"She needs to cut down the straw" — Loki	Perhaps remembered from recent Little Red Hen topic
Evaluation	What would you write if you could change the end of the story?	"They would all get messy" — M.T "They all went home. The witch went home and never came back again" — L.C "The witch would turn someone into a frog" — E.M "The bears would start hurting the boys" J.A "They would eat up all the pie, put the dish back in the kitchen, and then go home" L.R	Some lovely confident answers

- These sessions were 15–20 minutes long and took place at 1pm, after the children's lunch break, and at regular morning group time.
- It was part of the children's normal routine.
- The whole class participated – approx. 24 children in one group and 18 in the other. All children were aged between 3 and 4.
- Both groups contained approx. 8 EAL children – on average, 3 EAL children offered comments.
- The children enjoyed the story and the majority could handle the breaks in storytelling to answer questions.
- We noticed some of the EAL children became a little fidgety during the questioning.
- Sue's group had the story read to them first and then revisited it with questioning.
- Normally we wouldn't use so many questions in one story session.
- Having a prompt sheet with example questions helped enormously.
- We would like to continue questioning in this way with smaller groups and possibly with talking partners.
- This session went very well, the children made some interesting observations, and we could get a good sense of prior knowledge, misconceptions and targets for further learning as the session progressed.
- We felt that the majority of the class were thinking more deeply and creatively, felt more challenged and included in the session.

Fig. 8.2 *Nursery school use of Bloom's Taxonomy*

Two nursery teachers sent me an account of their experimentation with Bloom's taxonomy in their story sessions with 4 year olds (see Fig. 8.2). As they state at the end of this piece, their focused questions gave them insight about children's prior knowledge, their misconceptions, and targets for future learning. The children were thinking more deeply and creatively and felt more challenged and included.

De Bono's 'Thinking Hats'

Edward De Bono's *Thinking Hats* (1999) is his most famous creation. The hats, often literally used as such in the classroom, help channel children's thinking about a particular question. The six hats are described in Fig. 8.3.

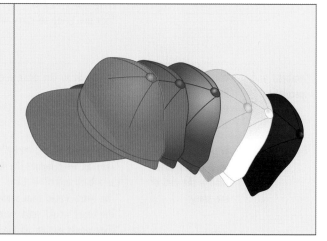

White: Information
(What are the facts?)
Red: Emotion
(What is my gut feeling about this?)
Black: Discernment
(What are the reasons to be cautious?)
Yellow: Optimistic response
(What are the benefits?)
Green: Provocation and investigation *(What are the possibilities, alternatives and new ideas?)*
Blue: Meta-cognition
(Are we managing the hat process properly?)

Fig. 8.3 *De Bono's 'Thinking Hats'*

Although teachers usually use the hats to help children think more deeply or in a specific way (*'This is a yellow hat question: Should we eat meat?'*), De Bono suggests a more structured approach. As a pre-cursor to a focus on writing balanced arguments, for instance, there would first be an extended session with the white hat, establishing the facts to create a shared vision of the issue being addressed. The other hats would then be used for a few minutes at a time, except the red hat, which is used for a very short time to ensure gut reactions rather than judgements. The rationale for the hats is that the brain thinks in a number of distinct ways which can be deliberately channelled and hence planned for use in a structured way, allowing us to develop tactics for thinking about particular issues.

Summary

- Continual questioning of individual pupils can help illuminate their understanding and so guide the direction of a lesson and the planning for individual needs.
- The configuration of tables in the room needs to facilitate teacher-to-child face-to-face discussion as well as a comfortable, non-distracting arrangement for pupils to be able to look to the front and be able to have paired and group discussions.
- Guiding questions through Bloom's Taxonomy or De Bono's Thinking Hats can also lead to deeper understanding on the part of the teacher and the pupil.

9   Feedback

So far...

The aim of formative assessment is to make learners independent enough to be able to confidently self- and peer assess and make subsequent improvements of their ongoing work. The preceding chapters have laid the foundations through the embedding of a *learning culture* and opportunities for much *mixed-ability paired and class discussion*. Lessons have *learning objectives* revealed, *prior knowledge* explored and *success criteria* generated or revisited. While the task is in hand, *ongoing questioning* gives pupils a chance to provide their feedback to the teacher so that the feedback they get from the teacher is appropriate. These conditions create capacity for the pupil to take control of the feedback stage and self- and peer assess, making ongoing improvements a matter of course.

Research findings

Hattie's effect-size for feedback is 0.73, or 9 months ahead, putting feedback within the top three of the 150 elements of education, ordered according to his extensive research synthesis. The Sutton Trust report (2011) summarises the research, defining feedback thus:

> *Feedback is information given to the learner and/or teacher about the learner's performance relative to the learning goals which then redirects or refocuses either the teacher's or the learners' actions to achieve the goal. Negative effects of feedback exist where feedback threatens self-esteem.*

To dismiss external rewards, or extrinsic motivation, appropriately, I first want to summarise the key research about their negative impact, via Hattie's effect-size round-up of the various studies. The effect-size is 0.4, so anything below that means its impact is low. If it reaches a negative value, it indicates regression:

> *Deci, Koestner and Ryan (1999) described tangible rewards (stickers, awards and so on). They found a negative correlation between extrinsic rewards and task performance (-0.34). Tangible rewards significantly undermined intrinsic motivation, particularly for interesting tasks (-0.68). Deci concluded that extrinsic rewards are typically negative because they "undermine people's responsibility for motivating or regulating themselves". Rather, extrinsic rewards are a controlling*

strategy that often leads to greater surveillance, evaluation and competition, all of which have been found to undermine enhanced engagement and regulation (Deci and Ryan, 1985). Verbal rewards appeared to produce (Cameron and Pierce, 1994) a positive effect and tangible rewards suggested a negative effect.

Kluger and DeNisi (1996) conducted the most systematic study of the various types of feedback. The highest impact occurs when goals are specific and challenging but when task complexity is low. Giving praise for completing a task appears to be ineffective, which is hardly surprising because it contains such little learning-related information. Feedback is more effective when there are perceived low rather than high levels of threat to self-esteem, because low threat conditions allow attention to be paid to the feedback.'

Hattie (2009)

Black and Wiliam's *Inside the Black Box* summary of their famous review of formative assessment literature contained a powerful message to teachers about the impact of external rewards, including grading – more about which will follow:

'Where the classroom culture focuses on rewards, gold stars, grades or place in the class rankings, then pupils look for the ways to obtain the best marks rather than at the needs of their learning which these marks ought to reflect. One reported consequence is that where they have any choice, pupils avoid difficult tasks. They also spend time and energy looking for clues to the "right answer". Many are reluctant to ask questions out of fear of failure. Pupils who encounter difficulties and poor results are led to believe that they lack ability, and this belief leads them to attribute their difficulties to a defect in themselves about which they cannot do a great deal. So they "retire hurt", avoid investing effort in learning which could only lead to disappointment and try to build up their self-esteem in other ways. Whilst the higher achievers can do well in such a culture, the overall effect is to enhance the frequency and the extent of underachievement.

Feedback to any pupil should be about the particular qualities of his or her work, with advice on what he or she can do to improve, and should avoid comparisons with other pupils.'

Black and Wiliam (1998b)

The rest of the Sutton Trust quote on page 121 focuses on the significance of the feedback flow, where information comes from student to teacher, teacher to student or student to student, and is developed further by Hattie, who has spent many years researching and exploring issues surrounding feedback:

> 'The mistake I made was seeing feedback as something teachers provided to students. I discovered that feedback is most powerful when it is from the student to the teacher. What they know, what they understand, where they make errors, when they have misconceptions, when they are not engaged – then teaching and learning can be synchronized and powerful. Feedback to teachers makes learning visible.'

Hattie (2012)

He reiterates, in *Visible Learning and the Science of How We Learn*, in his opening to the entire book:

> 'The overarching theme introduced through the initial Visible Learning book is that achievement in schools is maximized when teachers see learning through the eyes of students, and when students see learning through the eyes of themselves as teachers.'

Hattie and Yates (2014)

This emphasis on the importance of the information given to *the teacher* by the children synthesises perfectly with the spirit and practice of formative assessment. The constant quest to find out what children know characterised by prior-knowledge question starters, ongoing questioning and delving, frequent talk partner/class discussions and mid-lesson learning stops where individual children's work is critiqued by all leads to continual information being passed from pupils to teachers. The growth mindset learning culture reduces a fear of failure and encourages children to share their errors, to see them as learning opportunities, for it is when we make mistakes that we are given an opportunity to receive feedback. That feedback moves us further on in our learning. As Hattie (2012) reinforces:

> 'Feedback is most effective when students do not have proficiency or mastery – and thus it thrives when there is error or incomplete knowing and understanding. Errors invite opportunity. They should not be seen as embarrassments, signs of failure or something to be avoided. They are exciting, because they indicate a tension between what we now know and what we could know: they are signs of opportunities to learn and they are to be embraced.'

Practical applications of the feedback principles

'Closing the gap' principles of feedback

I have taken Sadler's three conditions for effective feedback to take place to illustrate how formative assessment can fulfil those principles (see Table 9.1). This is the big picture of the practical applications: how we help children to become confident self- and peer assessors, constantly and actively improving their learning, but also how the rationale of 'closing the gap' looks in practice. Feedback is not just a matter of oral and written marking, but a powerful jigsaw of actions and expectations.

Sadler's three conditions	How formative assessment fulfils them
Possess a concept of the goal being aimed for	➤ Be given the learning objective at the point at which it will affect performance *not to know* ➤ Have co-constructed success criteria for the skill in hand, using them to know what should or could be included and evaluating progress against them ➤ See more than one example of excellence in order to be able to apply the ingredients of excellence, without being constrained to one version only
Compare the actual level of performance with the goal	➤ Articulate to peers and to the teacher their understanding of the task and how it relates to the learning objective so far ➤ Have mid-lesson learning stops during which random examples are analysed under the visualiser for successes and 'even better ifs' and for 'magpieing' of ideas
Engage in some appropriate action which leads to some closure of the gap	➤ Be able to follow those up with self or cooperative improvement to one's own learning/product immediately, making review a constant activity

Table 9.1 *'Closing the gap' link with formative assessment*

We know that the more immediate the feedback the better, so we are now incorporating feedback into the very fabric of a lesson. The feedback, at its best, should result in greater understanding and therefore improvement of some kind. The questioning strategies covered in the last chapter provide one-to-one feedback from teacher to pupil throughout the day, although not every child will be reached in this way. However, over time, there are many episodes of quality feedback if the right questions are asked (e.g. *'What do you mean by that? Give me an example...').*

The paired discussions punctuating the day provide individual feedback to pupils from their partner about their thinking or their written work, and by articulating their thinking, intentions and reflections, pupils are more likely to see how they can change their strategy, improve their writing and so on.

Mid-lesson learning stops and cooperative marking enable pupils to actively improve their work by seeing excellent examples and discussing possible improvements. More detail about these powerful strategies are now described. They have had a significant influence on the quality and practice of feedback during lessons.

Mid-lesson learning stops

The advent of the visualiser or document camera has enabled teachers to stop at any time and ask the class to analyse ongoing work under the visualiser. The most effective technique within my teams has been to randomly pick a child using lollysticks or similar, so that everyone is focused, not knowing whose work will be picked. Anybody's work can be discussed if the same process is used, whether the highest or the lower achiever is the author. The routine tends to be as follows:

1 Ask the class to read through the piece first, look at it if art work, study it if mathematics, and so on.

2 They decide, in pairs, what are the best bits, either reflecting the success criteria or, if looking at narrative writing, looking beyond the success criteria. As discussed in Chapter 7, a piece might have very few technical aspects but be brilliant in other ways. Children give their opinions about the best bits and these are underlined and analysed as to why they are so good.

3 The class is then asked if there are any parts that could be improved or made even better. This might be how the piece could continue if there are no obvious improvement places. If a sentence feels right, even though there might not be spectacular adjectives, children need to keep it intact.

We don't want to improve things just for the sake of it. I once witnessed two children changing one really good sentence into a short sentence, taking out the good adjectives, simply because the success criteria listed short sentences for effect for a scary story. Pie Corbett talks about children needing to develop 'a nose' for quality by exposure to wonderful sentences and phrases in excellent texts, so that they feel the quality rather than itemise it.

4 After this modelling and possible magpieing of good ideas, words or phrases, children cooperatively, in pairs, working with one book at a time, discuss their own work in the same way, identifying good bits and discussing possible improvements.

> ## VIDEOCLIP TASTER #14 Mid-lesson learning stop
>
> Katie takes one child's writing at random for the class to analyse for 'best bits' and improvement needs. http://bit.ly/1fnZB5c
>
>

Cooperative feedback discussions versus swapping books

The general interpretation of peer marking or peer assessment has been the swapping of children's work. The pupil now becomes a teacher, working on their own, making comments on the work about what they liked and what could be improved. I have seen many examples of pieces marked by children in this way and, even at secondary level, the marking tends to be superficial and relatively unhelpful. *Cooperative feedback*, however, is an entirely different and more productive experience:

1 Both children read and discuss one of their pieces together, so *only one book between them*. The child whose work it is has control of the pen and ultimate say, unlike the swapping books scenario.

2 Together they decide the best bits, which they might disagree about, but reasons are given and those bits underlined, often pink for 'tickled pink' or a similar colour.

3 Then, together, they talk about improvements that could be made and the author makes them on the piece, there and then, writing the improvement in a new colour, often green. As the available space for improvements will be limited, many schools leave the left hand side of children's books blank, so that improvement can be written with no limits and retain legibility. No comments are written on the piece by either child, because this would take away precious time when the actual improvements could be made. Again, the author has the last word on the choice of improvement.

I once witnessed a discussion between two children about one of their scary story openings. The author read it out then described how she thought she had made the setting too obvious (a haunted house). She had the idea of improving it by setting it in a very safe and happy place, like Disneyworld, so that the horror would be more unexpected and therefore more effective. Her response partner said he thought she should set it in the jungle. Without any further discussion, she changed it to a jungle setting.... We need to make clear to children that their partner is only there to give them ideas, not to dictate, and this should be modelled – e.g. "Thank you, but I still prefer my idea."

The children then go through the same process with the other child's book.

VIDEOCLIP TASTER #15 Cooperative feedback

Two children cooperatively improve their writing.
http://bit.ly/1IZulrY

The steps detailed here relate to written work, but the cooperative improvement process can be used across all subjects. Instead of one book between them, they have one piece of mathematics, one piece of art work, one technology model and so on. The 'improvements' made might not be underlinings or written in a different colour, but, in order to make the process explicit to outside parties, children can label their practical learning to make explicit the process of discussion and improvement that took place (e.g. 23/2/14: *John and I liked the way I had used the watercolour wash for the sky but decided to add more...*).

This two-step practice of mid-lesson stops followed by cooperative feedback discussions leads to pupils working much harder than they used to, when the convention tended to be that work was mainly uninterrupted during lessons, then handed in for copious marking by the teacher, given back at a later time when the feedback was too late to do anything about, and was limited to written comments only. Of course there are times when children should not be interrupted in their writing, but when we are skill-building, constant review is more helpful than waiting till the product is finished then needing to go back and redo it.

One primary teacher created a 'cycle of success' as a poster (Fig. 9.1) for children to refer to, keeping them constantly aware of the 'big picture' of their learning from the learning objective through to the improvement stage.

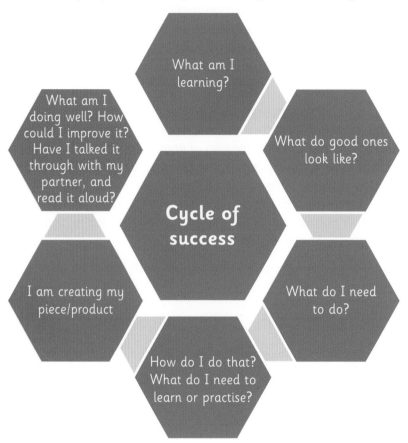

Fig. 9.1 *'Cycle of success' poster*

Using individually created success criteria for closed skills to probe understanding and give feedback

A recent interesting development in the feedback arena is the use of ***individually pupil-created*** success criteria for closed skills in mathematics and literacy skills (grammar and punctuation) which are then shared in mid-lesson learning stops followed by cooperative improvement. The criteria are written by the children *after the skill has been taught* to see how they are understanding the skill. The impact has been that it has given teachers and pupils an opportunity to see whether children have complete or incomplete understanding of the skill and to do something about that via the success criteria. Examples of this approach in action now follow.

Mathematics criteria used for seeking and developing understanding

This strategy works really well with children who can write fluently, so from about age 7 onwards. The steps are as follows:

1 Teach a new skill (e.g. how to calculate the range and mode) and have children practise it as a class.

2 Ask children to individually write their own success criteria for how to do the calculation, in whichever words will mean most to them. Walk around talking to individuals while this is happening, asking what they are going to write and get a feel for what they are all writing.

VIDEOCLIP TASTER #16 Individually created mathematics success criteria

After practising the skill, the class write their own individual success criteria for calculating the mode. http://bit.ly/1IZunjp

3 Take one child's success criteria at random and show them under the visualiser. Read through them and ask pairs to discuss first what is useful and secondly how the success criteria could be made even clearer. (It might sometimes be useful to 'fix' the lollystick, if there is one example you have noticed which contains a common error or omission and would be useful to share with the whole class.)

VIDEOCLIP TASTER #17 Analysing mathematics success criteria

One child's success criteria are analysed for identification of success and possible improvement needs. http://bit.ly/1h5Zbf8

4 Pairs then read out their success criteria to each other, cooperatively improving them.

5 Take one improved version and show it under the visualiser and give a little more time for children to improve their own versions again. These success criteria now become their reference every time they are presented with the skill.

A useful aid to this strategy is to reserve the left-hand side of the maths book for success criteria to be written, so that children know where to find them.

The following examples illustrate children's individual success criteria. Children's improvements are mainly answering the question *'Why do you have to do that step?'* Sometimes (e.g. Fig. 9.5) the teacher has jotted a question (*VF* for verbal feedback) as he is walking around while they are writing. Their responses reveal the extent of their understanding. Fig. 9.2 has all the right steps, but the wrong answer. The child has grasped the process, but has revealed misconceptions about division. Figs 9.3 and 9.4 have added explanations after feedback from the teacher, written on the spot.

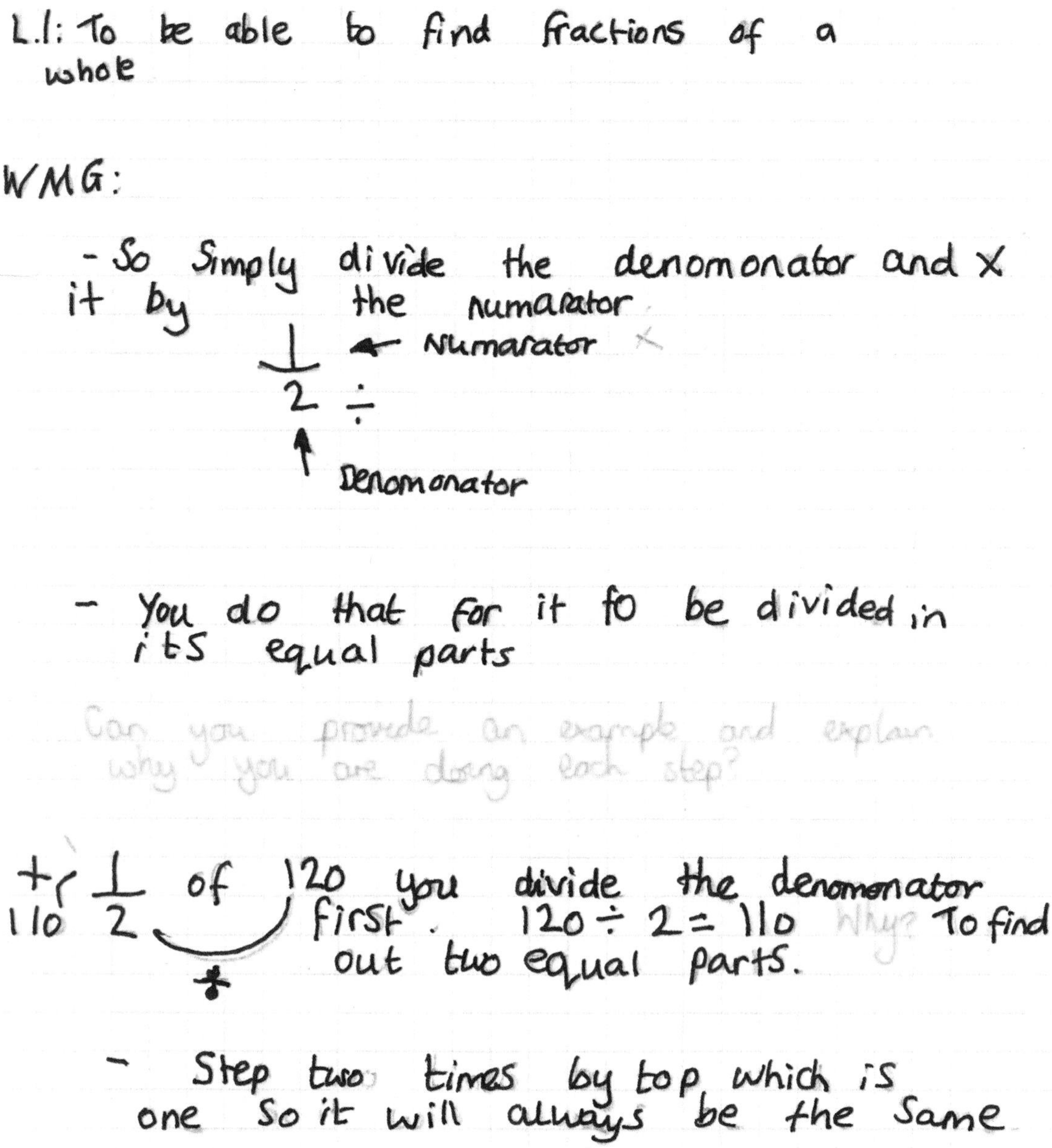

L.I: To be able to find fractions of a
whole

WMG:

- So simply divide the denomonator and X
  it by   the numarator
        1 ← Numarator ×
        ─
        2 ÷
        ↑
        Denomonator

- You do that for it to be divided in
  its equal parts

  Can you provide an example and explain
  why you are doing each step?

+r 1 of 120 you divide the denomonator
110 2   first. 120 ÷ 2 = 110 Why? To find
           out two equal parts.

- Step two times by top which is
  one so it will always be the same

Fig. 9.2 *Individual pupil success criteria – fractions*

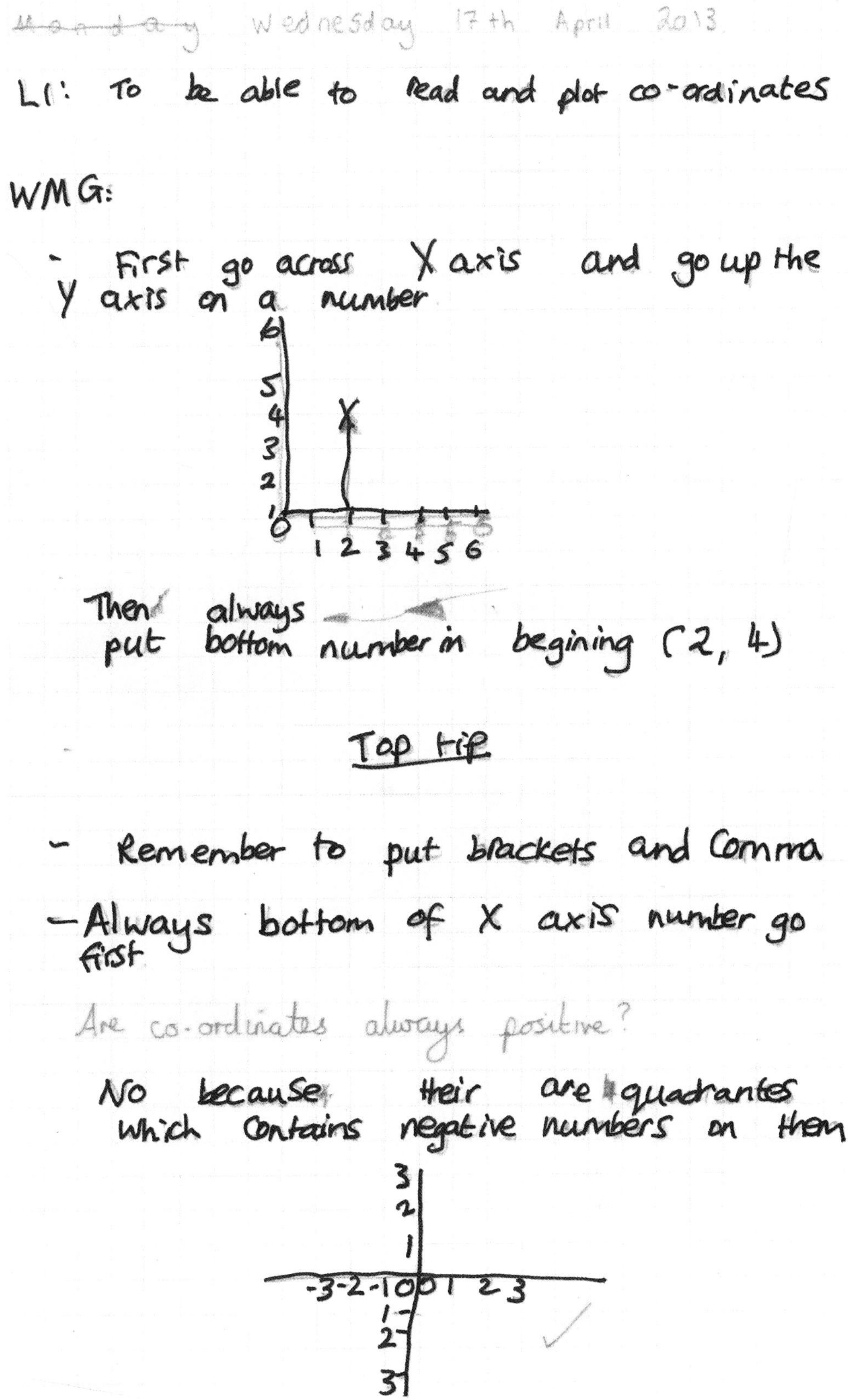

~~Monday~~ Wednesday 17th April 2013

LI: To be able to read and plot co-ordinates

WMG:

- First go across X axis and go up the y axis on a number

6
5
4   X
3
2
1
0 1 2 3 4 5 6

Then always
put bottom number in begining (2, 4)

Top tip

- Remember to put brackets and Comma

- Always bottom of X axis number go first

Are co-ordinates always positive?

No because their are quadrantes which Contains negative numbers on them

3
2
1
-3 -2 -1 0 0 1 2 3
1
2
3

Fig. 9.3 *Individual pupil success criteria – coordinates*

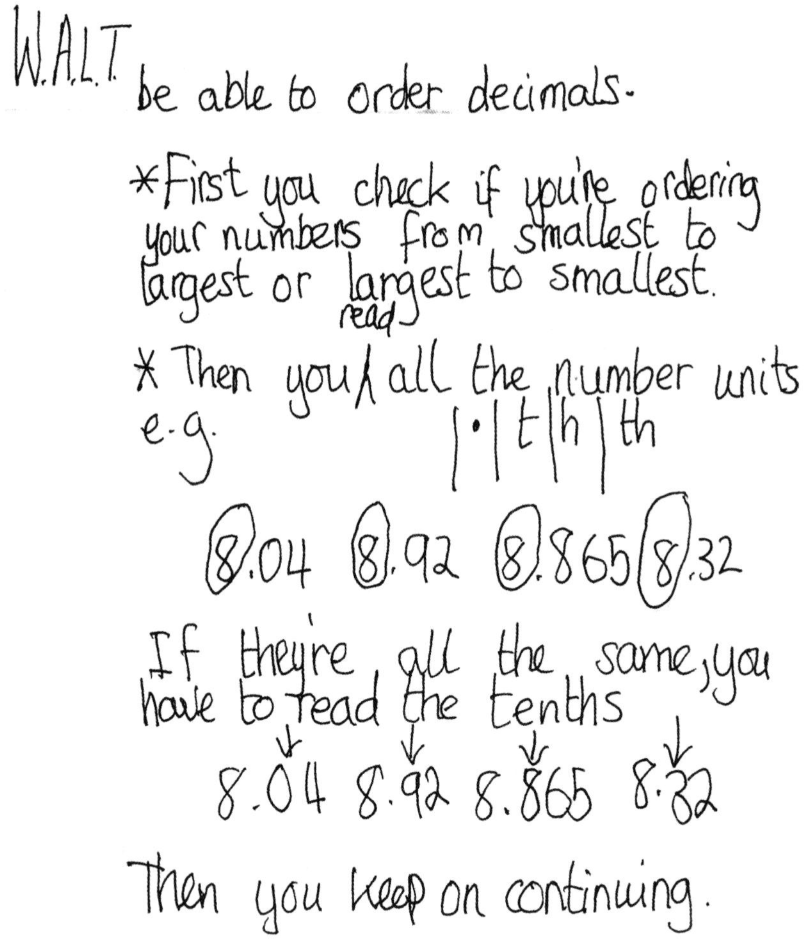

W.A.L.T be able to order decimals.

*First you check if you're ordering your numbers from smallest to largest or largest to smallest.

* Then you read all the number units
e.g.

| • | t | h | th

⑧.04 ⑧.92 ⑧.865 ⑧.32

If they're all the same, you have to read the tenths

8.04 8.92 8.865 8.32

Then you keep on continuing.

Fig. 9.4 *Individual pupil success criteria – decimals*

For young children the popular practice of *class-generated success criteria* for the steps involved in mathematics is most appropriate. However, children can be asked *why* each step is taken to see the extent to which they understand the process.

Grammar and punctuation criteria used for seeking and developing understanding

The same strategy described above works just as well with grammar and punctuation. The example shown in Fig. 9.5 reveals perfect understanding until the child provides an example. Then we see that all is definitely not perfect *(The boys' are playing football)*.

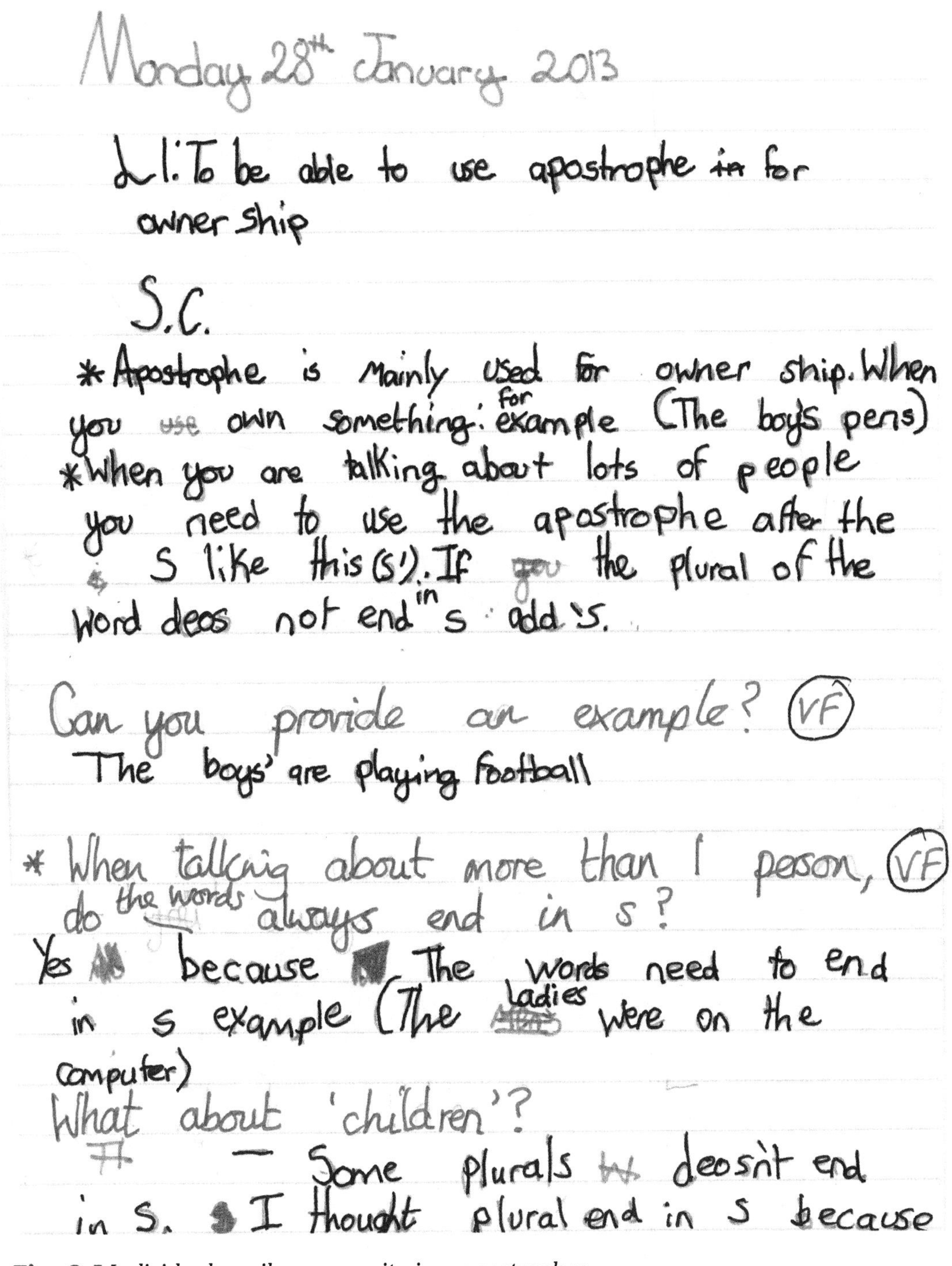

Monday 28th January 2013

L.I: To be able to use apostrophe in for owner ship

S.C.

* Apostrophe is mainly used for owner ship. When you use own something: for example (The boys pens)
* When you are talking about lots of people you need to use the apostrophe after the S like this (S'). If you the plural of the word deos not end in s add 's.

Can you provide an example? (VF)
The boys' are playing football

* When talking about more than 1 peson, (VF) do the words always end in s?
Yes because The words need to end in s example (The ladies were on the computer)
What about 'children'?
— Some plurals deosn't end in s. I thought plural end in s because

Fig. 9.5 *Individual pupil success criteria – apostrophes*

A closer look at marking

Marking tends to consist of grades or comments. One of the most quoted studies about the impact of these was conducted by Ruth Butler (1988). She set up three different forms of feedback for three different groups of same-age/achievement-level secondary pupils: grades only, comments only, and grades and comments together. The study revealed that learning gains measured by exam results were greater for the comment-only group, with the other two groups showing no gains. Where even positive comments accompanied grades, interviews with pupils revealed that they ignored the comments in favour of what the grade was telling them.

For some decades, the main form of feedback children received was written – away from them – and often gave advice about what to do in future. I have long believed that advice for the future is fairly futile. By the time the next similar context has arrived, the comment will have been forgotten, unless it is a constant reminder target.

Making the invisible feedback visible

Feedback at its best is much more immediate, with lots of oral interaction and cooperative peer marking. There is still, however, a strong requirement for teachers to annotate children's work in some way – for accountability purposes mainly – so interested parties can see that feedback has been given. Much of the 'marking', such as ongoing improvements made by pairs during a lesson, is invisible, yet it is the most valuable form of feedback, leading to a continual quest for improvement. Thinking in the action research teams has been that we need to bring these processes to people's attention in a more explicit way, so that they are not invisible. There are a number of good strategies for doing just that:

1 The use of codes to describe the type of feedback given:

> *VS* (visualiser stop)
>
> *VF* (verbal feedback)
>
> *CI* (cooperatively improved)
>
> *SA* (self-assessment).

2 Using a 'polishing pen' for improvements made in a different colour, or pinks and greens for best bits and improvements.

3 Giving children space for improvements to be made, such as the left-hand side of the book, so that improvements are not squashed in between the lines.

4 Getting *both* children to initial or write their names at the foot of cooperatively improved work.

5 Children drawing a line under their work at the visualiser stop so subsequent writing/learning can be compared.

6 Acknowledgement comments made by the teacher where work has been cooperatively improved in the lesson.

The examples shown in Figs 9.6–9.8 illustrate the problems of invisible feedback. Fig. 9.6 has space for adequate improvements. In fact, without the left-hand side of the book, I doubt that the child would have made such extensive revisions. The green highlighting makes clear the improvements, although a different coloured pen would be clearer. There is no indication that this was the result of cooperative discussion, so coding and children's initials would make that clear. A teacher's acknowledgement comment would provide the last piece in giving the child some feedback about the quality of the improvements (e.g. *'Good improvements. Especially liked the animal simile. I could really sense how starving you were.'*).

Fig. 9.7 is a great example of a persuasive letter. Although cooperative improvement took place, however, there is no explicit indication of this. The first asterix indicates a change from *'but on average'* to *'As a result of this'* – a good improvement. The second, hard-to-find asterix indicates an additional sentence, appealing for some empathy: *'How does that make you feel, Boris?'*, also a worthy improvement.

Imagine this piece with its improvements in a different colour on the left-hand side of the book, with children's initials, codes and a teacher's acknowledgement comment: so much more accessible information would be given about the process of feedback and the improvement that had taken place.

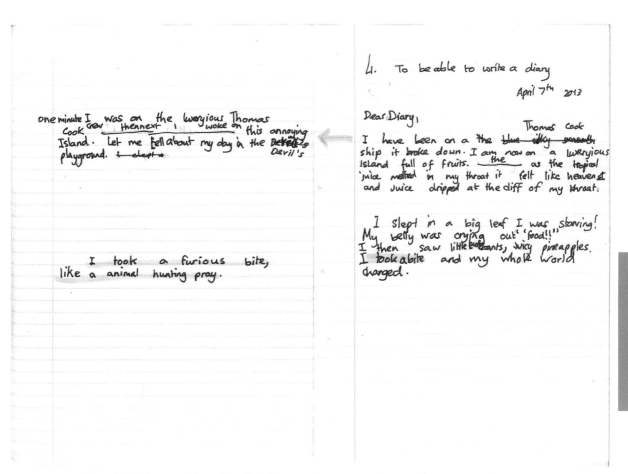

Fig. 9.6 *Diary writing: blank left page for comments and improvements*

> Windsor House 42-50
> Victoria Street London
> SW1H OTL
>
> Fernhead Road
> London W9 3EJ
>
> Monday 15th October 2012
>
> Dear Sir Boris,
>
> I am complaining to you about how late your buses are, other children that attend my school St. Luke's, are also being affected because of the truancy of your buses' departures. These children at St. Luke's are late almost every single day, *but on average* they're always given a late Pass. Your buses are affecting me and most St. Luke students, most of the children's parents are complaining to St Luke's that their child was not late because of their actions, Because of late transport!
>
> *As a result of this
>
> Your buses' punctuality affects other strangers aswell, especially ones with special appointments, these people get punished for being late to work and will have to pay it off with working overtime. People with doctor appointments suffer bad illnesses with the're bad health * How does that make you feel Boris?
> I want you to change your ways and be more organised in your work, Thank you.

Fig. 9.7 *A persuasive letter*

Fig. 9.8 shows a piece of instructional writing, with its success criteria, which has been self-assessed, then acknowledged by the teacher. This is a closed learning objective, instructional writing, where the ingredients can be ticked off.

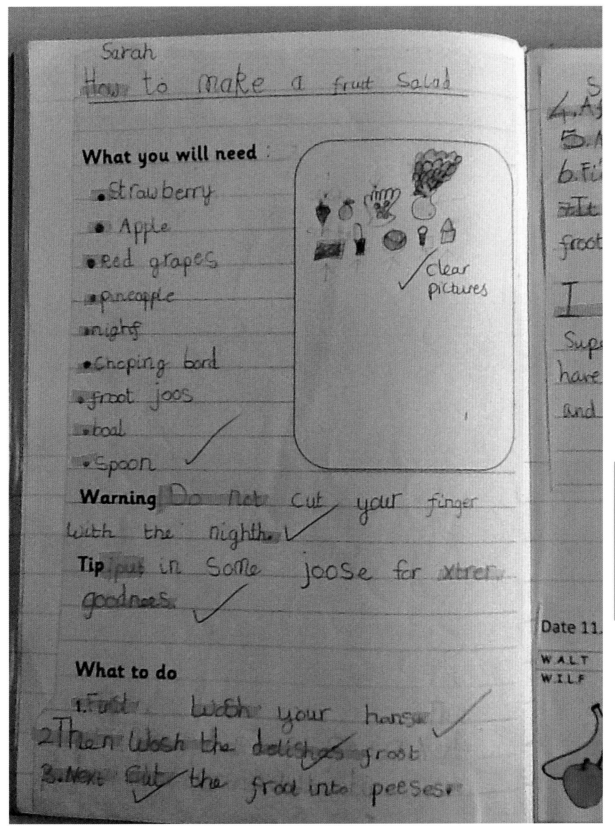

Fig. 9.8a *Instructional writing, with success highlighted*

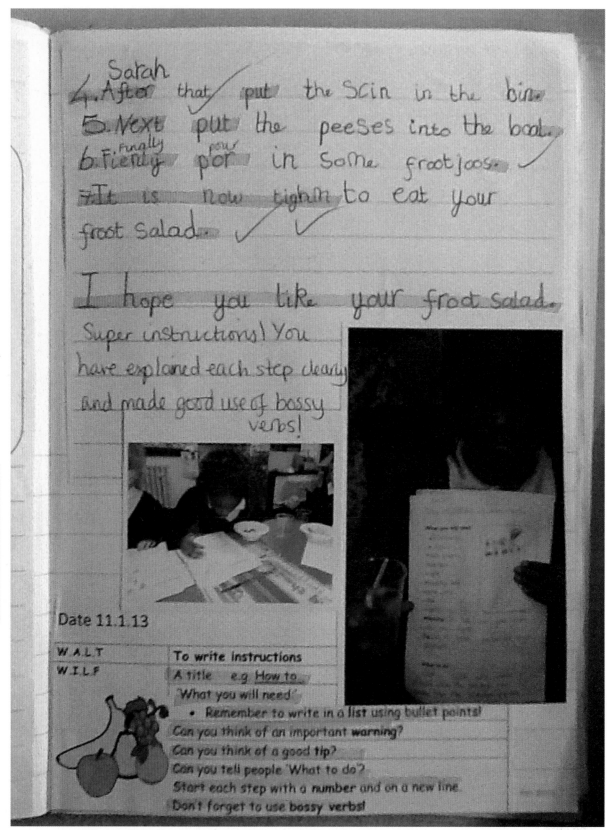

Sarah

4. After that put the scin in the bin

5. Next put the peeses into the bool

6. Fienlly finally por pour in some froot joose

7. It is now tighth to eat your froot salad

I hope you like your froot salad.

Super instructions! You have explained each step clearly and made good use of bossy verbs!

Date 11.1.13

W.A.L.T	To write instructions
W.I.L.F	A title e.g. How to...
	'What you will need'
	• Remember to write in a list using bullet points!
	Can you think of an important warning?
	Can you think of a good tip?
	Can you tell people 'What to do'?
	Start each step with a number and on a new line.
	Don't forget to use bossy verbs!

Fig. 9.8b *Instructional writing, with success highlighted*

We need to find ways of making our excellent practice visible rather than caving in to the accountability demands which can lead us to do things for the sake of doing them. By being more explicit in this way, we help all parties – including the children – to be more aware of the processes involved and the weight we are placing on them.

One of the teachers from the Doncaster Learning Team wrote the following case study, focusing on the impact of peer assessment:

Hexthorpe Primary School: Year 6, Class 14

FOCUS: PEER ASSESSMENT

AIMS: To improve pupils' confidence and understanding with Peer Assessment

Timescale: The study took place from February to November, therefore spanning two school/pupil intakes.

Background information

At Hexthorpe Primary School many AfL practices are embedded in our teaching and learning. However, like everything in life, there is always room for improvement or new innovations and ideas. So after being chosen to take part in the Shirley Clarke Action Research Project, I was open to anything new, but also going there with some prior knowledge of AfL.

Developing peer assessment was the area I focused on in school. Over the years I had used 'Two stars and a wish' as a peer assessment tool. Children knew the success criteria and read each other's work before filling in a 'Two stars and a wish' proforma. At the time I thought it was both worthwhile and useful. However after the input from Shirley Clarke, I realised that there were things I could do to make it much more effective.

Strategies used

Many of the elements introduced or developed in the Action Research Project influenced me on how to develop peer assessment, as well as making it an even more effective teaching and learning tool. These elements were:

- Modelling using a visualiser
- Talk partners
- Developing success criteria (both pupil and adults)

I approached the development of peer marking by establishing the three elements mentioned above. In class I went back to basics. I knocked down the building blocks to success and began rebuilding a stronger and better foundation. This was done so that the pupils had a clear view of what was expected of them, when they peer marked.

Firstly we went over what was meant by success criteria, making sure everyone understood the success criteria changed with every task/activity. Talk partners were used to discuss success criteria as well as what was expected from the pupils when they peer marked. Modelling, I saw as the key to success with peer marking. Pupils had to know what they were looking for. Even if the pupils said what the success criteria were, it was important to me and all the other adults in class to be sure the pupils could identify the success criteria in the piece of work.

Resources used

The piece of equipment which supported the modelling element was the visualiser. In the past I have used pieces of work that were typed and put on an IWB. However, using the visualiser gave greater impact, because of how instant it is. Pupils can look at pieces of work completed by their peers. Being able to show a piece of ongoing work directly onto the screen helps pupils in various ways:

- Modelling excellence as an aid to support others. If pupils see a piece of a high standard covering all the success criteria, they are aware of what to aim for.
- Identification of the elements of the success criteria.
- Highlighting areas of excellence/areas to develop.
- As part of a mini-plenary to support and develop pupils' work, whatever the subject area.

Once I had re-visited the elements, the class was ready to peer mark successfully. From the work done with Shirley Clarke, we approached peer marking in a slightly different way.

A peer-marking contract was discussed and each pairing adhered to it. This reinforced the idea of collaborative learning and the ideal that everyone's work is valued.

Peer marking took place in pairs. Each pair read each other's work then peer marked in partnership. This was done using the given success criteria, talk partners and 'Two stars and a wish' or 'Box and bubble' showing positives and areas to improve.

Talk partners: Pupils worked in mixed-ability pairings. Higher and middle achievers developed the lower achievers' understanding of the elements within the success criteria. This led to a reciprocal learning process. The higher and middle achievers articulated and extended their understanding by having to explain to others. Lower achievers, through repeated practice and verbal interaction, developed their ability to locate the elements of the success criteria within the task.

Impact of peer assessment

Right from the beginning I could see that the impact on the pupils' learning was going to be a positive one. The pupils were:

- more engaged in their own learning;
- aware of what constituted a successful piece of work;
- able to identify the success criteria in pieces of work and able to transfer knowledge from one task to another;
- more willing and confident to make comments upon a peer's work in a positive, constructive and often sensitive way.

All the adults who worked with me throughout the Research Project agree that peer marking has had an impact. The pupils' ability to be able to look critically at a piece of work and evaluate its success and its areas for development has had a great impact on their learning. It helps to develop the 'I can' culture, which leads to a more motivated and confident child.

Pupil quotes

'I like it when I know what I'm looking for.'

'It's great to get help from others.'

'I feel proud when my work is displayed for others to see.'

'When I look at someone else's work it gives me ideas to improve my own.'

'Working together helps me to understand what I'm looking for.'

Debbie Smith

Teacher marking

There are different types of teacher marking:

- Acknowledgement comments about the successes – which may or may not link to success criteria, if a narrative piece – and the quality of improvements made by children during lessons (e.g. 'I really liked the phrase... because...');
- Secretarial marking (e.g. underlining misspelt key words which need to be rewritten);
- Summary summative marking for class 'test' pieces or application of skills learnt (e.g. a paragraph of what that child can now do and what they need to target for the future);
- Response and review marking (e.g. the teacher points out successes and improvement points which are followed up the next day).

Response and review marking is very popular, as it satisfies inspectors and so on, but needs a number of issues to be considered. This is the practice of marking children's work away from them, highlighting the best bits and suggesting some improvements. These improvements are then done the next day at a dedicated time, often during registration at the beginning of the day. Considerations include:

- Can the child read and understand your suggestions?
- Do they have adequate time to make the improvement?
- Could the improvements be done cooperatively (not swapping books, but working together on one book at a time), so that children are not in isolation, missing out on each other's thoughts?
- Is your improvement suggestion really going to improve the piece or will it lead to overwritten descriptions (see Chapter 7)?
- Is there adequate room for appropriate improvement to be made – such as the left-hand side of the book?

My concern is that response and review marking on its own, while looking good to outside agencies, will not maximise the cooperative power of feedback after analysis and discussion of excellent examples. I wonder if the best marking is (a) paired cooperative improvement-making after mid-lesson learning stops with appropriate codes, etc., to make the process visible, followed by (b) teacher comments which applaud the best bits and may or may not suggest a further improvement, maybe picking up punctuation or spelling. As always, a meeting in the middle appears to be, perhaps, the best solution.

For an excellent example of teacher marking, see Fig. 7.3 on page 101, in which the improvement suggestion leads to a clear enhancement of the writing.

The shift to within-lesson quality feedback

Table 9.2 summarises the key changes we have made in developing effective feedback *within* lessons rather than after them.

From	To
Seeing best examples at the end	Seeing and analysing a range of excellent and not so good examples at the beginning and throughout
Hand it in after a cursory check	Constant review during the process
Written teacher feedback after the event	Learning partners cooperatively identifying success and making improvements during the process
Children swapping work for peer marking	Children cooperatively discussing one piece at a time
Not knowing how to improve something	Improvement-making modelled via random work discussed at the visualiser
Focusing on secretarial features	Focusing on one or more success criteria, looking for best bits and making improvements
In writing, focusing only on inclusion of success criteria	Acknowledge success criteria for the genre, but emphasise what makes writing engage the reader
Keeping your learning secret	Enjoying your learning being critiqued by the class
Reading the writing in your head	Frequently reading the writing aloud, to yourself or a partner
All your own work	Magpieing good ideas and words
Satisfied with first attempt	Striving for excellence
Teachers marking everything in detail	All work acknowledged, but comments only given if they can be followed up and are seen to have a positive impact
Marking seen as an accountability tool	Codes used to inform all interests of the process used (e.g. *VF* verbal feedback, *CI* cooperatively improved)

Table 9.2 *Feedback: changes in practice*

Teachers' comments

Teachers' comments about immediate feedback, mid-lesson learning stops and cooperative feedback discussions are typical of teachers' feedback and illustrate the impact on children's achievement and attitude to their learning.

5–7 year olds

➤ *One child cried because the visualiser in our class was broken. They are so proud of sharing their learning!*

➤ *One child who is always dreaming had his name picked and was very proud of his work under the visualiser. He began to concentrate more after that. Low achievers have their self-esteem boosted because the other children find positive things about their work. Children prefer the immediate feedback.*

➤ *Improving one child's work together has made the children more proud of their work. They are putting in more effort and focusing on the positive achievements in their learning. When any child's work can be chosen randomly for analysis, children work harder and are eager for their work to be chosen.*

➤ It is important for younger children to see the process of reviewing modelled lots of times with anonymous pieces of work.

➤ It is important in the culture of the classroom to talk about and model the zone of proximal development, making clear the comfort/stretch/stress zones. The language of learning has been developed and children feel happier about being stretched and want to challenge themselves.

➤ We started having collaborative marking sessions with the teacher. We began with work from a different class, using pink and green pens for best bits and improvement places. Then one person from the class was picked randomly to model the process. Now all the children want theirs to be chosen as the model. Children now have embedded reviewing skills: they continuously talk about their improvements in all lessons, not just when they are told to. They now don't mind making mistakes.

8–11 year olds

➤ Peer marking mid-lesson leads to good improvements within the session. There is a clear link with the growth mindset in demonstrating that anyone's work can be shown and improved. One teacher who stopped the children after 5 minutes to take one child's work at random said more work was completed in that 5 minutes than had ever been completed before! (8 year olds)

➤ Sometimes I choose which work is to be shown if I want to make a particular point. The focus should always be on quality, not quantity. Children really enjoy up-levelling and using a special colour to make those improvements.

➤ 'Stop share steal' is our motto for using our magpie books. This has had an immediate impact, with children then using their findings in their independent writing.

➤ We followed the process of mid-lesson learning stops and cooperative improvement, with one book on top of the other at a time. The process had improved quality, particularly in literacy. The random choice has been very motivating. Children are constantly having work read to them or reading their work aloud. Hearing their own mistakes rather than reading them is significantly easier. One 8 year old child said 'When I hear my work I can easily spot my mistakes.' Reading out loud for sense was key.

➤ Having children in mixed-ability pairs means that higher achievers treat lower achievers with complete respect, always looking for and finding positive elements. Learners are thus empowered regardless of their level.

➤ In my school we trialled all the techniques, including banning rubbers and using the left-hand side of the book for improvements. There needs to be a whole-school ethos for this to work well and for teachers to be trained. The impact has been that children are now going back to their work without being asked, adding new vocabulary and improving their writing independently.

➤ Cooperative improvement improves accuracy and leads to continual review. One child said 'It says "really nice work" in my book. What's wrong with that? It's no use to me. It doesn't tell me how to get better.'

➤ We introduced writers' journals as a school to encourage self-assessment and to magpie ideas, given a bank of good examples. There was also a feedback workshop with 'learning detectives' looking for success and next steps during mid-lesson learning stops *and improvement time within sessions. Children really understand the role of feedback and are more actively involved in their assessment.*

Secondary

➤ *I had learning walls with examples of peer-annotated student work, so that active learning was demonstrated and getting students to be experts, explaining, demonstrating how they learned and how they achieved something was powerful.*

➤ *I used old GCSE work to discuss – showing Year 10 what Year 11 did last year in health and social care. There was a positive student response. Combined with cooperative improvement strategies, the quality of work was much higher than last year and there were improved mock exam results.*

Feedback policy

The essence of any policy is that it should reflect the current practice. The following example of a marking and feedback policy is from Sheringham Primary School in Newham, a very large school with a majority of children having English as a second language. The school is embedded with formative assessment practice and ethos.

Sheringham Primary School
Marking and Feedback Policy; September 2013

Principles

Our Marking and Feedback Policy is based on the principles that:

- children have the right to have their work acknowledged, to be given feedback on their achievements and to be given advice for their future learning;
- feedback informs all participants in the learning process of the progress made and feeds into the next cycle of planning for teaching and learning;
- regular marking keeps the teacher in tune with the individual needs and abilities within the class and helps to raise standards.

Who is involved

Leadership Team: monitoring, evaluation and inset;

Partnership Teachers: modelling good practice;

Class Teachers: giving a range of feedback in a variety of forms;

Pupils: self-assessment and marking, peer assessment and marking and improving their own work;

Learning Support Staff: marking in line with the Learning Objective, commenting on assistance given;

Supply Teachers and Trainee Teachers are required to follow the policy.

Guidance for marking by teachers

Teacher marking is only effective if:

* it informs both the child and the teacher of what has been achieved and what needs to happen next;
* the child has an opportunity to read and respond to the marking;
* it is informing the teacher of learning needs which can be incorporated into future planning.

Remember that:

* marking is most effective in the presence of the child;
* children should be given time to read/reflect on/respond to marking;
* effort should be acknowledged alongside achievement.

Marking and feedback by teachers should take some of the following forms, as appropriate to the work:

* marking should be related directly to the learning objective/success criteria;
* in year groups, teachers to agree useful symbols to be understood by the class they are working with. These symbols should be shared with the children and displayed in the classroom;
* the use of **green** highlighter to promote positive aspects and **pink** highlighter to draw attention to errors or areas for development within a piece of work;
* positive comments and guidance to pupils for moving their learning forward;
* pose an open question specifically related to the learning objective to think about next steps;
* a correct example given by teacher;
* a request to do some corrections;
* verbal feedback to be acknowledged in books;
* use of continuous oral feedback;
* use of the visualiser and mini-plenaries to model and share good examples;
* asking children to check their work again referring to success criteria (with time given to do so);
* drawing attention to how children have moved on;
* LSAs working with groups can mark their work;
* time allocated for conferencing with pupils.

Notes:

Teachers' handwriting needs to be legible as a model for the child and in a contrasting colour to the child's work.

Not every incorrect spelling needs to be corrected by the teacher, but persistent errors should be commented on, and incorporated into the planning.

Guidance for peer/self-assessment

Peer and self-assessment have a key role to play in marking and feedback. They empower children to take control of their learning.

In line with AfL strategies, within most lessons children should have opportunities to assess their progress (or that of others) against agreed success criteria. Our teaching and learning policy reflects the need to be explicit about success criteria so that feedback can be specific and meaningful.

Children need to be trained in how to peer and self-assess meaningfully, in order that time spent in lessons, on this, is beneficial to the learning.

Some successful peer/self-assessment strategies include:

- two stars and a wish
- traffic lights systems
- thumbs up/thumbs down
- use of green (positive) and pink (development) highlighters

(Refer to Shirley Clarke, *Formative Assessment in Action*, Chapter 5)

Expectations

All pieces of work in books should be acknowledged in line with the approaches listed above: i.e. either through teacher marking, peer marking or self-assessment.

Detailed marking

- For Literacy and Maths, there should be *a fair balance* of teacher and child marking (see below).
- Teachers should also be conscious of checking the quality of peer and self-assessments made by children.
- For foundation subjects there should be evidence in Topic Books of teacher, peer and self-assessment. Comments written in the topic books by the teacher or pupils should reflect how children were successful in meeting elements of the success criteria, or achieving the learning objective. Children should be given opportunities to feed back their comments about other children's work in the topic books throughout the year.
- In each subject area, every child should have at least one piece of work marked in detail once every week.
- Cover/Supply teachers need to mark and initial all work.
- Relevant elements of detailed marking will be introduced during Reception, in preparation for KS1, although it is expected that children will be given more oral feedback at this stage.

Alternative ways of sharing/celebrating a child's success

- openings of lessons
- mini-plenaries – e.g. *Why is this good?* (refer to success criteria)
- plenaries and use of visualiser
- year group assemblies
- achievement awards
- display
- RM tutor – share work from laptops

Moderation

It is expected that cross-year group moderation will occur regularly throughout the academic year.

Monitoring

Marking and feedback will be monitored by senior management through taking in samples of books and through lesson observations.

Summary

- The most powerful form of feedback is that given to the teacher by the student.
- External rewards are negative forms of feedback which threaten self-esteem.
- Feedback relies on errors being revealed.
- Sadler's 'closing the gap' principles are fulfilled by formative assessment practices.
- Mid-lesson learning stops allow sharing of excellence and a modelling of the improvement process.
- Cooperative peer marking is more effective than swapping books, with both children deciding best bits and making improvements there and then.
- For *closed* mathematics and literacy skills, asking children to write their own version of success criteria reveals the extent to which they have real understanding.
- Most marking has little impact on pupil progress, and the more immediate the feedback, the better.
- Codes, coloured pens, children's initials and so on help to make the 'invisible' feedback processes visible to outside parties.

PART TWO
Lesson Culture and Structure

Effective ends to lessons

10 Summarising the learning

In this chapter I give some examples of effective ends to lessons, then explore the possible follow-up to what has been learnt about children's understanding.

Ends of lessons

Lessons typically end with some kind of round-up or summary of the learning, if they are not going to carry straight on after a break. Yet another opportunity is presented at ends of lesson to *(a)* probe children's level of understanding and also *(b)* encourage them to reflect on their learning.

Several strategies have emerged for getting a 'snapshot' of current understanding at the ends of lessons and also helping children reflect:

What did you learn?

Simply asking children to write on the end of their work what they have learnt, or to share with their talk partner, helps consolidate their thinking and remind them of the point of the lesson. Seeing what they wrote can illuminate the depth of their understanding. Similarly, children can be asked to select, from everything they learnt in a lesson, the one thing that they felt was most important for them. Again, this can give added feedback to the teacher, as their answers could range from elements of the skill or knowledge to use of a particular learning disposition.

Tell or ask

Children can be asked to write one question they have about the lesson – which could be a *'what if?'* or *'next could we ...?'* question – or another opportunity to 'tell' if there was an aspect they didn't understand.

Sticky notes

The pupils write advice on sticky notes to a fictitious pupil whose inaccurate work is up on the screen. Children write their names on the notes and stick them on the screen. Perusal of their comments gives an idea of how far children have understood the skill (maths, science, etc.) or developed an understanding of what makes quality in writing.

Exit cards

Exit cards are half-page proformas with a space for the child's name and a space for a final example of the skill being taught, to be carried out by the child (e.g. one calculation, one simile, an answer to a question, a diagram, etc.) as a summative test of what they have been learning. This recorded evidence is very useful if much of the lesson involved practical activity.

Exit cards can also be used for pupil evaluation of the lesson (e.g. *'How did you feel about working in small groups today?'*).

Phone templates

Children are given a phone template drawing and have to write a text message to the teacher explaining the success criteria in their own 'text speak' words. This could simply involve explaining how something is calculated, what the rules are for something, what matters with a particular skill or concept, and so on.

VIDEOCLIP TASTER #18 Summarising the learning

By putting their thinking into text speak, children summarise their understanding in a fun context. http://bit.ly/PKaYIr

Pupil self-reflections at the end of the work

After paired discussion, children can decide what they are most pleased with about their learning – which might be a learning power or an aspect of the learning objective. They also discuss and decide – often referring to the success criteria, if appropriate – what they could work on for that skill. Both ideas are recorded or articulated (e.g. *'I am proud of how I got each axis labelled on my line graph. I need to work on making sure my answer is accurate.'*). The teacher can ask pairs to randomly read out their 'proud ofs' and 'what I need to work ons', at the very end of the lesson.

Current understanding revealed and possible follow-up

A running theme throughout this book is the constant quest to understand children's understanding, minute by minute and at start and end points. The big question, however, is what should we *do* about what we discover? Too often, data (of any kind), and what it reveals, becomes the main focus, rather than what should be *done* about what has been discovered. 'Appropriate intervention' is too broad a remedy to be convincing. The range of possible follow-up activities, once the level of understanding has been revealed, indicate the complexity of such intervention, with the appropriate action to be decided on in the first place being the key dilemma.

A long discussion and brainstorm session with one of my Kentucky learning teams led us to compile a list of possible follow-up actions once misconceptions or errors have been revealed (Table 10.1). I have added some possible examples.

He/she needs ...	Example
To explain their own thinking	To explain, giving examples, of how they arrived at something
To watch or talk to their talk partner about the issue	Any error or misconception
Re-teaching by a peer tutor	Children are specifically paired for the misconception to be retaught by another child
To read aloud the question and break down the answer	A maths word problem, instructions for a task, a comprehension question
Visual or concrete examples, created by teacher or pupil	Excellent examples of any subject end-products shown, maths apparatus to represent the calculation or problem
To do a hands-on investigation which will prove the misconception wrong	Carry out the science investigation (e.g. what effect does sugar have on teeth)
To go back to something simpler	Smaller numbers in maths, fractions equivalent of decimals, easier reading book
To leave it alone and move on to new skills, returning at a later date	Place-value understanding can fall into place after experience of new mathematics
To apply the misconception as a rule through demonstration	Reading aloud to check for punctuation errors
A new strategy	A different way of multiplying or dividing, a new strategy for reading for sense
A mini-lesson in a group	Teacher, another adult or a pupil leads the teaching
More practice	Specific arithmetic procedures, number bonds, table facts, using punctuation, reading, catching a ball, etc.
More *application* of the skill rather than more practice	Write a paragraph in which apostrophes are used rather than practice sentences
To use the success criteria more closely	For closed tasks for steps to include (e.g. writing instructions) or for open tasks to consult the possible options (e.g. story ending)
A real-life link	Dividing by using real situations, such as sharing pencils between the class but linking with the associated notation to link the two
More life experiences	Some comprehension passages imply certain life experiences (e.g. a day at the zoo); some texts require more maturity for true empathy

Table 10.1 *Following up misconceptions*

Summary

A number of strategies can be explored to end lessons effectively which:

- enable pupils to reflect on their learning
- give feedback to the teacher about their level of understanding
- provide summative information.

Misconceptions revealed need a range of possible follow-up activities.

PART THREE
Whole-school Development

11 Lesson study: definitions and practice

Lesson study is a teacher development strategy from Japan for improving the quality of teaching and learning, which is becoming increasingly popular across the world and gradually taking root in the UK. Japan has well-established outstanding academic success and it seems that lesson study might be a major contributory factor, hence the reason for our interest in it. Before we look at the practical implementation of lesson study, it is – as always – important to first establish the underlying beliefs and principles governing its structure. If lesson study is minimised to 'watching someone teach and analysing it afterwards', it will probably do more harm than good – yet that is often the kind of shortcut that happens when schools are inundated and they hear about something new. Having watched the often complex principles and related strategies of formative assessment get reduced to notions of dogs and cats and stars and wishes, it is essential that we keep backtracking to the original thinking. Any implementation must keep those principles at the forefront and the detail as practical and as flexible as possible.

The Teaching Gap, by Stigler and Hiebert (1999), was my first introduction to lesson study and changed my way of thinking about staff development and the ways in which we teach, because it opened up completely new ways of seeing education. I believe in the last twenty years we have moved closer to the Japanese perception of learning, because we have been doing precisely what lesson study is all about: sharing our professional wisdom and knowledge for the greater good of all. Thus, Hattie's *Visible Learning* is exemplary in changing how teachers see their role and what makes a difference and what doesn't; Black and Wiliam's review of formative assessment redirected us to see that pupils need to control their learning and assessment; Carol Dweck and Guy Claxton alerted us all to growth and fixed mindsets and the vital ingredient of making *how* we learn as important as *what* we learn.

The Japanese perception

Individual differences between pupils are seen by Japanese teachers as a natural characteristic of a group and a marvellous resource, allowing different methods, strategies and ideas to be shared and compared. They accept that not all students will be prepared to learn the same things from each lesson, and the different methods that are shared allow each student to learn some things. We, on the other hand, often see mixed ability as a difficulty, a need for differentiation, although – as outlined throughout this book – the research about the negative effects of ability grouping and the advent of talk partners has gone a long way to changing our mindsets.

If we take mathematics, for instance, we tend to see lessons as a matter of learning a number of skills, practising them, then applying them. We keep the skills separate, keeping the focus on one at a time, in order to keep the attention level high. We try to make the practice as interesting as possible via real-life contexts or games. In Japan the teachers act as if mathematics, or any other subject for that matter, is inherently interesting and fascinating in its own right and don't feel the need to make it more engaging. They want children to think in a new way and see relationships between mathematical ideas above all else, so the sharing of methods and strategies is key.

We often try hard to reduce confusion by giving full information to children about how to solve any problems they might have, whereas a Japanese teacher will start with a challenge activity, watch children's methods and encourage them to keep going even if they are struggling. The methods are noted then shared with the class, picking out the successful elements as different methods are analysed. Many teachers steeped in formative assessment now begin lessons with a question or activity which is designed to establish prior knowledge (see Chapter 5), and using a visualiser to pick random children's work means that strategies are shared often throughout a lesson. Even ten years ago this was unusual in UK classrooms, yet now is very well established.

Although a smart board might be used in Japan, there is an all-important huge whiteboard on which the different methods, ideas or words are recorded throughout discussions, so that connections can be made more easily by the pupils. This whole-lesson record of everything that is contributed is something I have rarely seen in a classroom, yet, with an extra-wide whiteboard, it could help make connections for many children during the course of a lesson. Imagine all of the best phrases written as we go, or all of the mathematical strategies recorded, so that connections can be linked in some way.

Japanese teachers see lessons as sacrosanct – planned so all its parts flow – so that interruptions of any kind (such as PA announcements, classroom visitors, etc.) might destroy the connections gradually being made. Pete Dudley, the leading instigator of lesson study in the UK and the director of lessonstudy.co.uk, says:

'The Japanese say a lesson is like a fast flowing river, and teaching a lesson is like negotiating a canoe through rapids. You have a plan, but you need to make hundreds of decisions as you teach that you can't plan for.'

With *skills* practice, such as maths calculations, interruptions are less important, as they simply cut down the number of examples a pupil might be able to do, whereas the negative impact is potentially greater for more creative activities.

In the never-ending pursuit of improving the teaching profession, Stigler and Hiebert (1999) put forward a different way of thinking. We usually cite the higher salary and status that Far Eastern and other successful countries' teachers enjoy as a critical reason for their success and its accompanying respect and trust. They say, however, that simply adding these elements would lead us to *mistake the trappings for the profession*. They go on:

'A profession is not created by certificates and censures but by the existence of a substantive body of professional knowledge, as well as a mechanism for improving it, and by the genuine desire of the professions' members to improve their practice. Standing in the way is the teaching script.'

By the teaching script, they mean the way in which we teach, the roles we replay and don't question. Their answer is that the only way forward is collaboration, shared knowledge, watching learning happen and talking about what we see. The wisdom of the profession needs to be shared and validated. I often use the analogy of surgeons and how they have learnt, and continue to learn their trade, by watching other surgeons, discussing what happened and assisting, while constantly researching current thinking. We would not be too happy to be operated upon by someone who had only been to countless lectures, read books and talked about how to perform a procedure, yet we still have a culture of fear of being watched in the classroom and prefer to 'operate' on our own – caused in part by the various inspection and monitoring regimes carried out for decades by those in positions to make judgments.

Lesson study breaks through these barriers and, when carried out properly, results in rapid development, as it *'unlocks teacher practice knowledge and allows it to travel between classrooms'*, as Dudley says.

Stigler and Hiebert conclude:

'The star teachers of the future will be those who work together to infuse the best ideas into standard practice. They will be teachers who collaborate to build a system that has the goal of improving students' learning in the "average" classroom, who work to gradually improve standard classroom practices. In a true profession, the wisdom of the professions' members finds its way into the most common methods. The best that we know becomes the standard way of doing something. The star teachers of the twenty-first century will be teachers who work every day to improve teaching – not only their own but that of the whole profession.'

Lesson study – how it works

The traditional form of teacher staff development in much of the Western world consists of teachers attending courses or staff meetings, away from the classroom, listening to so-called experts, then trying things out in the classroom, followed by often-too-soon feedback sessions. The experimentation usually takes place by the teacher on his or her own in the classroom and the discussion about what happened is therefore based on words alone which we hope will communicate our results. The flaw in this is, of course, that we have no idea how each person firstly interprets the initial input, then how they translate that into practice, how they interpret the responses by the pupils, and what they mean by their feedback. We use the jargon of education ('focused', 'quality', 'self-esteem', 'ownership', etc.) to convey our thinking, with possibly very different meanings between us.

Lesson study is a form of action research, based on teachers watching lessons as the core activity for improvement and development, essentially enabling them to watch the learning in 'slow motion'. In Japan, the jointly planned lesson might be watched by many teachers, with follow-up discussion and analysis. In the UK and elsewhere a smaller group has been advocated. The basic format is as follows, although much variation is taking place:

1. A study group of research teachers is formed, of between two and four teachers.

2. They decide on a focus which has been identified as something children have found difficult and therefore needs improving (e.g. 9 year olds with fractions).

3. They plan a lesson together, first researching the subject matter thoroughly.

4. The lesson takes place, with teachers deciding who teaches the various parts of the lesson and the observers focusing on three case-study pupils or more, annotating what they see.

5. At the end of the lesson, the case-study pupils are asked for their views about the lesson.

6. After the lesson the teachers jigsaw their observations and conduct joint analysis, deciding what they agree about each pupil's and the class's learning.

7. Teachers decide, in explicit terms, what they have learned and the best way to disseminate their findings, linking theory with practical examples and observations. The aim is to help all teachers who are teaching the same skill to learn from the group's learning. In the Japanese method, student responses are noted but aggregated rather than left as individual (e.g. 60% of students used strategy 1, 20% strategy 2, etc.).

One teacher's comment about the impact of lesson study:

> 'The lesson-study was like a micro-observation of these pupils, rather than the quality of teaching, so it was very different (to being observed as a teacher). Teachers found it very liberating and interesting. The quality of feedback we got was so powerful and it helped the group bond as a team. We knew our solution wasn't just someone else's idea. We found out the information ourselves and we know it will work for our children and our school.'
>
> Sue Teague, Caddington Village School, Luton

There are many implications for the model of lesson study – mainly the commitment of a school to allocate time for the intensive planning, teaching and discussion time needed. Teachers need to construct ground rules for risk taking and joint ownership of the research lessons, where it is recognised that learning is from what goes *wrong* as well as right. The use of video cameras or software such as *Irisconnect* are invaluable in allowing teachers to play back their own lessons, pause and rewind sections or for teachers to be remotely involved. There are many variations on lesson study, as teachers wrestle to cope with the practical issues, but the key focus is on the *learning* first, hence the identification of case-study pupils across the current achievement range. The analysis of what happened leads, of course, to what worked and what didn't, but more is learnt from seeing how the learners react than thinking about how well we taught.

Lessonstudy.co.uk is a wonderful, comprehensive website, including video and a downloadable handbook outlining everything a school would need to begin lesson study.

Pete Dudley concludes:

> Because a lesson is jointly owned, it is OK if aspects go wrong. You learn from that. Teachers must be able to bare their souls to each other if they are going to improve. They must not criticize each other. They must create a safe space, where there are ground rules for discussion. Teachers often find they learn profoundly new things about how their pupils are learning and have to make significant reassessments of them as learners. Lesson study allows schools to create a culture of teacher learning through talk, of detailed thinking and reflection about learning and teaching that leads to real improvement for pupils.

John Gardner, professor of education at the University of Stirling, adds:

> It creates a focus within schools – the solutions come from teachers themselves and not from an expert telling them what to do. There is no way the teachers perceive lesson study as a method for monitoring their performance because they have designed the lesson. The observation is carried out by others who have designed the lesson. And the teacher knows they could be next to teach it.

In the next chapter, we continue the improvement journey by learning about a similar model of sharing teacher practice – outlined by the headteacher of Sheringham Primary School, Newham, in London – in which the most experienced teachers work jointly with other teachers rather than having their own classes, leading to a school which has been consistently deemed by all as outstanding and creating a culture of teachers who are continually striving to improve their practice.

Summary

Lesson study is an action research-based strategy in which teachers jointly plan a lesson then teach and analyse their observations of identified pupils. By opening up a dialogue about learning based on lesson observation, teaching and learning improves.

The background to successful lesson study, a Japanese invention, is a culture of sharing practice and collaborative thinking. Mixed ability is seen as a gift because pupils can learn from one another and subjects are seen as intrinsically interesting in their own right, uninterrupted so that connections can be developed, recorded and made throughout the flow of a lesson. Pupils are encouraged to have a growth mindset.

12 Whole-school accounts

This chapter focuses on whole-school development and the embedding of formative assessment. Although I have included a number of accounts throughout the book, dealing with specific aspects, these stories describe how schools went about developing a whole-school approach to formative assessment.

The first section was contributed by Paula Hill, from Milby Primary School, Warwickshire. Having introduced formative assessment over time, she devised a pupil survey as the means to see how it had impacted on children's learning and where there was a need for improvement.

The second section consists of three schools' accounts of their journeys as they went about embedding formative assessment.

Pupil survey: Milby Primary School, Nuneaton, Warwickshire

Paula Hill, from Milby School, decided to survey the 430 children in the school to see how well formative assessment was being developed in the school and, most importantly, to see how children were perceiving these new elements of their learning. Three examples of completed surveys across the age range can be seen in Figs 12.1–12.3. Their replies reflect the growth mindset culture *('I like to challenge myself')*, the collaborative approach *('help other people')* and the involvement in planning *('we tell her what would help us')*. I particularly like the 10 year old's comment that good learning for him/her is *'when the work has been explained to me properly and I understand it'*. The continual references in this book to the never-ending quest to understand how children are *understanding* are manifested in this sentence. If both clarity of explanation and understanding exist together, it seems that success can more or less be guaranteed.

The pupil survey scores were first tallied by each teacher and then by Paula (Fig. 12.4), and followed by a letter to all staff about her findings (Fig. 12.5).

Aged 6

Formative Assessment Survey.

Please answer as many questions as you can.

Please tick a face. 😊 Always. Sometimes. 😊 Never.

Then give an example if you can.

I am a good learner.		😊	X	X
I am a good learner when I ~~everything~~ always				
I help my teacher plan my learning.		😊	X	X
I have planned ...to describe something and to help other people aswell				
I know what to do to help myself if I am stuck.		😊		
I can... think ASK a friend have a go have another go use the class room				
I enjoy having a talk partner.		😊		
Because they give you ideas				

Fig. 12.1 *Excerpt from a 6 year old's survey*

Aged 9   4 J

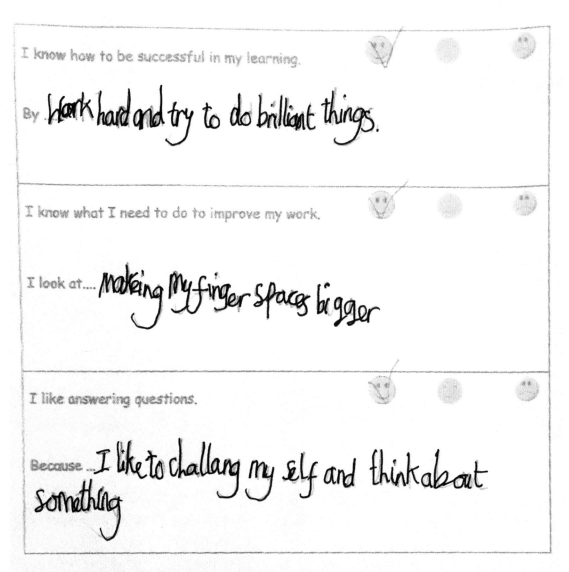

I know how to be successful in my learning.

By Work hard and try to do brilliant things.

I know what I need to do to improve my work.

I look at.... Making my finger spaces bigger

I like answering questions.

Because ...I like to challang my self and think about something

Thank you for taking the time to fill in this survey.

Please return to Mrs. Hill.

Fig. 12.2 *Excerpt from a 9 year old's survey*

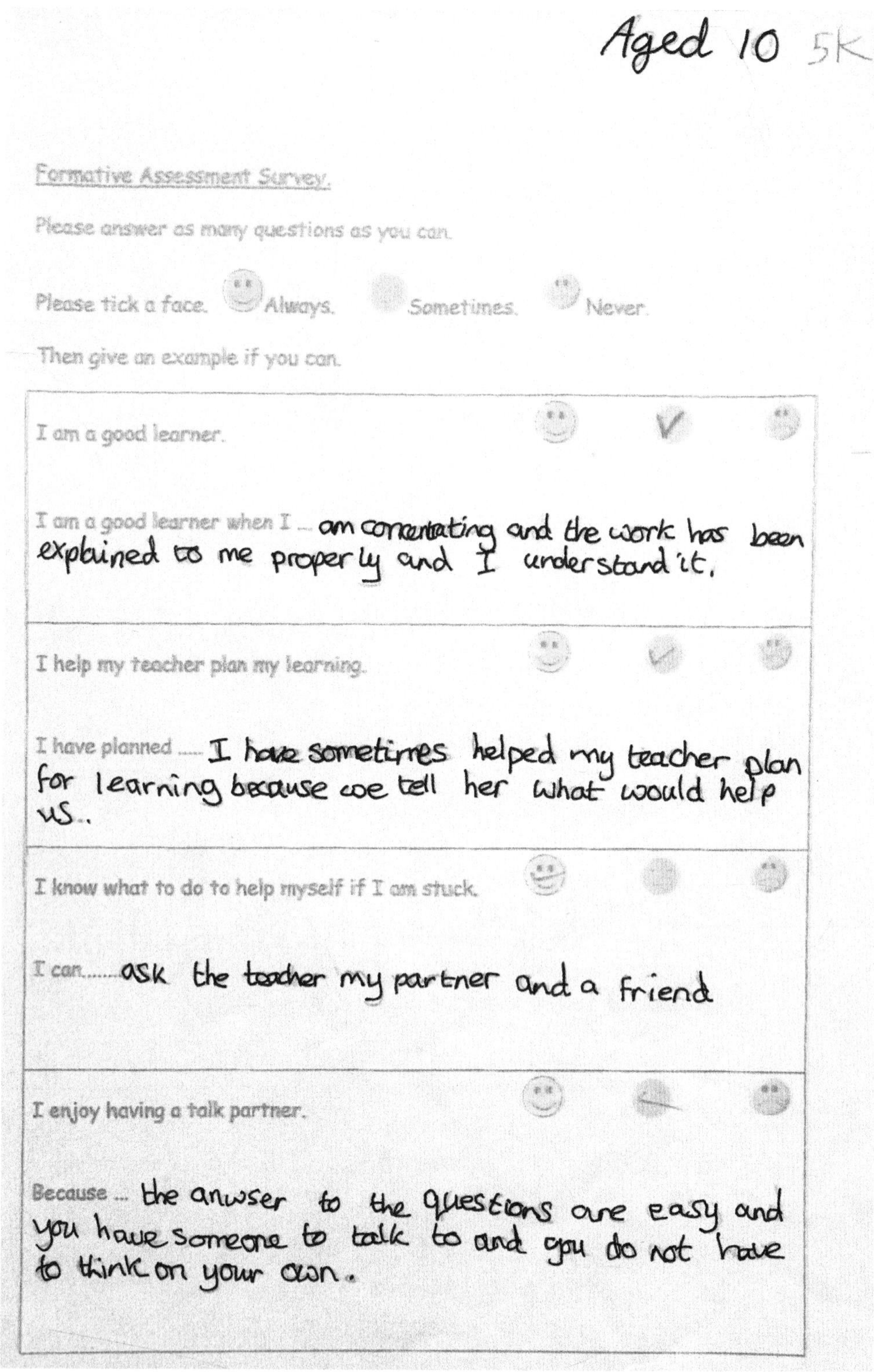

Aged 10 5K

Formative Assessment Survey.

Please answer as many questions as you can.

Please tick a face. 😊 Always. 😐 Sometimes. 😟 Never.

Then give an example if you can.

I am a good learner.	😊	✓	😟

I am a good learner when I — am concentrating and the work has been explained to me properly and I understand it.

I help my teacher plan my learning.	😊	✓	😟

I have planned — I have sometimes helped my teacher plan for learning because we tell her what would help us..

I know what to do to help myself if I am stuck.	😊		😟

I can — ask the teacher my partner and a friend

I enjoy having a talk partner.	😊	←	😟

Because — the anwser to the questions are easy and you have someone to talk to and you do not have to think on your own.

Fig. 12.3 *Excerpt from a 10 year old's survey*

School Survey Results

	Always						Sometimes						Never					
I am a good learner.	Y1	Y2	Y3	Y4	Y5	Y6	Y1	Y2	Y3	Y4	Y5	Y6	Y1	Y2	Y3	Y4	Y5	Y6
	22	15	20	18	22	16	6	14	9	8	10	14	0	0	0	1	0	0
	23	24	24	20	25	16	6	6	6	8	6	13	0	0	1	1	0	0
I help my teacher plan.	Y1	Y2	Y3	Y4	Y5	Y6	Y1	Y2	Y3	Y4	Y5	Y6	Y1	Y2	Y3	Y4	Y5	Y6
	22	16	9	1	5	1	10	11	14	8	27	28	5	3	6	18	0	1
	13	23	8	0	1	6	4	7	15	5	26	22	2	0	8	22	4	1
I know what to do when I am stuck.	Y1	Y2	Y3	Y4	Y5	Y6	Y1	Y2	Y3	Y4	Y5	Y6	Y1	Y2	Y3	Y4	Y5	Y6
	24	19	20	17	31	25	7	10	9	9	1	5	1	2	0	2	0	0
	21	26	28	25	24	20	4	4	3	2	6	9	0	0	0	0	1	0
I enjoy having a talk partner.	Y1	Y2	Y3	Y4	Y5	Y6	Y1	Y2	Y3	Y4	Y5	Y6	Y1	Y2	Y3	Y4	Y5	Y6
	17	19	12	16	22	17	8	10	10	9	9	12	5	2	7	3	0	1
	15	21	20	11	22	18	9	8	11	8	7	8	2	1	0	3	2	3
I know how to be successful in my learning.	Y1	Y2	Y3	Y4	Y5	Y6	Y1	Y2	Y3	Y4	Y5	Y6	Y1	Y2	Y3	Y4	Y5	Y6
	24	17	16	15	27	19	4	13	12	12	6	11	1	0	1	1	0	0
	24	24	26	23	27	19	4	6	4	3	4	10	0	0	1	1	0	0
I know what to do to improve my work.	Y1	Y2	Y3	Y4	Y5	Y6	Y1	Y2	Y3	Y4	Y5	Y6	Y1	Y2	Y3	Y4	Y5	Y6
	23	21	21	16	29	19	7	9	8	11	8	11	0	0	0	1	0	0
	22	21	24	23	23	14	3	9	6	3	8	15	1	0	1	1	0	0
I like answering questions.	Y1	Y2	Y3	Y4	Y5	Y6	Y1	Y2	Y3	Y4	Y5	Y6	Y1	Y2	Y3	Y4	Y5	Y6
	22	16	17	16	21	10	1	14	8	10	11	19	4	0	4	2	0	1
	24	24	19	18	16	16	1	3	9	8	14	12	4	3	3	1	1	2
	Y1	Y2	Y3	Y4	Y5	Y6	Y1	Y2	Y3	Y4	Y5	Y6	Y1	Y2	Y3	Y4	Y5	Y6

Fig. 12.4 *Pupil survey tally*

Survey results: What does this mean for our school?

Firstly thank you so much for completing the surveys. I have read every one and they make very interesting reading.

We have a school of children who understand what it is to be a learner, and to varying degrees they know what to do to help themselves achieve. This is obviously vitally important for them if they are to develop autonomy over their own learning.

When looking at the survey results, you can see that they were very positive about being a good learner and hardly anyone said that they did not consider themselves to be a good learner. Some children obviously saw that there was some room for improvement, but many listed the requirements – concentrating and listening being the points most often named. Now children could look at other learning muscles and think about how they may use those a little more to help them learn.

'I know what to do when I am stuck' was another area that most children felt confident to answer and here they talked about asking for help or using the working walls or stuck learner prompts. Not many negatives, and fewer answered 'sometimes'. Again the children could share what they do when they are stuck and why.

Another two areas which scored well were how to be a successful learner and what to do to improve. Many positive ideas: looking at the success criteria, working walls, looking at their own work to see where they could improve. This is another area where the children could share more ideas and think about what else makes them successful.

Areas as a school that we could work on varied from class to class. For example, some classes did not see the benefits of a talk partner as well as others. So one class could share these with another, or model what you do with your talk partner. Some classes liked to answer questions and found this a very positive activity. Other children did not understand why they were questioned or how this helped them to learn.

The main area that as a school we could all develop is the children's perception of their learning being planned for them and not something that they have input into or is shaped to meet their needs and interests. This is a quick-fix area and I know many people have started to look at this in their own classrooms. I think the more children feel involved and see the need for their learning, the easier it will be to get them to learn.

So now we have completed the survey and we can see areas to celebrate and keep going and areas we could develop, I wondered what our next steps should be. I am conscious that I have not done detailed feedback on all areas yet and I would like to share 'questioning', as this is an area we could think more about. I would also like to do a mini-feedback to the children and tell them what we have done about the survey and what we have decided.

What about you as a staff? Do you feel the survey was useful? Would you do it again?

Would you change it? Will you be changing the way you teach or plan or start off in September? What are the benefits?

Fig. 12.5 *Survey results letter to staff*

The emphasis on learning from children's perceptions resonates with the lesson study approach, where we step back and look at the learning rather than the teaching. The conclusions drawn are focused on how we can *improve pupil learning via the teaching* rather than improving the teaching to impact the learning – a significant, liberating difference. All teachers want to improve children's learning, but few want to be told what to do.

Paula ran a staff meeting to discuss her findings and sent me details of what happened next:

> 'Following this meeting…
>
> * Staff said they found it particularly useful to look at the survey with relation to what children with SEN know and what they use to support themselves.
> * They said they would love to use the survey again at the beginning of the year so they know what they need to do with their next class, as the classes mix.
> * A lot of the staff wanted to use induction day to plan the first term back and involve the children in the planning.
> * Many staff wanted to go over each area again, so they could reinforce, practise and improve in September.'
>
> Paula Hill, Milby Primary School

Three schools' journeys in formative assessment

The schools

Sheringham Primary School, in Newham, London, is a large school with almost all pupils having English as an additional language, a high proportion of children on free school meals, and many with special educational needs. The last three Ofsted inspections have deemed the school 'outstanding' for every element. A number of sample school documents have been provided by the school at the end of the account.

Rudyard Kipling Primary School, in Brighton and Hove, Sussex, is also a large school, with almost all pupils having white British backgrounds, and higher than average free school meals and special educational needs. Two teachers from the school had been in my Brighton and Hove action research learning team two years before they wrote this account. The headteacher adds her thoughts about why the development in the school has been so successful.

St Luke's C of E Primary School, in Westminster, London, is a smaller than average school with more than half the pupils having English as an additional language, with sixteen different ethnic groups represented. Half of the pupils are eligible for free school meals and the number having special educational needs is average. Seamus Gibbons – mentioned throughout this book – had been the deputy headteacher for one year when he wrote this account, so he outlines in great detail the steps they took as a staff, giving us a 'close up' view of their development.

After each school's account, I discuss what appear to be the significant factors involved in the success of their development. It is interesting also to see common and different approaches between the schools. Just as it is informative for pupils to see several different versions of excellence, we need to see different approaches to school development, or we can be led to believe that there is only one way and that making the development our own will somehow not be possible. By sharing different versions of school development in this way, we are encouraged to magpie ideas, but also to more easily think of new or 'even better' strategies for our own context.

School 1: Sheringham Primary School, Newham

Sheringham: our journey (told by Gary Wilkie, headteacher)

The beginning

When I started as headteacher at Sheringham in 2000 the school was sadly stuck in the past. The emphasis was on what the children were going to do, but with little structure. Much of my first few years at the school were spent reinvigorating teachers, enhancing teacher subject knowledge (this was at the peak of the National Literacy and Numeracy Strategies) and introducing schemes of work. My time had to be spent telling staff what to do and helping them to judge their progress in teaching against a set of criteria.

Partnership teaching – the way forward

I soon realised that some teachers made rapid progress and that others needed to see good practice in action rather than have it described to them. That's when we started with a philosophy that has continued until this day – the development of **partnership teaching**. Since that moment I've always had some of my best teachers based not with their own class but working alongside others. The Sheringham model of partnership teaching is not about team-teaching individual lessons but, instead, working alongside teachers in one subject for a period of *at least a half-term*, properly sharing responsibility and accountability for the progress that the pupils make in that time, but also with an ongoing dialogue between the teachers about the impact that their pedagogy is having upon the pupils.

By about 2005, by the criteria of the day, teaching at Sheringham was consistently good, but we still felt there was so much more that we could do. Our best teachers had it absolutely clear what they wanted the pupils to learn, how they were going to guide them towards that learning, how the pupils were going to complete a task that supported the learning and how they were going to tell the pupils whether they had succeeded in the task and what they needed to do to be even better. This wasn't universal, though, as in many lessons one of these elements was missing. It had, however, become clear that teachers can only move a certain distance by being told what to do, and the partnership teaching model of teachers working together to improve their practice was having a real impact.

Using *Formative Assessment in Action* as a development focus

I knew of colleagues who had started working with groups of their staff, working together on areas of school life, and realised that this was an approach that I wanted to take. It was at that time that I read a review in the *TES* of Shirley's book *Formative Assessment in Action*. I seem to remember that the review was positive, but more importantly it struck a chord with where the school was. I had worked with Shirley on a number of her courses at the Institute of Education, University of London, in the early nineties, and had always felt that the work that we did then had heavily influenced me when I was a classroom teacher.

I bought the book and it taught me some things that I hadn't considered – but, far more importantly, it articulated some of the things that I was trying to say to staff far better than I ever could. One of the challenges of improving learning in a school is getting a shared language – even at the surface you have different terms with similar or exactly the same meaning: *formative assessment* or *assessment for learning*, *learning intentions* or *learning objectives*. I realise that if we had a shared understanding of the book, we also had a shared staffroom language of learning.

Using Shirley's book as a key source material for what we were doing also added credibility to how I wanted to move things forward. For years I had been (and still am) very critical of the wording of the learning objectives in QCA schemes of work and National Strategies materials, feeling that they often didn't really describe what the teacher wanted the pupils to learn. After the staff had read the book, people realised that I wasn't on a one-person mad crusade!

The structure of staff development for each element of formative assessment

The key shift that was needed in teachers was the change from including a range of strategies in your lessons– because that's what Ofsted are looking for – to **understanding what makes a difference to pupils' learning and becoming a facilitator of this learning**. We had to start simply, though, and we decided that we also had to build upon the strengths of the existing teachers. We also decided that we wanted to get good at one element of AfL, then concentrate on the next area, and move things systematically, so we essentially worked through the book one question at a time. We've used the approach below several times since we first started using it and it has been refined over the years. Essentially the pattern has been:

1. Read the chapter.

2. Meet in groups to discuss what is described in the chapter, with each teacher indicating whether they recognise what is being described.

3. Discussing some approaches to trialling something new in classes.

4. Every group member deciding on one element of their practice over the next two or three weeks to focus on.

5. Set up opportunities for a group member to observe one of the other staff – it's important that nothing is written down and given to senior managers at this point, as this should be one colleague honestly saying to another *'I'm going to try this today – can you please let me know whether I'm actually doing what I think I'm doing, and whether you can spot whether it is having an impact upon the pupils.'*

6. Feed back as a group and then as a whole staff.

7. Consider whether there are things that we now think *all* staff should be doing, and others that could be optional.

Only once the research period has taken place do we start to think about what our written policy might look like, changing the section of the teaching and learning policy to reflect everyone's thinking.

Non-negotiables

There were a few strategies that we introduced across the school without using action research:

- As soon as I arrived at the school I stressed the importance of having a language-rich classroom, particularly because of the large number of pupils at the school with English as an additional language.

- We started encouraging staff to use talk partners to get pupils to work together. We even did some work in the early 2000s on what makes a good talk partner. This has been an area where we have told staff how to apply the strategies in the classroom, although things have constantly evolved as staff have developed new ideas, particularly because senior staff are continually working alongside others in partnerships. Talk partners became *learning partners* and we then became quite regimented about how regularly they would be changed in classrooms and how they are displayed in a very uniform manner as you move around the school.

Introducing meta-cognition

Another shift that happened at Sheringham, directly after seeing one of Shirley's conferences, is our emphasis upon children knowing what makes a good learner. This certainly does not focus on asking the children to define themselves as a learner using one of the many definitions that there are. Our work has been based upon children understanding what makes a good learner, and the habits that a good learner gets into. This is, of course, all intertwined with them having good success criteria to follow and check against. After experimenting over several years, we have now developed a very regimented and formatted approach to the start of the school year in every classroom, as outlined in Example 1. Experience has shown us that investing three or four days in re-training the children each year has a very positive impact. It also provides classroom display materials that can themselves be continually used to support learning.

Current experimentation with iPads and Apple TV

We have always been keen to embrace new technologies at Sheringham, sometimes being prepared to invest in them before we were really clear about what impact they would have on learning. When we purchased our first visualisers, for example, they were given to a few staff to explore how they might use them in their classrooms. Our initial thinking was that they would mainly be used for showing worksheets or for use at the end of the lesson. It was once this technology was in the hands of teachers that their full potential became realised. Staff started to develop mini-plenaries and use visualisers to display models of excellence. I believe that we are once again at this stage with iPads and mobile technology. We have invested in iPads and Apple TV display technology in each classroom and we are at the stage where staff are exploring how to use them with children to enhance learning. This might be a bit haphazard at the moment, but by regularly talking to each other we will soon develop a menu of quality uses for them.

New teachers

One of the most interesting parts of our journey has been to see how new teachers have dealt with moving to Sheringham. There are a number of examples of highly competent experienced teachers, who were highly rated at their previous school, struggling a few terms into their time with us. They find it relatively easy to start using lollipop sticks and learning partners, but are often used to being at the forefront of the lesson. These teachers have often had a clear idea in their own mind what they want the pupils to learn, but more often than not they have been more worried about their teaching than the children's learning. It appears that these staff need to deconstruct how they teach, to allow them to really find out what really makes a difference to learning. Usually this is them taking a back seat and letting the children get on with it! Getting the balance right between a clear introduction with a level of modelling that supports the pupil progress, using models of excellence/high quality success criteria and using mini-plenaries, discussion of pupil work on the visualisers and conferencing with pupils, is incredibly difficult. I've certainly learned that even the best experienced teachers need to spend some time working alongside a Sheringhamised teacher before they really get it!

What matters

The most significant learning that I've had during our journey is that we are on a journey with no destination! Teachers are all different and we should use their strengths and weaknesses. I believe that almost all teachers want to be the best that they can be, but they don't want to be told what to do. They want to believe what they are doing makes a difference. I think this can only come from a culture where the questioning and challenge doesn't come from the leadership within the school, but from a culture where everyone is continually questioning and challenging themselves and others, and by creating a school where it is OK to fail, as long as from that failing there is learning.

Gary Wilkie, Headteacher, Sheringham Primary School, Newham

EXAMPLE 1: Agreed non-negotiables for the beginning of every school year for Years 4 and 5 (9 and 10 year olds)

	Reception	Year 1	Year 2	Year 3	Year 4	Year 5	Year 6
General for ALL year groups	Class Rules, rules for 'standards' – e.g. **presentation** (more advice to follow from standards team), classroom talk (use of standard English, 'banned words' board, striving to be a good speaker tips…) Learning power story – reminder about characters (provide some learning power activities for chn to do); choose your focus creatures based on the learning attributes you would like the children to develop. What does 'learning in harmony' (the school's 'motto') mean? Election of school council rep – some work on 'an ideal candidate' How I learn in Y1/Y2/Y3/Y4… Learning partner rules (this should be appropriate to year group – and referred to throughout the year) First piece of extended writing (decide as a Year group or may be signposted by the Literacy team) Find out about reading attitudes – begin reading a 'class book' A maths-related activity (to be confirmed by maths team) Reflection on 'targets' for the year (start a 'learning journal'?), what are the children's personal targets – can they be drilled down to more learning related than 'to improve my handwriting' and associated discussion…? Consider first two(?) blocks to be taught – KWL [what the child *knows*, *wants* to know, and has *learnt*] to aid child-centred planning (Curriculum team to advise)						
Year-group specific	Home visits	Use of Rainbow fish to explore kind behaviours	Use 'Secrets of Success' materials (ebook on WP)		Use of *Towards Successful Learning* (Diane Pardoe) book/materials		ELLI Profiles – complete individual learning profiles with children Team points for charity

EXAMPLE 2: Evaluation sheet completed by staff after a focus on learning intentions and observations

Learning Intentions Staff Meeting and Action Research

Evaluation Sheet

Completed by:

Were the aims of the meetings and research time made clear to you?

Did you find the opportunity to talk through one of your lessons and to hear the experiences of others (in the meeting on October 2nd) valuable?

Were you clear about what was expected of you before you observed/were observed?

What did you learn from observing/being observed that you will bring into your own practice?

What did you learn from people's feedback from observing/being observed?

Next half-term we plan to work on use of success criteria. Would you be in favour of using this model of working again? How could we make it even better next time?

Would you be prepared to be part of a small working group looking at how we integrate our findings from the action research on learning intentions into policy and practice?

EXAMPLE 3: Mid-year reports guidance and an example of the completed 'Learning Powers' section

Mid-Year Reports Guidance

Reports have changed in 2012/13 from an end-of-year report with a summative focus, to a mid-year report with a more formative focus. Please read the following guidance to help you complete your reports, but if you require any support please talk to any person in the hub, your year group leader or NQT mentor.

Important Dates:

27th February: Teacher Assessments are due in reading, writing and maths.

4th March: Targets need to be drafted for all children in reading, writing and maths for discussion in Pupil Progress meetings.

18th March: Reports due to SMT.

22nd March: Reports sent out to parents.

26th and 27th March: Progress Review Meetings in the evening with parents.

Technical Information:

- Reports should be written in Trebuchet font, size 12.
- They will be stored in the year group folders (on the left) in the reports room. The link for this room is on the Staff Entrance page.

- Reports will be backed up regularly but you should also back up your own reports/comments. One way some teachers do this is by writing their comments in a separate doc and cutting and pasting them into the Fronter doc.
- Please make sure your comments fit inside the existing box, so the whole report stays on 3 pages and the formatting is neat and tidy!

Maths, Reading and Writing Comments:

- The Maths comment and target will be written by the maths set teacher (where applicable).
- The Writing comment and target will be written by the literacy set teacher (where applicable).
- The Reading comment and target will be written by the base class teacher (where applicable) following conversations with the literacy teacher and/or RWI teacher.
- The comment will be about what they have learned or achieved so far, and their strengths and weaknesses in this area. The focus should be on skills rather than knowledge/content. It may be appropriate to include some comment about learning behaviour and attitudes to the subject.
- The child's attainment relative to national standards must be referred to in the conversation with parents.

Maths, Reading and Writing Targets:

- Each area will need one or two targets, each as a new bullet point.
- Targets should be taken from the Reading, Writing and Maths APP materials, although the Criterion Scale may also be used if more applicable.
- Targets should be phrased in the same way as an LO, 'To <verb> …', but should be rephrased in child/parent-friendly language.
- They should be targets that will be challenging but attainable to reach by the end of summer (Academic Review Day).

Learning Power Check Boxes

- These judgements are relative to their year group level, so the expectations for a Year 6 in terms of strategic thinking are far greater than for a Year 2. This will be done again in the end-of-year report to see if progress has been made.
- These will be done by the base class teacher but shared with set teachers who may have opinions to add.

General comments

- These should include some comment on the following, in any order:
- Learning behaviour (if further elaboration of the tick boxes is needed).
- Strengths, weaknesses and interests in foundation subjects. Don't comment on *every* area of the curriculum.
- Speaking and listening.
- Learning partner/group work.
- Behaviour/motivation/attitude.
- Social comments.
- Extracurricular activities (where important).

In Year 6, how is my child learning?

Resilience	Is persistent and doesn't give up when faced with things that are difficult. Tries different approaches to find what works.	☐☐☐☐☒☐☐ ☹ ☺
Independence	Can work well alone, focusing on the task and ignoring disruptions. Is self-confident and can make their own decisions.	☐☐☐☐☐☒☐ ☹ ☺
Cooperation	Works well in a team or with a partner, sharing ideas and compromising where needed. They are supportive of others and a good listener.	☐☐☒☐☐☐☐ ☹ ☺
Creativity	Is imaginative and comes up with original ideas. They are adaptable and will think of alternative suggestions to problems.	☐☐☐☐☒☐☐ ☹ ☺
Curiosity	Asks lots of questions and is keen to find out the answer to problems. Enjoys discovering and exploring new things.	☐☐☒☐☐☐☐ ☹ ☺
Making Links	Makes links between ideas and spots similarities and relationships. Can apply their learning to different settings.	☐☐☐☒☐☐☐ ☹ ☺
Changing and Learning	Enjoys a challenge and has a belief that they can learn and improve with effort. Is open-minded and flexible.	☐☐☐☒☐☐☐ ☹ ☺
Strategic Thinking	Makes plans and follows them, thinking carefully about the next steps. Is organised, prepared and analytical.	☐☐☒☐☐☐☐ ☹ ☺

General Comment

Xxxx has been a willing and polite member of year 6. Xxxx has had a difficult start to the year due to his regular absences from school but when he came back he was eager to catch up with his peers. Since being back at school full time he has worked hard to keep up with his peers. He has worked most effectively within partner discussions as he shares his ideas freely. Also when working independently he remains focused on the task at hand. However, when working in groups he can be shy and intimidated by other peers, he must understand that his points are valuable and his group would benefit from his views. Xxxx has shown parts of his creative side during our Strong Structures topic as he was able to be imaginative and creative in building his structure.

EXAMPLE 4: *Teaching and Learning Policy*

Sheringham Primary School

Teaching and Learning Policy: September 2013

Aims/Rationale

At Sheringham Primary School we recognise that quality classroom practice is the key to improving learning and pupil achievement. This policy is not designed to be a comprehensive 'recipe' of how to teach at Sheringham, but it aims to outline the fundamental principles which underpin all Learning and Teaching at our school. This policy has been developed by Sheringham Primary teachers after much staff development and action research into using formative assessment strategies in previous academic years. The aim is both to reflect the current good practice in the school, and to encourage further development of interactive and formative assessment strategies.

This policy does not stand alone: to be effective it must be embedded into our classroom practice and other related policies. Therefore, this policy is linked to:

- Behaviour Policy
- Planning Policy
- Marking and Feedback Policy
- Curriculum Map

and will also refer to other materials where they have contributed to our shared understanding of good practice.

Learning Objectives

Lesson design needs to begin with selecting appropriate learning objectives according to the needs of the class, based on prior learning and understanding. More detail surrounding the planning of lessons can be found in the planning policy; however, it is important to note:

Learning objectives should:

- set challenging expectations;
- be used as an assessment tool for future learning;
- support learning outcomes, in that each learning objective is a small step in arriving at what the learner is supposed to know or be able to do;
- aid the selection and design of activities to be undertaken in a lesson/series of lessons.

Learning objectives should not:

- simply describe that activity that children are doing.

Teaching Strategies

Our school has a very high proportion of EAL children, SEN children and children with a wide range of barriers to learning. To ensure motivation, engagement and challenge of all children, a variety of learning experiences should be used.

1. Whole-Class Teaching

Learning Partners

A key element in teaching at Sheringham is the use of learning partners. We recognise the importance of speaking and listening in all areas of the curriculum, and the need for all learners to articulate and therefore extend their learning.

Learning partners should:

- be organised and change regularly in set classes and base classes;
- be displayed in classrooms;
- have good speaking and listening modelled for them, including the development and constant review of 'what makes a good learning partner'.

(For further information, refer to Shirley Clarke, *Formative Assessment in Action*, p. 55)

Interactive Strategies

There are numerous interactive strategies that can be used in whole-class teaching to engage learners. Such strategies often provide teachers with AfL information, including:

- Thumbs up, thumbs down to show agreement/understanding
- Mini-whiteboards/show me
- True/false sorting activities
- Cards/number fans
- Use of 'no hands up' random selection after talk partners have discussed (i.e. names on lolly-sticks)
- Use of drama/role play
- Hot-seating

Alongside these, there is enormous scope for using ICT resources (interactive whiteboards, Apple TV and visualisers) to ensure children are engaged with their learning. The information gained from these strategies should be used to determine a shift in lesson pathway immediately, or in subsequent lessons, for particular groups or all children, in order to challenge their potential and ensure learning time is maximised.

Modelling and Success Criteria

A key aspect of the teaching should be the clear and specific modelling of the task that children are required to do. Shirley Clarke is specific about providing high quality models to guide and inspire children. A recommended strategy is to use a good model to analyse and generate success criteria from. These success criteria are then a tool to guide children through their own piece of work. Assessment (self/peer/teacher) and plenaries are the opportunity to reflect on success and next steps, referring to the success criteria. Teachers should have a clear idea (i.e. on planning) which success criteria are important for the learning.

Effective Questioning

Effective questioning means challenging children to deepen their thinking. Teachers need to take time to plan effective questions which go beyond straight recall with strategies. Teachers' responses to effective questioning should inform lesson adaptation to suit the needs of the learners:

- Giving a range of answers for discussion
- Turning the question into a statement
- Finding opposites – why does one work, one doesn't?
- Giving the answer and asking how it was arrived at
- Asking a question from an opposing standing

(Refer to Shirley Clarke, *Weaving the Elements Together*, Focus Education materials: Mount Cognito)

2. Group/Independent work strategies

As the promotion of speaking and listening is a key priority in our curriculum, children should be given opportunities to work collaboratively, or to share their ideas with others, regularly. Specific strategies for collaborative learning (which help make the curriculum accessible for all learners) include:

- Snowballing (talk partners first, then share with another pair/group – do you agree?)
- Jigsaw (groups research one aspect of a topic, becoming 'experts'. Re-organise into home groups to complete task using expertise of each member)
- Matching/sorting
- Diamond ranking
- Mind/concept mapping
- Using speaking frames
- Drama/roleplay

Differentiation

As stated earlier, the children at our school have diverse learning needs. Differentiation is therefore essential in matching learning opportunities with individual learning needs.

Differentiation can occur in:

- the **content** delivered – teachers being clear about the knowledge, skills and attitudes they want groups or individuals to learn;
- the **learning process** – varying learning activities or strategies to provide appropriate methods for students to explore the concepts;
- the **product** – varying the complexity of the product (which means teachers setting clear expectations for the quality of the work expected, not just accepting a range of outcomes);
- varying the **environment** in the classroom – using different teaching styles, groupings, levels of support.

We must ensure that we offer all children access to an appropriate curriculum. In some instances it may mean an individual curriculum, although more often it means personalising learning by using some of the following strategies:

- providing resources which are appropriate: careful selection and evaluation is required;
- planning for support of groups or individuals by additional adults or the teacher;
- being aware of groupings to support children (see below);
- providing writing frames appropriate to the capabilities of the child;
- scaffolding support as appropriate to support the child;
- adapting activities as appropriate;
- providing word banks/pictures;
- adapting/renegotiating success criteria (this could be used to further the challenge for higher achievers);
- utilising 'cut-away' groups;
- promoting independent choice;
- providing alternating methods of recording work (e.g. ICT, including iPads and talking tins).

It is key to recognise the link between effective formative assessment and effective differentiation: in order to differentiate effectively, teachers must have a clear understanding of exactly where the children are at.

Pupil Groupings

Teachers should plan opportunities for children to work collaboratively with others in a range of different groupings to enrich their learning experiences and opportunities. Grouping should be fluid and be relevant for pupils, according to their next learning steps. Teachers should keep the following criteria for groupings in mind when planning and ensure groupings are appropriate to the activity:

- mixed-ability or similar ability groups
- gender ratio
- children's home languages
- levels of English
- teacher chosen or self-chosen
- children's social behaviour
- individual leadership qualities.

Resources

At Sheringham we recognise that it is key to provide carefully chosen, clear, visually stimulating resources to support EAL, SEN and all learners. We have a wealth of ICT resources to engage learners: the use of these should be incorporated into planning.

Good and Outstanding Lessons observed at Sheringham Primary School have included a range of the following:

- Learning objective made explicit to the pupils
- Learning put into a wider context – why are we learning this?
- Models of good work shared and used to generate success criteria
- A range of question types
- Range of interactive strategies, not dominated by teacher talking

- Clear, appropriate differentiation
- Activities which match the Learning Intention and fully engage the children
- Stimulating resources to support independent learning
- Children are asked to justify their opinions
- Success criteria referred to during lesson and in plenary
- Self- or peer assessment related to success criteria
- Time for children to improve their work in lessons.

As we strive to keep developing the quality of our teaching and learning, this policy will be reviewed in the academic year 2013/14 to consider how to best incorporate ideologies on lesson structure and learning power.

Parents' Guide

How we learn at Sheringham Primary School

The way your child learns may be quite different to how you learnt at school!
At Sheringham Primary we make sure our teachers keep up to date with the latest developments in teaching and learning…this is what your child may tell you about their learning:

> In lessons we decide on **Success Criteria**. This helps me to know how I can be successful in my learning and how to make my work even better.

> I often work with my '**Learning Partner**'. We share our ideas; plan our work; and reflect on our learning together. This helps us both. My Learning Partner might be different in maths, literacy and topic. We change partners regularly and they're chosen randomly.

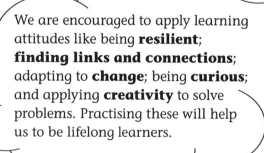

> We are encouraged to apply learning attitudes like being **resilient**; **finding links and connections**; adapting to **change**; being **curious**; and applying **creativity** to solve problems. Practising these will help us to be lifelong learners.

Learning can happen inside and outside of the classroom. Sometimes I might go to different parts of the school to learn, or even to the local park!

We also go on educational visits throughout the year.

I do my work in different ways. Sometimes I work **independently**, sometimes **with my learning partner**, sometimes in **groups with other children** and sometimes in **groups with the teacher**. All of these are good ways to learn.

I know that it's OK if I make a mistake in my work. If I got everything right, that would probably mean the work was too easy for me anyway!

In reception we learn through **play and exploration**, in a free flow environment. The way we learn supports our communication and language development, physical development and personal, social and emotional development.

In most lessons the teacher uses the **interactive whiteboard** to support our learning. Other technology is used to support and record our learning, including cameras, iPads and visualisers.

My teacher will often use **lolly sticks** to randomly select someone to share their ideas.

I know exactly what I am learning about, or learning how to do because we have '**Learning Objectives**'.

My teacher doesn't mark every piece of work in my book – sometimes I have to evaluate how well I have done using the success criteria, or my learning partner will help me decide what I can improve.

A visualiser is a special kind of projector. My teacher uses this to show my work to the class.

I can show what I have learnt in different ways. Sometimes I will have work in my book but there are other ways to show what I have learnt, these include: work on a mini-whiteboard; discussion in small groups; activities on a laptop or iPad; presenting to my teacher or the class; games or activities with my learning partner; or work in our class topic book.

Commentary

Having visited Sheringham school, the aspect I was most struck with was the 'partnership teaching' model. Instead of teachers all being assigned to individual classes, the most experienced Sheringham teachers, called partnership teachers, are not assigned to a class, but instead work for a half-term at a time with different classes, focusing on one subject with each class. The partnership teacher and the class teacher each time share responsibility for the learning in that half-term, plan the lessons together, teach them together and discuss how they went after each lesson. The radical move made by Gary in order to fund this approach was to decide to only have a small number of teaching assistants in the school. Comparing the impact of a teaching assistant to partnership teaching led him to believe that this would be a wise move, confirmed by the excellence throughout the school. Teachers who are new to the school – whether new to teaching or very experienced – all become linked with a partnership teacher, but, within a few years, they become the partnership teachers themselves.

Interviewing teachers in the school was fascinating, because, try as I did, I heard no evidence of teachers feeling they were being monitored, observed or 'manipulated' to teach in a particular way. Instead, they enjoyed the continual dialogue they were engaged in about the learning, a rare event in most schools. One partnership teacher talked about how both teachers always learnt as much as each other for the half-term, but clearly the partnership teacher – by being observed by the less experienced teacher as they share the teaching – was modelling formative assessment in action. In every class I visited, I saw consistency of practice, but with individuality. So, all teachers had mid-lesson learning stops, focused on success and improvement, had success criteria and learning partners and so on, but they had their own way of using them.

Throughout the examples given, and through Gary's account, the collaborative staff approach is tangible. The staff are empowered as a group, fully owning decision making, not being told what to do, but always experimenting, moving forward and making policy together. Having said that, Gary's leadership is strong, in that his vision for the school is clear and passionate, and where prescription is found – such as the non-negotiables and report writing guidance – this only supports the staff in fulfilling the decisions they have already made.

School 2: Rudyard Kipling Primary School, Brighton and Hove

Formative Assessment at Rudyard Kipling (told by Ben Massey and Jenny Aldridge)

Since Anna and I took part in the Shirley Clarke Action Research group, Rudyard Kipling has adopted many of the practices and principles of formative assessment and the positive effects of this are evident across every part of the school.

Following a number of meetings and INSETs to introduce the ideas to all of the staff at Rudyard, teachers and learning support assistants recently took part in an in-school AFL Action Research project to look into how formative assessment was impacting on staff and children, and to identify areas for development.

Growth Mindset

Teachers across the school introduced the idea of fixed and growth mindsets to the children and the whole school has contributed to displays. The growth mindset has been successfully incorporated into the school's green (for 'great') and orange (for 'on the way') mark scheme.

Impact:

The language of 'Growth Mindset' is evident in every year group and all teachers regularly give out *'Ask me how I have grown my brain'* stickers to encourage children to discuss their learning. Children are learning to 'act on orange' and use their marking to identify their own ways forward. In some classes, this has extended to children choosing their own targets based on their progress, and this ownership has resulted in a clear increase in enthusiasm towards achieving their targets. *'I couldn't and now I can'* is now a common phrase in Year 1!

Learning Muscles

We held a school-wide competition for children to design characters to represent each aspect of the eight learning muscles. Each year group submitted a winner and these were used to create posters. Characters were introduced in weekly whole-school assemblies and each class focused on the traits of that character throughout the week.

Impact:

Children across the whole school are taking an active interest in the ways they learn and are able to explain in detail what character they have been learning like and why. They are developing a clearer awareness of how they learn and how their learning can develop.

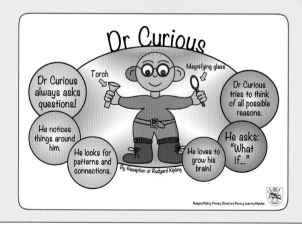

Talk Partners and Self- and Peer Assessment

The school has encouraged the use of Talk Partners – including celebrating positive Talk Partner work – and random questioning for quite a long time now and the practice has had a very positive effect on the attitudes of children of all abilities. The use of visualisers has been especially successful and has made it easy to offer real-time feedback and model the use of the school's mark-scheme to children.

Impact:

Children are eager to share their work on the visualiser and are increasingly confident to carry out self- and peer assessment. Through shared peer assessment, children know and can celebrate what they have done well and are developing a clearer understanding of how to achieve their targets as well as to pinpoint new targets and ways forward for their classmates.

Worthwhile Questioning

All planning now contains worthwhile questions, which encourage children to discuss answers and be confident that there is no 'wrong' or 'right' answer, as well as making lessons more engaging and fun!

Impact:

Less confident children are more willing to take part in discussions without the fear of being wrong. Children come up with their own thoughtful and engaging ideas and have started to generate questions of their own which can feed back into planning. Children are able to share their Talk Partners' ideas and support each other. It has given them more confidence to express their ideas and extend their thinking.

Child-centred Planning

Increasingly, children are being involved in the planning of sequences of work and reviewing and magpieing from their prior knowledge.

Impact:

Initially, children came up with thoughts and suggestions of what they would like to learn about, which fed into planning. More recently, the process has been developed in some classes to include asking the children how they would like to learn *about* things, which in turn helps to develop their thinking and questioning skills.

Child-generated Success Criteria

Through analysis of texts and examples of excellence, children in every group play an active role in generating their own 'remember' and 'choose' success criteria for every lesson. Actions and games are used to embed the success criteria.

Year groups have developed age-appropriate *'every time we read and write'* success criteria, which show progression throughout the school.

Impact:

Children have more ownership of their learning, know what they need to do and are able to assess their achievements against their own success criteria. They find out what they need to do for themselves and are increasingly able to quickly analyse examples of work to generate their success criteria.

Working Walls

Literacy and Maths Working Walls are being used across the school to support learning. Stepping stones, learning intentions, resources, prompts, success criteria and examples of marked work are updated in line with progress through units of work and are a constant reference point for teachers and children.

Impact:

Working Walls put work in context for children and teachers. Children are more aware of what they have learned so far, where they are headed and the steps they are taking to get there. Literacy walls have been particularly successful for displaying sequences of work.

Conclusion

The impact of formative assessment on learning and the children's understanding of why, what and how they are learning has been massively significant across the school. Children show a genuine pride in having 'grown their brains'. They are able to discuss their achievements and are eager to share and act on their 'oranges' (ways forward). Modelling, use of the visualiser and the active involvement of children in assessing their own and their peers' work is beginning to have a really positive influence on progress and attitudes to learning.

Ben Massey

Key factors in the success of the process:

- The opportunity to take part in the Action Research Team.
- The enthusiasm, creativity, drive and persistence of the two teachers taking part in the Action Research Team.
- Non-contact time for these teachers to plan and trial strategies.
- Creation of a Lead Literacy Group to which a range of staff belonged – distributed leadership.
- Ensuring the implementation of strategies was part of whole-school development: in our case it was one of the Themes of our RAP (Raising Attainment Plan), so INSET and staff meetings were planned.
- Involvement of all teaching staff and support staff – ownership of developments/strategies.
- Marking and feedback – a simple and logical system 'on the way orange', 'green is great', understandable for all children across the primary range. Creating a 'can do' culture.
- Key 'scripts' used by all adults in school, vocalised by the children:

  Ask me how I've grown my brain today! How have you grown your brain today?
  I'm showing a 'growth mindset' today.

- Moving onto meta-cognition, a natural progression from 'Growth Mindset' principles.
- Children as key partners in developing the characters to represent each Learning Muscle and in identifying the characteristics for each of these.
- Introducing the 'Learning Muscle' posters in whole-school assembly; then displaying the posters around the school.
- Adults referring to Learning Muscles when referring to children's learning: *'You were just like Perseverance Pete and Co-operating Clara when you did that writing!'*
- Making reference to the Learning Muscles in marking and feedback and on displays, e.g. 'Which Learning Muscles did Jamie use when making this model?'
- Seeing a real impact on children's learning, both in mindset and attitude and in improved outcomes/achievement.

Jenny Aldridge, Headteacher

Commentary

Developing a growth mindset was the first step at Rudyard Kipling, with time spent on making sure as many different ways as possible had been explored. The school lives and breathes the growth mindset and the learning powers, with everyone using the shared language Gary Wilkie spoke of. The culture of the school has to be consistent for every child to develop a growth mindset. Having stickers saying *'Ask me how I have grown my brain!'* and having a competition for the learning power characters has given children ownership and power over their mindsets. The headteacher mentions 'key scripts' used by all teachers, again sharing agreed language across the school, so that consistency of approach is achieved. As with Sheringham, there is a juxtaposition of teacher autonomy with prescription to support the decisions made by the staff. If we've all agreed to use the same growth mindset praise language, for instance, then it can only be helpful to have similar posters in every class as a prompt.

The inclusion of the headteacher's remarks illustrates how committed she is to a school with embedded formative assessment. To that end, she made sure that teachers were freed up for trialling and discussion and that formative assessment was integrated into the school development plan. Without this support from the top, meaningful development across a school is unlikely to happen. Like Gary, Jenny has a clear and committed vision for her school and for children's learning.

School 3: St Luke's C of E Primary School, Westminster, London

St Luke's journey, told by Seamus Gibbons

After taking on the role of deputy head at St Luke's C of E Primary School, Westminster, I and the other members of the senior leadership team aimed to create a culture of assessment for learning across the whole school. While our journey is not yet complete, this is how we approached AfL in our school.

Key Starting Point: All members of SLT need to be singing from the same hymn sheet

I don't think there is a single teacher in the country who has not had some form of training which has mentioned assessment for learning – but how often do different trainers say different things when it comes to AfL? With this in mind, we knew it was essential that we all had expert AfL training and a unified vision of what AfL meant, so I, my headteacher and assistant head all attended Shirley's conference together. Throughout the day we made notes and compared our reflections. Following a full day of inspiring training, we spent the next few SLT meetings creating a whole-school 'Learning Plan' (see below) outlining what our approach would be.

It would start out with a full-day INSET and then for one whole term every staff meeting would be focused around AfL. We agreed that no matter what else comes up, our staff meetings would stay focused on learning and we would not let anything else distract us from this.

STAGE 1: Whole-day INSET to launch AfL journey

Morning session 9:15 – 11:00

On our first day back from the Christmas break (January 2013), we set up the hall for all members of staff (teachers, teaching assistants, learning mentors, etc.) for a day of training together. We knew it was important that we all got trained together and shared the same vision.

We began the day with a celebration of how far we had come so far – we reflected on how we have moved from being in 'special measures' to 'good', and how we were going to build on this success with a whole-school approach to AfL.

We knew that the starting point was having a unified definition of AfL, so we began with the question 'What is Assessment for Learning?' After some discussion, here is a sample of some of the answers we got:

'How you mark a child's work'

'Using assessment information to move learning on'

'Setting targets for children'

'Using success criteria in learning'

While the above is only a sample of the many different answers, it was clear already that assessment for learning meant something different to all of us. While none of the responses were by no means 'wrong', we wanted AfL to mean something much bigger in our school. We wanted AfL to represent a culture of learning and not a 'tick list' of strategies. We, therefore presented some key principles (in no particular order) which would define AfL in our school:

- AfL should include the expectation that children will become autonomous learners (Davies, 2009).
- AfL should include elements of enquiry (Davies, 2009) and challenge.
- A culture of positive self-belief that intelligence is not fixed (Dweck, 2011).
- Should foster motivation (Assessment Reform Group, 2002).
- Should include learners in knowing how to improve, as well as the ability to explain their learning and their peer's learning.
- Learners should know what 'excellence' looks like and strive to do better.
- Success criteria should be generated with the children, including them in understanding why each step is carried out.
- Feedback should be clear, concise and move learning forward.

It was important that all staff viewed AfL as an effective way of creating a school with children who learnt how to learn and develop autonomy. We wanted this to become a culture that would underpin all we do in our school. It was also important that we wanted all staff to be part of the agreed principles underlying AfL in our school, but we did not want our teachers to be clones of each other. We wanted all staff to have a shared vision, but provided them with the autonomy and ability to be creative and individual in how they brought the principles of AfL to life. Therefore, you will notice that lots of the training is exposure, discussion and reflection about AfL and none of it dictates how a teacher should teach.

Once this was shared and agreed, we began by discussing how we can create the right learning culture in our school.

THE RIGHT LEARNING CULTURE

Teachers were asked to draw their ideal classroom, with children and adults. This proved to be not only a fun starting point, but also very useful, as it really meant all members of staff had to focus on what the classroom looked like. It was interesting to look at things like table layout, whether the children were collaborating, where was the teacher, etc. Another interesting thing was to compare the teaching assistant working in that classroom with the teacher's picture of that class, where had they placed themselves and the teacher? Staff shared their pictures and made annotations and, once this was done, we put the pictures to the side and told staff they would have time to re-visit their picture at the end of the session.

Growth Mindset *vs* Fixed Mindset

We know that in order for AfL to work, the classroom *culture* needs to be right, as this underpins all the principles of AfL. This is why we began with exploring growth and fixed mindset. All that we needed to know about fixed and growth mindset could be found in Shirley's book *Active Learning through Formative Assessment* and this was further developed when we attended Shirley's conference. We also found useful information on Carol Dweck's www.mindsetworks.com website.

One of the real benefits of launching this training in January was that the teachers now knew their classes, and as we discussed the different mindsets, teachers could match the traits associated with them with children in their class.

Fixed Mindset	
Fixed mindset	**Impact on learning**
– Believe that ability leads to success	– Focused on results, not learning
– Seek satisfaction from doing better than others	– Believe that intelligence is fixed, effort is not important
– Emphasise competition	– Avoid challenges and will pick easiest task
– Don't want to be seen as ever being 'stuck'	– See peers as obstacles to success
– When a task is difficult, they display helplessness	– Ignore feedback
	– Plateau early and achieve less than full potential

We shared the above with the staff and took time to reflect as a school on the following question.

'What are some of the things we may do as teachers which might encourage a fixed mindset?'

This opened a big discussion. Teachers worked together, scribing on big sheets of sugar paper. We discussed many things – from, on a larger scale, issues such as how in the UK our school data is compared nationally and league tables are often a factor in judging the quality of schools sharing levels, to everyday issues such as sharing levels, grouping by ability, when we get lesson feedback do we focus on the grade or feedback for improvement, etc. These conversations were important to have, as it allowed people to reflect on some of the bigger issues which could encourage a fixed mindset. We had a big dialogue about the use of the word 'work' in our school and whether this word encourages a growth or fixed mindset. Some of what our team said:

When you think of the word 'work' you think of

'something for someone else'

'laborious'

'not personal'

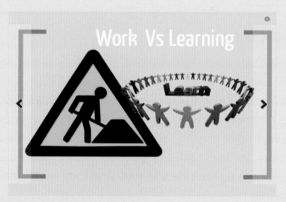

When you think of the word 'learning' you think of

'something personal and meaningful'

'room for improvement'

'OK to make mistakes'

Some changes we discussed
Team work or Team learning?
Let me see your work or Let me see your learning?
Have you finished your work or Have you finished your learning?
Homework or Home learning?

Growth Mindset	
Growth mindset	**Impact on learning**
– Embrace challenges – Resilient in the face of difficulty – Effort is the path to mastery – Learn from critical feedback – See other learners as aids to their own learning – Find lessons and inspiration in the success of others	Played a 90-second video of Carol Dweck discussing the benefits of a growth mindset, found at: www.mindsetworks.com/webnav/ videogallery.aspx

After sharing the research about Growth Mindset learners, we moved on to thinking about how we support the learners in our school in developing a Growth Mindset. We looked at Shirley Clarke's DVD and watched the section about creating the right learning culture. After each clip we allowed discussion time and shared all the good practice we had seen. We suggested the following steps would be a good starting point for creating the right learning culture

STEP 1:	**HOW YOU COULD DO THIS:**
Find out what mindsets already exist in your classroom.	– Ask the children when they feel clever – does it reflect a growth or fixed mindset? – Provide the learners with 3 challenges, all of which vary in difficulty, such as 3 different mazes and 3 different jigsaws. Which one do they choose? – Chris Watkins has a useful learning questionnaire and the 'mindsetworks' website has one also.
STEP 2: Show some inspirational success stories reflecting a Growth Mindset and allow pupils time to reflect on this. Open up discussions on intelligence and Growth Mindset (lots of good examples on Shirley's DVD). Ensure we praise 'effort'.	– If you put 'famous failures' into a search on *YouTube* you can get some fantastic inspirational videos about famous people which reflect a Growth Mindset. – Circle-time discussions – Are you born intelligent? What does intelligence mean? Show a selection of famous people and ask children to order from most to least intelligent (this idea is on the DVD). – Guided reading activities based around brain research, in child-friendly language.
STEP 3: Have a whole-school vision on what a 'good' learner is.	(See below)

STEP 4: Refer to 'Growth' mindset and our school learning muscles across the curriculum.	– How are our learning muscles being referred to in subjects such as PE and Art? – How does the learning environment encourage a growth mindset…? What do learners see when they look around?

FINALLY

The above are only suggested steps and there are many more ways a growth mindset can be developed, so any other ideas you have feel free to use in your class and bring to share with the rest of the team at our staff meeting. You know your children best.

Developing the best possible learning culture is something which is continuously developing and becoming embedded and will not happen overnight. Watch out for those learners who may switch mindsets in different lessons!

What makes a good learner?

We felt as a school that it was important to have a unified vision of what makes a good learner/ successful learning. So we began the session by asking teachers to trace around their hand and in 60 seconds write in the five fingers, five things which made a good learner. Once time was up, they were asked to find someone in the room they had yet to partner with and shake their hand or high-five and then both sit beside each other and share what they felt made a good learner.

After attending Shirley's conference, we found the table she provided us with on Successful Learning (see page 34) had covered everything mentioned and we wanted to now make this personal to our school.

Inspired by the table, we created our own to make it more personal to our school. It reflected the same message as the table mentioned above, but – being a Church of England school – we wanted the learning muscles to incorporate some Christian ethos. Following this INSET day, we asked our local vicar to help us link the learning muscles with Bible stories. We also felt that if the learning muscles felt more unique to our school it would make it more meaningful. With this in mind we made the table below.

St Luke's Learning Muscles

Stay resilient Story of the persistent widow – Luke 18:1–8	Learn hard Practise lots Keep going in the face of difficulty Try new strategies Ask for help Start again Take a brain break

Think hard Joseph suggests a plan for the famine in Egypt – Genesis 41:33–40	Manage distractions Get lost in the task Break things down Plan and think it through Draw diagrams, jot down thoughts or things which help you think
Learn from our mistakes Story of the prodigal son – Luke 15:11–24	Respond to all feedback Reflect on your learning Don't worry if things go wrong Have a growth mindset Make every piece of learning better than the last
Unite Nehemiah gets everyone together to rebuild the walls of Jerusalem – Nehemiah 4:6–23	Learn as a team Co-operate with other learners Listen to others Say when you don't understand Be kind when you disagree Explain things to help others Remember that everybody has something to contribute Be tolerant
Keep improving Jethro Moses Father in Law who makes some suggestions about how to govern people, which Moses puts into practice – Exodus 18:13–27	Keep reviewing your learning Identify your best bits Improve one thing first Try to be better than the last time Listen to feedback Don't compare yourself to others, only yourself Take small steps
Enjoy learning Jesus teaches about the excitement and possibility of faith – Luke 17:5–6	Feel proud of your achievements Feel you neurons connecting Imagine your intelligence growing by the minute! Be creative Let you imagination go Use what you have learnt in real life Know that you can do it, if you practise

Show curiosity Samaritan woman asking questions of Jesus – John 4:7–26	Ask questions Notice things Look for patterns and connections Problem solve Think of possible reasons Research Ask 'What if…?'

Once we had established these, we wanted posters professionally made and framed in classrooms and around the school so our learning message was consistent to all learners in the building. We made contact with a design company and got the posters below designed:

NB: The children love the posters and understand that the posters represent learning muscles and what makes a good learner. We spoke as a staff that we would not name or personify the characters in the posters. They were simply visual representations of the learning muscles and we were never learning to 'please' the *character*. We wanted children to be learning for *themselves* and not for something else.

Reflection Journals

We finished our morning session off by introducing learning journals. We felt it was extremely important that every learner in the school had time for reflection on their learning – and by every learner, this included all members of staff also. We provided every member of staff with a reflection journal and explained that this reflection journal needed to come to every staff meeting, as it would become an important part of their professional development. We finished the morning session with the following reflection thoughts:

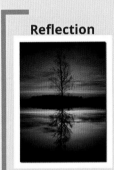

Reflection

What changes will you make?
Thinking points:
- **Work Vs Learning**
- **Find out who has a growth mindset**
- **The DVD footage observed**
- **Strategies to promote a growth mindset**
- **St. Luke's learning muscles – how will you promote these?**
- **Reflecting on learning**
- **How will you give learners more choice?**
- **What changes would you make to your picture?**

We give people the choice to share their reflections, but don't ask them to do this. The decision is theirs.

Revisit reflections from last meeting – how do your reflections and your current situation match?	What has worked well in your class, and what good practice can you share?	What issues have arisen and what support might you need? Share possible solutions or re-visit next week, if needed.	Any new aspect of AfL introduced/ revisited and developed.	Reflection time on the learning during the session.

Since these meetings, there have been many more staff meetings introducing paired talk, success criteria, questioning and more meetings on the classroom culture and learning muscles, reflection and feedback.

Our formative assessment staff meetings are held every other week and the focus is now on revising and developing (e.g. creating talk partner success criteria and how the pairs communicate and cooperatively improve learning).

All staff completed an anonymous online questionnaire (through the SurveyMonkey website) which meant they were brutally honest. As a result we are revisiting their reflection journals and looking at excellent examples, as there was confusion about how best to use them.

We are now working on bringing parents on board. Each of the seven learning muscles is in a bag and each teacher will choose one and host a specific activity in their class which reflects that muscle clearly, and we are going to do a whole-school carousel so every teacher teaches every child on a set 'Learning Day'. This will be filmed and put on our website. Parents and teaching assistants will be encouraged to visit.

Last words

1. When planning the whole-day INSET we asked the following questions beforehand:
   - Do all members of the Senior Leadership Team have the same vision?
   - Is there a clear definition of what AfL means?

2. Practise what you preach – conduct training in the AfL style that you want to see in the classroom.

3. Take an AfL approach to monitoring.

Seamus Gibbons, Deputy Headteacher

VIDEOCLIP TASTER #19 Seamus reflects

Seamus's thoughts about the power of formative assessment.
http://bit.ly/1rwrOH6

Commentary

As with the other two schools, the vision is clear for what the head and the deputy want for their school. It is also clear that the culture has to be one of staff being fully involved and not *told* what to do. As Seamus says, they did not want to dictate how teachers should teach or try to create clones – a sentiment echoed in the other two schools.

Clearing all the staff meetings was a significant act, something many schools feel unable to do with the immense pressure to accommodate new initiatives – almost every week, it seems. Staff meetings on formative assessment on alternative weeks allowed the other things to be tackled in parallel, but the dedicated time for formative assessment gave not only space for discussion and experimentation but also a strong message that this is a worthwhile pursuit.

Seamus places great emphasis on reflection, and by giving the staff reflection journals they are encouraged to stop and think about how they are reacting to new ideas and what is working well or not. Recording in this way is relatively unusual, so it was not surprising that the anonymous survey revealed some problems with its purpose.

The focus on the growth mindset and the learning culture, as at Rudyard Kipling, was tackled first and seen as the most important aspect of formative assessment. Unlike most schools introducing the learning powers or muscles, the staff of St Luke's decided that they did not want characters attached to the powers, because they didn't want the children to be pleasing a character. The key here is how accessible we make the concepts we want to become embedded in children's thinking. By having the special posters printed and linking with Bible stories, of great importance in a church school, children were given that access.

Bringing parents in for a fun carousel of learning powers is an innovative way of sharing the values of the school. By posting a video of the day on the website, parental exposure to them is maximised.

I particularly like the way in which Seamus emphasises that there should be a parallel with what we expect from children in what we do as a staff. Not mentioned in his account, he tells me he picks random lollysticks for each staff meeting for who will be sitting next to who, just as we randomly select children's talk partners. The same rule applies: we can't get too cosy with our friends and we will experience, over time, a range of different learning partners, some of who might challenge our thinking or present us with new ideas and attitudes.

13 The impact of formative assessment, and conclusion

The following comments are typical of what teachers say at the end of a year as a member of an action research team, and usefully summarise the impact of formative assessment. I have included the thoughts of one teacher and then those of two of the teams.

One teacher's comments about what she had introduced and its impact:

What worked?

- Focusing the learning objective;
- Giving pupils a choice of task in lessons;
- Use of traffic lighting to reflect on their understanding of the learning objectives at the beginning and end of lessons;
- Providing choice in the level of challenge in mathematics;
- Co-constructed success criteria;
- Use of highlighting great examples and the visualiser to provide instant feedback;
- Peer and self-assessment during the mini-plenaries;
- Split screen lessons with compulsory and optional success criteria;
- Use of good and average models to compare;
- Application of pupil generated success criteria in other curriculum areas.

Impact

- Pupils are able to access their learning more effectively and areas of misconceptions can be identified more easily (starting question and focus on learning objectives).
- Clarity for pupils – they know what they have to achieve and can choose how to demonstrate their understanding and achievement.
- Adjustments can be made quickly to ensure all children are being stretched and given appropriate learning opportunities with progress monitored throughout the lesson.
- Most pupils attempted more challenging work as they want to stretch themselves, with lower achievers often attaining more in these lessons than they would have (differentiated maths challenge choices).
- Children do more work than the teacher!

- Modelling excellence supports all, especially lower achievers. Everyone can achieve during a lesson.
- Pupils become increasingly able to verbalise their understanding and ways to improve their own work.

One team's collection of only one word or phrase each to describe the main impact of formative assessment:

- Confidence
- Engaged
- Enthusiasm
- Excitement
- Awareness
- Higher expectations
- More progress
- Improved achievement
- Pupil control
- Ownership
- Support
- Motivation
- Resilience
- Challenging
- Reassuring
- Culture of improvement

- Independence
- Taking responsibility
- Pride
- Respect
- Reflection
- Inclusive
- Inspiration
- Perseverance
- Striving for excellence
- Quality
- Transferrable skills
- Power shift
- Partnership
- Flexible
- Cooperation
- Positive ethos

Another team's final thoughts:

- Huge impact on self-esteem
- A learning ethos
- Children are more engaged
- Teacher confidence in planning
- More flexibility to use our professional judgement
- Effective talk and quality discussions
- Better use of talk partners
- Less teacher talk
- Positive praise instead of rewards
- Better questions
- Identification of excellence and how to achieve it
- Reduced marking workload as children are more involved
- Increased enjoyment for all
- Higher quality feedback

- Children are checking and improving their work
- They know what to do to improve
- Improved social skills
- More reflective teaching
- More independent thinking and learning
- Children are being challenged further
- Increased pace and progress in a lesson
- Children have more opportunity to learn with a range of children and achievement levels
- Use of success criteria has raised quality
- Children can now contribute in planning
- Children more willing to have a go
- Children are lifelong learners – their skills are embedded for life
- We got outstanding teaching and learning from Ofsted

'It has brought my lessons alive. The children are excited to find out what our new topic will be and they think we don't do work anymore but instead have fun. I have learned not to be constrained by rules or stick to time limits but to take risks and do what my heart feels is right.'

Passion

Of all the ingredients a teacher should have, there is one that marks out the most successful and is usually plain to see: *passion*. Passion about children's learning can make you seem intense at times – something levelled at me occasionally(!) – but it is the driving force to be continually seeking improvement and criticism. I have been told by countless people to take notice only of the 95% good evaluations on my courses and throw the rest away. On the contrary, I actively seek out any criticism, painful as it might be. One person's thoughts might be representative of many who didn't want to say, or only one person might have the insight to hit the nail on the head. The initial defence mechanism doesn't last and every criticism is helpful as it makes you reflect, rethink or confirm – it is *our* feedback, the most significant aspect of formative assessment.

John Hattie's (2009) views on what is needed to create a learning environment embedded with formative assessment:

❛To facilitate such an environment, to command a range of learning strategies, and to be cognitively aware of the pedagogical means to enable the student to learn, requires dedicated, passionate people. Such teachers need to be aware of which of their teaching strategies are working or not, be prepared to understand and adapt to the learner(s) and their situations, contexts and prior learning, and need to share the experience of learning in this manner in an open, forthright and enjoyable way with their students and their colleagues. We rarely talk about passion in education, as if doing so makes the work of teachers seem less serious, more emotional than cognitive, somewhat biased or of lesser import.'

The teachers who have contributed to this book are the ones to applaud. Because of their passion, thousands of children's and teachers' lives have been turned around forever. By reading this book and watching the videoclips of passionate teachers in action, I hope that many more will be inspired and motivated to introduce formative assessment into their own classrooms when they have read exactly how it can be achieved. By being clear about the principles, by seeing models of excellence and by having a real stake in the process, any teacher with passion about children's learning can do what they have done. Profound change is never easy and their stories show their dedication to the cause, gradually learning about each aspect of formative assessment in turn and being excited by the transformation witnessed in the classroom by their own efforts. It is simply my privilege to be the receiver of so many inspirational examples and stories, and to be able to give them back to the teaching profession.

What next for formative assessment? Whenever I think everything that could have been said must now have been said, it somehow moves on, as we keep learning more about children's learning. The ever-developing practice of formative assessment runs parallel to our understanding of learning, so, as Gary Wilkie said at the end of his account: *'We are on a journey with no destination.'* Our destination is not fixed, but we know what it must embody – the empowerment of children to confidently know how to learn, how to self-assess, how to improve and to thrive on challenge.

References and resources

Adey, P. and Dillon, J. (2012) 'From fixed IQ to multiple intelligences', in Adey, P. and Dillon, J. (Eds) *Bad Education*, McGraw Hill.

Alexander, R. (2004) *Towards Dialogic Teaching*, Dialogos UK.

Ames, C. and Ames, R. (1984) 'Systems of student and teacher motivation: toward a qualitative definition', *Journal of Educational Psychology, 76*, 535–56.

Assessment Reform Group (2002) *Assessment for Learning: Ten Principles*, www.assessment-reform-group.org.uk

Ausubel, D. P., Novak, J. and Hanesian, H. (1978) *Educational Psychology: A cognitive view*, Holt, Rinehart and Winston.

Baines, E. (2012) 'Grouping pupils by ability in school', in Adey, P. and Dillon, J. (Eds) *Bad Education*, McGraw Hill.

Birkhead, J. – *see* Ginnis (2010)

Black, P. and Wiliam, D. (1998a) 'Assessment and classroom learning', *Assessment in Education: Principles, Policy and Practice, 5*(1), 7–73.

Black, P. and Wiliam, D. (1998b*) Inside the Black Box: Raising standards through classroom assessment*, King's College London School of Education.

Bloom, B. S. (1969) 'Some theoretical issues relating to educational evaluation', in Tyler, R. W. (Ed.) *Educational Evaluation: new roles, new means: the 63rd yearbook of the National Society for the Study of Education* (part 11), *69*, 2, 26–50, University of Chicago Press.

Butler, R. (1988) 'Enhancing and undermining intrinsic motivation; the effects of task-involving and ego-involving evaluation on interest and performance', *British Journal of Educational Psychology, 58*, 1–14.

Cameron, J. and Pierce, W. D. (1994) 'Reinforcement, reward and intrinsic motivation: A meta-analysis', *Review of Educational Research, 64* (3), 363–423.

Clarke, S. (2008) *Active Learning through Formative Assessment*, Hodder Education.

Claxton, G. (2002) *Building Learning Power*, TLO Limited, Bristol.

Cohen, A. D. (1987) 'Student processing of feedback on their composition', in Wenden, A. L. and Rubin, J. (Eds), *Learner Strategies in Language Learning*, Englewood Cliffs, Prentice Hall International.

Corbett, P. (2013) *Formative Assessment in Literacy*, Teach First magazine: www.teachfirst.org.uk

Costa, A. L. and Kallick, B. (2008) *Learning and Leading with Habits of Mind: 16 essential characteristics for success,* Association for Supervision and Curriculum Development, VA.

Crooks, T. (1988) 'The impact of classroom evaluation practices on students', *Review of Educational Research, 58* (4), 438–81.

Davies, A. (2009) *Making Classroom Assessment Work*, Perfect Paperback.

De Bono, E. (1999) *Six Thinking Hats*, Penguin.

Deci, E. L., Koestner, R. and Ryan, R. M. (1999) 'A meta-analytic review of experiments examining the effects of extrinsic rewards on intrinsic motivation', *Psychological Bulletin, 125* (6), 627–68.

Deci, E. L. and Ryan, R. M. (1985) *Intrinsic Motivation and Self-determination in Human Behavior,* Plenum.

Delaney, R., Day, L. and Chambers, M. R. (2006) *Learning Power Heroes,* TLO Limited, Bristol.

DFE Education White Paper (2010).

Dudley, P. – Director of www.lessonstudy.co.uk

Dweck, C. S. (2000) *Self-Theories: their role in motivation, personality and development,* Psychology Press.

Dweck, C. S. (2006) *Mindset,* Random House.

Dweck, C. S. (2011) 'You can grow your intelligence', article on www.mindsetworks.com

Flynn, J. R. (2007) *What is Intelligence?,* Cambridge University Press.

Gardner, J. (1983) *Frames of Mind,* Basic Books.

Ginnis, P. (2010) from his website www.ginnis.eu and quoted in his address to Ireland's Principals: Tim Birkhead, University of Sheffield, and Jonathan Kestenbaum, Chief Executive, National Endowment for Science, Technology and the Arts.

Hargreaves, E. (2005) 'Assessment for Learning? Thinking outside the (black) box', *Cambridge Journal of Education, 35,* 2, 213–24.

Hattie, J. (2009) *Visible Learning,* Routledge.

Hattie, J. (2012) *Visible Learning for Teachers,* Routledge.

Hattie, J. and Yates, G. (2014) *Visible Learning and the Science of How We Learn,* Routledge.

Hillocks, G. Jr (1986) 'Research on written composition: new directions for teaching', National Conference on Research in English, Urbana, Illinois.

Kestenbaum, J. – *see* Ginnis (2010).

Kluger, A. N. and DeNisi, A. (1996) 'The effects of feedback interventions on performance: A historical review, a meta-analysis, and a preliminary feedback intervention theory', *Psychological Bulletin, 119* (2), 254.

Leahy, S., Lyon, C., Thompson, M. and Wiliam, D. (2005) 'Classroom assessment: minute by minute, day by day', *Education Leadership, 63* (3).

North Gillingham EAZ (DfES)/Institute of Education (2001) Three Reports of the Gillingham Formative Assessment Project.

Outstanding Formative Assessment, DVD from www.shirleyclarke-education.org

Programme for International Student Assessment (2007) *PISA 2006: Science competences for tomorrow's world* (Vol.1), Paris: Organisation for Economic Co-operation and Development.

Quigley, C. (2010) *Secrets of Success,* Chris Quigley Education.

Reid, C. and Anderson, M. (2012) 'Left-brain, right-brain, brain games and beanbags: neuromyths in education', in Adey, P. and Dillon, J. (Eds) *Bad Education,* McGraw Hill.

Rowe, M. B. (1974) 'Relation of wait-time and rewards to the development of language, logic and fate control', *Journal of Research in Science Teaching, 11,* 4, 292.

Sadler, R. (1989) 'Formative assessment and the design of instructional systems', *Instructional Science, 18,* 119–44.

Scannell, V. (2002) *New and Collected Poems 1950–80,* Robson Books (for the poem *Nettles*).

Stiggins, R. J. (2005) 'From formative assessment to assessment for learning: a path to success in standards-based schools', *Phi Delta Kappan, 87* (4), 324–8.

Stigler, J. W. and Hiebert, J. (1999) *The Teaching Gap,* The Free Press.

Sutton Trust (2011) *Education Endowment Foundation Teaching and Learning Toolkit.*

The Power of Formative Assessment, DVD from www.shirleyclarke-education.org

White, J. (2005) 'The myth of Howard Gardner's multiple intelligences', *ioelife, 1, 9,* London: Institute of Education.

Wiliam, D. (2011) *Embedded Formative Assessment,* Solution Tree Press.

Woollett, K. and Maguire, E. A. (2012) 'Exploring anterograde associative memory in London taxi drivers', *Neuroreport, 23,* 15, 885–8.

Zellermayer, M. (1989) 'The study of teachers' written feedback to students' writing: changes in theoretical considerations and the expansion of research contexts', *Instructional Science, 18,* 145–65.

Other resources

Growth mindset:

I Can't Do This, by K. J. Walton (buy at www.growthmindset.org and see how to use the book)

Giraffes Can't Dance, by Giles Andrae and Guy Parker-Rees

All Kinds of Ways to Be Smart, by Judy Lalli

Your Fantastic Elastic Brain, by JoAnn Deak

Angelina Ballerina, by Katharine Holabird

The Dot, by Peter Reynolds

Rosie Revere Engineer, by Andrea Beaty

Ryan the Spy and : the SuperHero Secret, by Jason Rago

Cindersilly, by Diana B. Thompson

www.growthmindset.org
www.mindsetworks.com
www.practicalsavvy.com
www.zazzle.com
www.tpet.co.uk

YouTube clips: famous failures, Carol Dweck interviews, neurons connecting taxi drivers' brains, Charlie and Lola

Effects of grading: see *The Report Card,* by Andrew Clements (2004), Aladdin Paperbacks

Immersion resource: www.historyoffthepage.co.uk

Immersion resource: www.thehistoryman.org.uk

Randomiser: www.harmonyhollow.net

TASC: www.tascwheel.com

Video resource: www.irisconnect.com